America's New
Swing Region

America's New Swing Region

Changing Politics and Demographics in the Mountain West

Ruy Teixeira

editor

BROOKINGS INSTITUTION PRESS
Washington, D.C.

Library of Congress Cataloging-in-Publication data
America's new swing region : changing politics and demographics in the Mountain
West / Ruy Teixeira, editor.
   p. cm.
Includes bibliographical references and index.
Summary: "Analyzes effects of the increase in minorities, younger residents,
educational levels, and urbanization on the traditionally Republican politics of six
states in the Mountain West, comparing changes in voting patterns from 1988 to
2008. Discusses possible ramifications of those changes and the 2010 mid-term
elections on the 2012 presidential election"—Provided by publisher.
   ISBN 978-0-8157-2286-1 (pbk. : alk. paper)
   1. Party affiliation—Rocky Mountains Region. 2. Demography—Political aspects—
Rocky Mountains Region. 3. Population geography—Political aspects—Rocky
Mountains Region. 4. Apportionment (Election law)—Rocky Mountains Region.
5. Rocky Mountains Region—Politics and government. I. Teixeira, Ruy A.
   JK2271.A64 2012
   324.978093—dc23   2011052455

9 8 7 6 5 4 3 2 1

Printed on acid-free paper

Typeset in Minion

Composition by Cynthia Stock
Silver Spring, Maryland

Printed by R. R. Donnelley
Harrisonburg, Virginia

Contents

Foreword

Brookings Mountain West is a partnership between the University of Nevada, Las Vegas (UNLV) and the Brookings Institution, the world's leading public policy think tank, based in Washington, D.C. Brookings Mountain West brings Brookings's high-quality, independent, and high-impact research to a wide range of issues facing the dynamic Intermountain West region, building on the work of the Brookings Metropolitan Policy Program, which focuses on helping metropolitan areas, such as Las Vegas, grow in robust, inclusive, and sustainable ways.

Brookings Mountain West faculty and staff, in both Las Vegas and Washington, D.C., conduct research; publish data and analyses; host conferences, meetings, and public lectures; and facilitate collaboration between local, state, and regional leaders and organizations with Brookings experts. Brookings scholars are regular and frequent visitors to the UNLV campus and the region, engaging with local scholars and experts on a wide range of public policy issues.

As a regional public policy think tank, Brookings Mountain West is committed to improving the quality of life in the Mountain West, which includes Arizona, Colorado, Idaho, Nevada, New Mexico, and Utah. These states constitute the new swing region in American politics, yet many national observers and commentators have only a superficial understanding of the profound economic, political, and social changes that continue to reshape the region. Prior to the Great Recession, this region was the fastest-growing area of the

United States. Conversely, no region of the nation has suffered more economic distress or lagged behind national recovery indicators longer than these six states.

On October 8, 2010, Brookings Mountain West hosted a conference, "The Political Demography and Geography of the Intermountain West," on the UNLV campus, during which a gathering of notable scholars and public policy researchers presented a series of contemporary research papers on topics critical to this region. The presentations covered such topics as recent demographic trends that have altered the region and its politics; an analysis of the metropolitan politics that define the region; and a public opinion survey exploring attitudes on state and national politics, alternative energy, education, deficits, health care, immigration, and other topics essential to understanding the political landscape of this region on the eve of the 2010 elections and in advance of the 2012 presidential race.

Following the conference, Brookings Mountain West asked selected contributors to revise their observations and findings in light of the 2010 congressional elections and to consider the implications for the 2012 presidential election. An additional paper that explores the implications of the 2010 census and multistate congressional redistricting plans is also included in this volume.

Brookings Mountain West would like to acknowledge the many people who contributed to the October 8, 2010, conference and to this volume. Individuals worthy of special recognition include Neal Smatresk, president of UNLV; Rebecca Boulton, former Brookings Mountain West business manager; Alexandra Nikolich, current Brookings Mountain West business manager; Lucy Klinkhammer, associate vice president for community relations, the Lincy Institute; Lee Bernick, dean, Greenspun College of Urban Affairs; Laurie Fruth, general manager, UNLV TV; Daniel Grimes, manager, instructional production and engineering, UNLV TV; and our invaluable UNLV student assistants and volunteers.

ROBERT E. LANG,
UNLV Director,
and
WILLIAM E. BROWN JR.,
Director of Planning and Communication,
Brookings Mountain West

November 2011

America's New Swing Region

introduction
America's New Swing Region

Ruy Teixeira

The United States is experiencing a period of rapid demographic change, and nowhere is the speed of change more rapid than in the Mountain West, which includes the states of Arizona, Colorado, Idaho, Nevada, New Mexico, and Utah.* As this region has changed, its politics have changed as well. It should no longer be considered a reliably conservative and Republican area but rather a new swing region of the country. In the 2008 presidential election, Colorado, Nevada, and New Mexico all went for Democrat Barack Obama, and these states are all sure to be hotly contested by the parties in 2012. It seems likely that Arizona will be added to that list in the near future.

How did this happen? How did a region where no state voted Democratic in any presidential election between 1968 and 1988, a region supposedly imbued with an unshakable libertarian ethos and a reverence for Reagan-style politics, become America's new swing region? The answer lies in ongoing processes that have dramatically increased the minority share of the region's population, brought in millions of new residents from outside the region, raised educational levels, replaced older with younger generations, and powered the rise of dynamic metropolitan areas where the overwhelming majority of the Mountain West population now lives.

---

*We do not discuss the smaller Mountain West states of Montana and Wyoming in this volume. When we refer to the Mountain West region in this book, we always exclude these states and focus on Arizona, Colorado, Idaho, Nevada, New Mexico, and Utah.

In this volume, these processes of change are outlined in detail and connected directly to the shifting political terrain in the Mountain West. The chapters include

—a detailed examination of the political demography and geography of all six states (William Frey and Ruy Teixeira)

—an analysis of shifting voting patterns in five primary metros—Albuquerque, Denver, Las Vegas, Phoenix, and Salt Lake—that are the locus of growth and change in their respective states (Robert Lang and Thomas Sanchez)

—an assessment of race-ethnic changes in the Mountain West, especially the surge in the Hispanic population, and the political effects of those changes (Frey)

—a close look at the rising Millennial generation in the Mountain West and how it compares with both its counterparts in the rest of the country and older generations in its own region (Scott Keeter)

—a report on a unique 2010 survey of Mountain West residents in all six states, allowing comparisons across states of views on issue priorities; federal legislation like the health care, economic stimulus, and financial regulation bills; social issues like gay marriage; the role of government; the distinctive characteristics of Mountain West life; and much more (Karlyn Bowman and Teixeira)

—a detailed consideration of reapportionment and redistricting in the Mountain West and how their outcomes are being shaped by ongoing processes of rapid demographic and geographic change (David Damore).

Here are a few of the many findings from these chapters, selected to highlight the scale and dynamism of the changes transforming the Mountain West and its politics. In chapter 1, "America's New Swing Region: The Political Demography and Geography of the Mountain West," demographer William Frey and political scientist Ruy Teixeira provide detailed analyses of trends in Arizona, Colorado, Idaho, Nevada, New Mexico, and Utah. Trends are analyzed at the state level and by regions within states using specially created regions that permit analysis of eligible voter populations.

In Arizona, Frey and Teixeira find that the minority share of the state's eligible voters, currently 31 percent, is rising fast (up 6 points over the 2000–10 period), while the working-age, white working-class (non-college-educated) share of eligible voters, currently 37 percent, is declining almost as fast. The rise of minority voters is sharpest in the Phoenix metro, where 66 percent of the state's population resides.

While GOP candidate John McCain did carry Arizona in the 2008 presidential election, his 8-point margin would likely have been less without his favorite son status, and it pales in comparison with the average 26-point margin Republican presidential candidates enjoyed in the 1968–88 period. This shift toward the Democrats has been strongest in the fast-growing Phoenix metro (a 19-point margin gain for the Democrats). Across the state, with the exception of the West region, higher population growth rates tend to correlate with increased Democratic voting.

In Colorado, the minority share of the state's eligible voters, currently 22 percent, is rising (up 3 points in the last decade), but so too is the share of working-age, white college graduates, up 2 points to 27 percent. In contrast, the white working-class share of eligible voters is declining very fast, down 6 points over the decade to 39 percent. The rise of minorities and decline of the white working class is sharpest in the Denver inner suburbs, while the rise of white college graduates is fastest in the city of Denver.

After voting Republican in every presidential election between 1968 and 1988, with an average GOP margin of 18 points, Colorado voted Democratic in 1992 by 4 points and again in 2008 by a margin of 9 points. The biggest gains since 1988 have come in the Denver inner suburbs (25-point margin gain), Denver city (29 points) and the Boulder metro area (38 points). Almost all Democratic-shifting counties over this period have grown in the last decade, while Republican-shifting counties tend to be a mix of growing and declining counties, especially in the East region.

In Idaho, Frey and Teixeira found that the minority share of the state's eligible voters, currently just 10 percent, is rising (up 3 points in the last decade) but—as in Colorado—so too is the white college graduate share, up 2 points to 18 percent. The white working-class share of eligible voters is declining fast, down 6 points over the decade, but at 55 percent, it is still very high. The rise of minorities and decline of the white working class are strongest in the Boise metro, where two-fifths of the state's population resides.

Idaho has voted Republican in every presidential election since 1964, typically by very wide margins. Unlike in Arizona and Colorado, the overall change since 1988 has been minimal—the GOP margin was 26 points in 1988 and 25 points in 2008. However, there have been countervailing changes within the state that have canceled one another out. The fast-growing Boise metro has seen a strong shift toward the Democrats since 1988 (14 points) while the much slower-growing Panhandle region has experienced an 18-point shift toward the GOP.

In Nevada, the fastest-growing state in the nation, the minority share of the state's eligible voters, currently 34 percent, is rising very rapidly (up 10 points in the last decade). The white working-class share of eligible voters is declining just as fast, down 10 points over the decade. The rise of minorities and the decline of the white working class are sharpest in the Las Vegas metro area, where almost three-quarters of the state's population resides.

After voting Republican in every presidential election between 1968 and 1988, with an average GOP margin of 22 points, Nevada voted Democratic narrowly in 1992, by 3 points, and in 1996, by 1 point; it voted Democratic more authoritatively in 2008, by 12 points. The biggest gains since 1988 have come in the very fast-growing Las Vegas metro area (35-point margin shift toward the Democrats) and in the Reno metro (also a 35-point shift). The slowest-growing part of the state, the rural heartland, experienced the smallest shift toward the Democrats (15 points).

In New Mexico, Frey and Teixeira found that the minority share of the state's eligible voters, currently just over a majority (52 percent), is rising fairly rapidly (up 4 points in the last decade), with an almost equivalent decline in the white working-class share of eligible voters. The rise of minorities and the decline of the white working class are sharpest in the Albuquerque metro area, where 43 percent of the state's population resides.

After voting Republican in every presidential election between 1968 and 1988, though by a comparatively modest average margin of 14 points, New Mexico has voted Democratic in four of the last five presidential elections. The Democrats' largest margin, 15 points, came in 2008. The biggest gains since 1988 have come in the Albuquerque metro area, by far the fastest-growing area of the state (26-point margin shift toward the Democrats).

In Utah, the minority share of the state's eligible voters, currently just 12 percent, is rising moderately fast (up 3 points in the last decade), and, unusually, the white college graduate share is rising at about the same pace, up 3 points to 21 percent. The white working-class share of eligible voters is declining rapidly, down 6 points over the decade, but at 54 percent, it is still dominant. The rise of minorities and the decline of the white working class are strongest in the Salt Lake metro area, where two-fifths of the state's population resides, while the rise of white college graduates is strongest in the Ogden and North area.

Utah has voted Republican in every presidential election since 1964, typically by very wide margins, with an average GOP margin of 38 points in the 1968–88 period. By that standard, McCain's 28-point victory in 2008 represented some improvement for the Democrats, driven almost entirely by a substantial Democratic shift in the Salt Lake metro area (19-point margin gain since 1988). However, the rest of Utah, which is faster growing than the Salt Lake metro area, has either remained the same (Ogden and North region) or moved slightly more toward the GOP (Provo and South).

The overall pattern of change is clear. Across the region, minorities and white college graduates are gaining while the white working class is declining rapidly. Typically, the shifts are sharpest in the large, dynamic metropolitan areas of the states in the region. And it is those metro areas that are playing the leading role in changing the politics of Mountain West states, turning Colorado, Nevada, and New Mexico into accessible states for Democrats and moving Arizona rapidly in the same direction.

In chapter 2, "Metropolitan Voting Patterns in the Mountain West: The New and Old Political Heartlands," geographers Robert Lang and Thomas Sanchez take a close look at the evolving politics of the region's large metro areas. They point out that, counter-intuitively, the Mountain West is among the most urbanized areas in the United States, with an especially strong concentration of population in five rapidly diversifying "Moutain Mega" metro areas: Phoenix (66 percent of the state population); Denver (51 percent); Las Vegas (72 percent); Albuquerque (43 percent); and Salt Lake (41 percent). Population growth inside these metro areas, both overall and among minorities, is considerably outpacing growth outside.

Lang and Sanchez find that there was a consistent trend toward voting Democratic over the last decade in these metro areas, both in U.S. House elections (2000–10) and presidential elections (2000–08). Trends toward the Democrats have been noticeably more consistent within these areas than outside them, especially in House elections. The authors observe that while in 2000 all five metros voted Republican for the House, in 2010—a very good year for Republicans—only two of them did, and in one of them (Denver), the margin was a razor-thin .4 percentage points.

Lang and Sanchez conclude that the voting behavior of these five metro areas is shifting from its Republican foundations. In so doing, these areas have played a leading role in turning the "New Heartland" states of Nevada, Colorado, and New Mexico into a critical swing bloc that has more electoral votes (20) than Ohio (18) and that could decide the next presidential election. Moreover, trends toward urbanization and diversification will reinforce these states' swing status and likely add Arizona to the mix. Lang and Sanchez emphasize the centrality of rising Hispanic voters to this transformation. They remark: "These voters are to the New Heartland of the twenty-first century what white ethnic voters from southern and eastern Europe were to the Old Heartland in the twentieth century. They are now the potential deciding voters in any toss-up presidential election."

In chapter 3, demographer William Frey focuses on the role of minority, especially Hispanic, voters in Mountain West politics. He starts by reviewing the effects of race-ethnic change on the nation as a whole, in particular by comparing fast-growing with slow-growing purple states. Fast-growing purple states are located in the Mountain West (including Arizona, Colorado, New Mexico, and Nevada) and the Southeast, and they feature larger minority shares of eligible voters and much faster growth of minority voters than their slow-growing counterparts. Frey points out that in 2008 minorities delivered to Barack Obama seven states where minorities did not make the difference in 2004 and that five of these were fast-growing purple states.

Frey cautions that the political effect of rapid minority growth in purple states is blunted by the "translation gap" between the number of eligible voters and the total population. For example, 77 of 100 whites in the national population are eligible to vote, while just 42 of 100 Hispanics are eligible. This is because the Hispanic population is younger and, especially, because of the large share of noncitizens among Hispanics. The translation gap heavily affects the Mountain West purple states of Arizona, Colorado, Nevada, and New Mexico. However, as Frey also shows, the race-ethnic voter profiles of these states still feature significant shares of minority voters that are growing fast despite the translation gap.

That growth will have a considerable effect on the politics of these states, including the overall structure of public opinion. Drawing on a special survey of Mountain West residents conducted for this volume, Frey shows that in addition to favoring a far softer line on immigration, Hispanic residents are far more favorable to President Obama, far more supportive of the new health reform law, and considerably more supportive of increased government involvement in areas like schools, health, and the environment. Frey concludes that

> as young minority residents advance to voting age and make up ever larger shares of eligible voters, candidates for national, state, and local offices will need to cater to their interests in government solutions for the economy, good schools, affordable health care, and the environment. With respect to the political effects of minorities' increased electoral clout, "demography is destiny." In the short run, however, politicians will have to strike a delicate balance between the interests of minority populations and those of the typically larger white, Republican-leaning population.

In chapter 4, survey researcher Scott Keeter examines the rising Millennial generation in the Mountain West and compares it with both its counterparts in the rest of the country and older generations in its own region. Drawing on a rich store of data from the Pew Research Center as well as the survey of Mountain West residents conducted for this volume, Keeter finds that just as Millennials in the rest of the country are, Mountain West Millennials are more politically liberal than older generations in a variety of ways. They are more supportive of activist government, the social safety net, regulation, environmental protection, and the Democratic health care reform legislation. They also are more accepting of same-sex marriage and interracial dating and marriage and significantly less likely than older people to identify with a religious tradition.

The attitudes and values of Mountain West Millennials tend to be very close to those of Millennials in the rest of the country, but they tend to differ from those of Millennials outside the Mountain West on party affiliation and voting behavior. That is, while Mountain West Millennials are indeed less Republican than their elders, as one would expect from their attitudes and values, they are nevertheless considerably more Republican than their generation outside the region. For example, while 18- to 29-year-olds outside the region favored Obama in the 2008 election by 67 to 31, 18- to 29-year-olds in the Mountain West favored him by only 51 to 47. With respect to party identification, 18- to 29-year-olds outside the region gave the Democratic Party a 49-to-31 advantage over the Republicans in 2011, while Mountain West 18- to 29-year-olds were split about evenly (39 percent Democratic/40 percent Republican).

Keeter points out that Millennials were a positive factor for Democrats in the Mountain West in the 2010 election, helping Harry Reid keep his Senate seat and voting significantly less Republican than their elders in the Arizona races for U.S. Senate and governor. But he expects the loyalties of this group to be hotly contested in the upcoming 2012 election, given the possible large role of at least three states—Colorado, Nevada, and New Mexico—in a tight presidential contest and the fact that despite the seemingly liberal attitudes of Mountain West Millennials, they remain relatively open to GOP appeals.

Keeter concludes that while the region's Millennials will likely be more Democratic in their voting than previous generations, their political distinctiveness will be felt beyond the polling place. The Mountain West's libertarian instinct will survive in this generation, but it will go hand in hand with support for environmental protection and the regulation that accompanies it. Mountain West Millennials will also be more welcoming to immigrants and less likely to become embroiled in "culture war" conflicts over social issues. In that respect, Keeter argues, even conservative members of this cohort may be more true to their Western roots and libertarian tendencies than older generations in the region.

In chapter 5, survey researcher Karlyn Bowman and Ruy Teixeira report on a unique 2010 survey of Mountain West residents in all six states covered by this volume. The survey found that healthy majorities of Mountain West residents see themselves as more likely than other Americans to have a number of characteristics, including a tendency to engage with the outdoors (ranked first) and to support renewable energy (ranked third). Consistent with that ethos, Mountain West residents felt—by more than a 2-to-1 majority regionwide and with strong majorities in every state—that their state was better off "investing in wind and solar energy solutions that will generate clean, renewable energy sources and jobs for years to come" than "investing in proven technologies like clean coal and nuclear energy sources because they are guaranteed to produce jobs now."

The second-ranked characteristic on the list was having to deal with the effects of immigration, and here too the survey found evidence that the issue tied the region together. Across the region and in five of the six states, immigration was the area where the most residents wanted to see more federal government involvement. And across the region and in every state, majorities of Mountain West residents felt that the new Arizona immigration law was either about right or did not go far enough. Nevertheless, residents across the region and in every state also felt that immigrants make a positive contribution to the country and supported a path to citizenship for illegal immigrants.

The survey also found some evidence of a libertarian bent, especially on gun rights, consistent with Mountain West residents' view of themselves as being skeptical of federal government power. But other findings from the survey confounded the libertarian stereotype, as strong majorities across the region said that they wanted more federal and state government involvement in areas like protecting the environment, promoting renewable energy sources, cracking down on crime and drugs, guaranteeing quality public education, and creating jobs. The last two areas were also the top two issues—overall and in most states—that residents wanted their state elected officials to address. Regional residents also supported the idea that government regulation of business is necessary.

Moreover, Mountain West residents did not appear to be as tax sensitive as would be suggested by the libertarian stereotype. Regionwide and in every state, majorities or pluralities felt that their federal taxes were "about right" and said that they did not mind paying federal taxes "because we each have a responsibility to contribute to the common good and to support those who can't support themselves."

Bowman and Teixeira note that the ongoing process of demographic change in the Mountain West should produce gradual shifts in public opinion across the region, given the internal demographics revealed by the poll, especially the differences between the Millennials and older generations, between minorities and whites, and among whites, between college-educated and working-class residents. Shifts include more support for government involvement in areas like education, energy, and the environment; less tax sensitivity; warmer attitudes toward immigrants and a path to citizenship for illegal residents; more support for free trade; and less support for socially conservative positions such as opposition to gay marriage. But they stress that the public opinion profile of the Mountain West will remain complex and contradictory, even in the relatively liberal states of Colorado, Nevada, and New Mexico, which will be heavily targeted by the parties in 2012. They conclude that the region confronts the parties with "very challenging political terrain where nothing should be taken for granted and where conventional stereotypes about the Mountain West should be treated very, very cautiously."

In chapter 6, political scientist David Damore takes a detailed look at the redistricting and reapportionment process in the Mountain West and at how outcomes are being shaped by ongoing demographic and geographic change. Damore notes that in the last decade no region in the United States experienced the magnitude of demographic and geographic change that swept through the Mountain West. The diversification and increased density of Mountain West populations have favored Democrats, turning a traditional Republican stronghold into a partisan battleground.

But will these changes be reflected in the reapportionment and redistricting processes set in motion by the 2010 census? That is where things start to get complicated. These processes are of Byzantine complexity, and there are many political and legal channels through which parties can influence outcomes. Thus, the extent to which demographic and geographic change is embodied in reapportionment and redistricting is highly contingent on partisan and legal maneuvering and is vigorously contested, as Damore shows for the outcomes of the 2001 redistricting process. Damore expects the final outcomes of the 2011 process to be just as vigorously contested, if not more so, because the issues raised by demographic and geographic change are sharper.

Further muddying these waters is the fact that while Democrats made considerable progress in the region over the decade, a good chunk of their gains was lost to the GOP in 2010. Particularly pertinent to the redistricting process was the Democrats' loss in 2010 of unified legislative and executive control in two states (Colorado and New Mexico), leaving them without unified control in any state. Republicans now have unified control in three states (Arizona, Idaho, and Utah) while three states have divided control (Colorado, Nevada, and New Mexico). As Damore notes, "the Democrats' ability to use reapportionment and redistricting to solidify their gains in 2011 is likely to be limited; it is the Republicans who are better positioned to minimize the effects (at least temporarily) of the demographic forces working against the party in the region."

But Damore does believe that regardless of which party gains an advantage in a state's redistricting process, the real and undisputed loser will be rural interests. These interests have been overrepresented for too long, and their position is no longer sustainable under any process. Urban interests are on the rise, and ranching interests (in Idaho and Utah) and mining interests (in Colorado and Nevada) are likely to see their influence wane. Damore believes that the void created by the decline of rural legislators will be filled by minorities, particularly Hispanics. The question now is "whether all of these politicians will be taking office with a 'D' next to their names or whether some will be elected as Republicans."

All the chapters in this volume tell different aspects of the same story. This is not, as it were, your father's Mountain West. The demographic and geographic changes detailed throughout the volume have made the Mountain West the new swing region of the United States, a new reality that is unlikely to change anytime soon. Indeed, these studies suggest that the process of change will continue to unfold in this decade and that the contests between the parties will become only more intense and widespread.

one

America's New Swing Region:

THE POLITICAL DEMOGRAPHY AND
GEOGRAPHY OF THE MOUNTAIN WEST

WILLIAM H. FREY AND RUY TEIXEIRA

This chapter on the political demography and geography of six Mountain West states—Arizona, Colorado, Idaho Nevada, New Mexico, and Utah—focuses on a demographically dynamic part of the country where the current balance of political forces is in flux. Demographic and geographic trends are constantly testing the political balance in these states, as was evident in the 2008 presidential election when three of the states turned from "red" to "blue" and the other three remained red. This chapter provides a guide to the trends that are currently reshaping the balance of forces in these states, with considerable implications for the states' long-range political trajectories.

The dramatic growth of these states is shown in table A-1. Over the 2000–10 decade, Nevada and Arizona ranked first and second among the states in growth, increasing their total populations by 35 and 25 percent, respectively. Utah was third, Idaho was fourth, Colorado was ninth, and New Mexico, the slowest growing of the six, still grew faster than the nation as a whole. For the most part, growth in these states is linked to new Western economies tied to growing "megapolitan regions" and industries such as information technology, financial services, energy, and tourism.[1]

For each state, we start by delineating our regions of analysis and discussing population growth patterns for the state as whole and for each region. We then provide demographic and growth profiles for the state and each region, focusing particularly on four key demographics: minorities; white, working-age college graduates; the white, working-age, working-class population; and white

Table A-1. Population Growth, Economic, and Political Indicators for the United States and Selected Mountain West States

Indicator	United States	Arizona	Colorado	Idaho	Nevada	New Mexico	Utah
Growth and economic indicators							
Population growth rate, percent, 2000–10 (state rank)	9.7	24.6 (2)	16.9 (9)	21.1 (4)	35.1 (1)	13.2 (15)	23.8 (3)
Median household income, 2010 (state rank)	50,046	46,789 (28)	54,046 (15)	43,490 (38)	51,001 (19)	42,090 (42)	54,744 (13)
Percent of persons in poverty, 2010 (state rank)	15.3	17.4 (13)	13.4 (32)	15.7 (20)	14.9 (24)	20.4 (2)	13.2 (34)
State political indicators							
Number of Democratic/ Republican House members		3D/5R	3D/4R	2R	1D/2R	2D/1R	1D/2R
Number of Democratic/ Republican senators		2R	2D	2R	1D/1R	2D	2R
Democratic or Republican governor		R	D	R	R	R	R
Democratic margin, 2008 presidential election		−9	9	−26	12	15	−29

Source: Authors' analysis of data from the 2000 and 2010 U.S. decennial censuses, the 2010 American Community Survey, and state election returns.

seniors. We then describe the demographic voting patterns within the state and continue with an extensive discussion of how different regions within the state have trended politically since 1988. We conclude the analysis of each state with an assessment of the key trends and groups to watch for in the 2012 election and beyond. Together our analyses show how these states shifted from a heavily Republican bloc to a new swing region in U.S. politics.

Data Sources and Definitions

The demographic, polling, and voting statistics presented in this chapter are the latest available from authoritative sources. The demographic profiles of states and their regions are drawn from the U.S. decennial censuses through 2010 and the Public Use Microdata Sample (PUMS) of the Census Bureau's 2010 American Community Survey. Polling data are drawn from CBS/New York Times (1988) and National Election Pool (2004 and 2008) state exit polls. Presidential and congressional election data are drawn from official county-level election returns for the six states.

Our analysis of eligible voters—citizens ages 18 and older—draws on data from the 2010 American Community Survey and the 2000 census to examine these voters with respect to several social and demographic attributes. Special emphasis is given to four key demographic segments of eligible voters: *minorities*—all persons stating something other than "non-Hispanic white alone" as their race/ethnicity; *white seniors*—non-Hispanic whites ages 65 and older; *working-age, white college graduates*—non-Hispanic whites ages 18 to 64 having a four-year college degree; and *working-age, working-class whites*—non–college-educated non-Hispanic whites ages 18 to 64.

The substate regional definitions that we employ are discussed and displayed on maps in each state-specific section. They are typically based on counties or groups thereof that make up metropolitan areas or other regions that are strategically important in terms of their recent demographic shifts or voting trends. These regions will be used to identify substate trends drawn from U.S. census county data and county-level election returns. Regions delineated for the analysis of eligible voter demographics in each state-specific section sometimes deviate slightly from the regional definitions that we employ. This is due to the geographic limitations of data available with the 2010 American Community Survey PUMS, which is used in these analyses. Details about these slight differences in regional definition are available from the authors.

Arizona

Arizona was the second-fastest-growing state for 2000–10, after Nevada. It has gobbled up electoral college votes, adding one vote after each of the censuses from 1960 though 1990 and two votes after 2000. Despite a sharp slowdown in growth in the last few years, it still gained one vote after the 2010 census, and its new total of eleven votes can make a difference in a close election. Arizona is the home of Barry Goldwater and a conservative Republican tradition; nonetheless, its dramatically shifting demographics prompted many observers to contend that it would have been strongly in play in 2008 had Arizona senator John McCain not become the Republican presidential standard-bearer.

Regions of Arizona

The regions for Arizona are shown in map B-1 (see color insert after page 22); related population and growth statistics are shown in map B-2 and table B-1. The regions are as follows:

Table B-1. 2010 Population and 2000–10 Growth Rate for Arizona Regions

| Region | 2010 population | | Growth rate (percent) |
	Number	Percent of state	
Phoenix	4,192,887	65.6	28.9
Tucson	980,263	15.3	16.2
North	313,388	4.9	10.7
West	627,459	9.8	25.0
Southeast	278,020	4.3	11.5
Arizona total	6,392,017	100.0	24.6

Source: Authors' analysis of data from the 2000 and 2010 U.S. decennial censuses.

—*Phoenix:* Maricopa and Pinal counties, coincident with the Phoenix–Mesa–Scottsdale metropolitan area. Metropolitan Phoenix, with a population of 4.1 million, accounts for 66 percent of the state population, and it has grown 29 percent in the last decade, faster than the state as a whole

—*Tucson:* Pima County, coincident with the Tucson metropolitan area, which is the state's second largest, with a population of nearly 1 million. The home of the University of Arizona, it accounts for 15 percent of the state's population. Its growth rate has been 16 percent since 2000, lower than that for Phoenix or the state as a whole, but it continues to attract both immigrants and domestic migrants.

— *North:* Includes Coconino County, which coincides with the Flagstaff metropolitan area, along with Apache and Navajo counties. It contains a substantial Native American population. The North region accounts for only about 5 percent of the state's population; it grew a modest 10.7 percent in 2000–10.

—*West:* Consists of rapidly growing Yavapai County, coincident with the Prescott metropolitan area, as well as equally fast-growing Mohave County, LaPaz County on the western border, and Yuma County, bordering Mexico and coincident with the Yuma metropolitan area. Due to the very rapid growth in the northwest part of this region, which borders both Nevada and California, the West region increased its population by 25 percent between 2000 and 2010. It accounts for nearly 10 percent of the state's population.

—*Southeast:* Consists of Graham, Gila, Greenlee, Cochise, and Santa Cruz counties, all located in the southeastern part of the state bordering New Mexico and Mexico. The region, which accounts for just 4 percent of the state's population, has grown at 11.5 percent since 2000.

Overall, it is the rapidly growing metropolitan Phoenix region that has the greatest potential for affecting statewide election results as well as longer-term political trends in Arizona.

Arizona's Eligible Voters

Arizona's profile is similar to Nevada's in its percentage of minority eligible voters (31 percent) and white, working-age, working-class eligible voters (37 percent). (See tables A-2A and A-2B.) Arizona, however, has slightly higher percentages of white college graduates and white seniors than Nevada does. Another similarity between the two is the very large shift in the minority share of eligible voters in each state; still another similarity is the high share of eligible voters in each state who were born out of state. Both have shown especially fast growth among voters born in California and outside the United States. Still, statewide patterns do not hold in all regions, and there is considerable divergence in the demographic profile of individual regions. (See table B-2A.) For example, both the Phoenix and Tucson metro areas have significantly larger shares of white college graduates than other regions.

The North region, on the other hand, is heavily minority, due to its very large Native American population; most of the "minority white" population is working-class white. The small Southeast region also shows a substantial minority share, mostly composed of Hispanics. In contrast, the West is the "whitest" of all regions, with white seniors making up a quarter of eligible voters and the white working class outnumbering white college graduates almost 5 to 1.

In terms of recent changes in shares of eligible voters, the Phoenix and Tucson metro areas as well as the West region are quite consistent with state-wide patterns, showing a substantial decline in the share of working-class whites and a similar gain for minorities (see table B-2B). In contrast, in the Native American–dominated North region, white seniors showed the highest gains in share in 2000–10. In the smaller Southeast region, white seniors also showed a noticeable gain in share. Overall, due to relatively slow growth rates, white working-class voters are declining as a share of voters in the state as a whole and in every region. It is especially noteworthy that Phoenix and Tucson have seen substantial declines in the white working-class share of the electorate, and both metros now have a large presence of minorities and white, college-graduate eligible voters. These trends are likely to make these areas friendlier territory for Democrats.

Table A-2A. 2010 Share of Eligible Voters by Demographic Segment and Attribute for Selected Mountain West States

Percent

Demographic segment/attribute	Arizona	Colorado	Idaho	Nevada	New Mexico	Utah
Segment						
All minorities	31	22	10	34	52	12
Whites, age 65+	17	13	17	14	12	13
Whites, working-age college graduate	16	27	18	12	13	21
Whites, working-age non–college graduate	37	39	55	40	24	54
Age						
18–29	22	22	22	21	22	29
30–44	24	26	25	26	23	28
45–64	34	36	34	35	36	30
65+	20	15	18	18	19	14
Race/ethnicity						
White	69	78	90	66	48	88
Black	4	4	0	8	2	1
Hispanic	19	14	6	15	39	7
All other	8	4	3	10	11	4
Gender/marital status						
Male	49	50	50	50	49	49
Female, married	25	26	29	24	24	30
Female, not married	26	24	21	26	27	20
Education						
High school graduate or less	37	32	40	43	41	33
Some college	38	34	38	37	35	41
College graduate	25	35	23	20	23	26
Male occupation						
Managerial/professional	36	40	33	29	34	36
All other	64	60	67	71	66	64
Place of birth						
Same state	28	35	40	14	47	57
California	12	7	13	23	6	9
Other Western state	9	8	23	11	9	14
Rest of United States	45	45	22	40	33	16
Abroad	7	5	3	12	5	4

Source: Authors' analysis of data from the 2010 American Community Survey.

Table A-2B. 2000–10 Change in Share of Eligible Voters by Demographic Segment and Attribute for Selected Mountain West States

Percent

Demographic segment/attribute	Arizona	Colorado	Idaho	Nevada	New Mexico	Utah
Segment						
All minorities	5.9	2.9	2.5	10.3	3.9	2.9
Whites, age 65+	−0.1	1.0	1.1	−0.1	0.6	0.4
Whites, working-age college graduate	−0.3	2.0	1.9	−0.1	−0.8	2.6
Whites, working-age non–college graduate	−5.4	−5.9	−5.5	−10.1	−3.6	−5.8
Age						
18–29	0.4	−0.3	−1.0	1.6	0.5	−2.9
30–44	−5.4	−6.9	−4.4	−6.1	−7.0	−1.7
45–64	4.4	5.7	3.9	3.0	4.7	4.0
65+	0.6	1.5	1.5	1.6	1.7	0.6
Race/ethnicity						
White	−5.9	−2.9	−2.5	−10.3	−3.9	−2.9
Black	1.0	0.0	0.0	1.7	0.3	0.1
Hispanic	4.2	2.2	2.4	5.5	3.0	2.2
All other	0.7	0.7	0.1	3.1	0.6	0.6
Gender/marital status						
Male	0.4	0.0	0.0	−0.1	0.7	0.2
Female, married	−3.3	−2.1	−2.2	−3.2	−3.9	−1.5
Female, not married	2.9	2.2	2.2	3.3	3.2	1.4
Education						
High school graduate or less	−4.6	−4.8	−4.5	−4.5	−5.8	−4.2
Some college	2.2	0.3	1.0	1.3	4.3	−0.1
College graduate	2.4	4.6	3.6	3.2	1.5	4.3
Male occupation						
Managerial/professional	2.6	1.9	1.9	3.1	1.3	2.3
All other	−2.6	−1.9	−1.9	−3.1	−1.3	−2.3
Place of birth						
Same state	3.5	1.3	−1.0	2.2	2.1	−0.9
California	2.3	0.9	2.0	2.9	1.3	0.7
Other Western state	−0.1	0.4	1.1	-1.9	−0.1	−0.2
Rest of United States	−7.2	−3.8	−2.5	-6.6	−4.1	−0.4
Abroad	1.5	1.1	0.4	3.3	0.8	0.7

Source: Authors' analysis of data from the 2010 American Community Survey and the 2000 U.S. decennial census.

Table B-2A. 2010 Share of Eligible Voters by Demographic Segment and Attribute for Arizona Regions

Percent

Demographic segment/attribute	Phoenix	Tucson	North	West	Southeast	Total
Segment						
All minorities	29	35	51	23	41	31
Whites, age 65+	16	17	9	26	15	17
Whites, working-age college graduate	17	16	12	8	10	16
Whites, working-age non–college graduate	38	32	28	43	33	37
Age						
18–29	22	23	27	17	22	22
30–44	26	22	23	18	23	24
45–64	33	34	35	36	34	34
65+	18	21	16	29	21	20
Race/ethnicity						
White	71	65	49	77	59	69
Black	5	3	1	1	3	4
Hispanic	18	26	8	18	33	19
All other	6	6	42	4	5	8
Gender/marital status						
Male	49	48	49	50	51	49
Female, married	25	24	21	27	26	25
Female, not married	26	27	30	22	23	26
Education						
High school graduate or less	36	34	45	44	42	37
Some college	38	38	36	40	40	38
College graduate	26	28	19	16	19	25
Male occupation						
Managerial/professional	37	38	28	27	35	36
All other	63	62	72	73	65	64
Place of birth						
Same state	26	30	53	17	34	28
California	11	9	8	22	10	12
Other Western state	8	8	13	12	9	9
Rest of United States	47	45	23	42	36	45
Abroad	7	7	2	7	10	7

Source: Authors' analysis of data from the 2010 American Community Survey.

Table B-2B. 2000–10 Change in Share of Eligible Voters by Demographic Segment and Attribute for Arizona Regions

Percent

Demographic segment/attribute	Phoenix	Tucson	North	West	Southeast	Total state
Segment						
All minorities	6.9	5.7	−0.4	5.9	2.3	5.9
Whites, age 65+	−0.4	0.1	2.3	−0.2	1.0	−0.1
Whites, working-age college graduate	−0.4	−0.5	0.2	−0.8	−0.2	−0.3
Whites, working-age non–college graduate	−6.2	−5.3	−2.2	−4.9	−3.1	−5.4
Age						
18–29	0.3	0.2	0.4	1.1	1.0	0.4
30–44	−5.2	−5.7	−7.8	−5.1	−5.0	−5.4
45–64	4.7	4.5	3.6	3.7	2.5	4.4
65+	0.3	1.0	3.7	0.3	1.5	0.6
Race/ethnicity						
White	−6.9	−5.7	0.4	−5.9	−2.3	−5.9
Black	1.4	0.4	0.0	0.0	0.4	1.0
Hispanic	4.2	4.6	1.6	5.9	2.4	4.2
All other	1.3	0.7	−2.0	0.0	−0.5	0.7
Gender/marital status						
Male	0.1	0.9	0.3	1.0	0.7	0.4
Female, married	−3.2	−2.6	−6.0	−3.3	−3.6	−3.3
Female, not married	3.1	1.7	5.7	2.2	3.0	2.9
Education						
High school graduate or less	−3.7	−4.8	−6.3	−7.7	−7.9	−4.6
Some college	1.5	1.3	4.5	6.1	4.9	2.2
College graduate	2.3	3.4	1.8	1.6	3.1	2.4
Male occupation						
Managerial/professional	2.3	3.2	0.1	3.4	7.4	2.6
All other	−2.3	−3.2	−0.1	−3.4	−7.4	−2.6
Place of birth						
Same state	4.2	4.5	0.3	1.2	1.7	3.5
California	2.4	1.5	0.6	3.5	2.7	2.3
Other Western state	−0.3	0.5	0.9	0.0	0.4	−0.1
Rest of United States	−8.1	−7.3	−2.4	−6.3	−4.4	−7.2
Abroad	1.8	0.8	0.6	1.7	−0.5	1.5

Source: Authors' analysis of data from the 2010 American Community Survey and the 2000 U.S. decennial census.

Table B-3. Arizona Voting in the 2008 Presidential Election for Selected
Demographic Groups

Percent

Group	Democratic	Republican	Democratic-Republican
White	40	59	−19
Black	90	9	81
Hispanic	56	41	15
Other	55	40	15
Men	45	53	−8
Women	45	54	−9
White men	39	60	−21
White women	41	58	−17
High school dropout	46	53	−7
High school graduate	43	56	−13
Some college	48	51	−3
College graduate	43	55	−12
Postgraduate	45	55	−10
White non-college	39	60	−21
White college	41	58	−17
18–29	52	48	4
30–39	48	49	−1
40–49	40	59	−19
50–64	44	54	−10
65+	43	56	−3
All	45	53	−8

Source: Authors' analysis of data from the 2008 National Election Pool Arizona state exit poll.

Demographic Voting Trends in Arizona

We now turn to how Arizonans have been voting in recent elections. Table
B-3 displays some basic exit poll data from the 2008 presidential election.
In 2008, Arizona voted solidly Republican, by 53 to 45 percent. McCain's
8-percentage-point margin in the state was only slightly less than Bush's
10-point margin in 2004, despite the big pro-Democratic shift in neighboring states like Colorado, New Mexico, and Nevada. No doubt that reflected
McCain's status as a favorite son presidential candidate.

According to the exit polls, McCain's victory was based on 59 percent
to 40 percent support from white voters, who were 76 percent of all voters.[2] That more than made up for McCain's 25-point loss (36 to 61 percent)

among minority voters, driven by a 9–90 percent deficit among blacks (4 percent of voters) and by a 41–56 percent deficit among Hispanics (16 percent of voters).

McCain carried male voters by 8 points and female voters by 9 points—essentially no gender gap. However, a slight gender gap can be seen when comparing white men and white women, whom McCain carried by 21 and 17 points, respectively. McCain carried every education group. His best showing was among high school graduates (+13 points) followed by college graduates (+12). He also carried all age groups, except young voters, whom he lost by 4 points. Arizona white working-class voters supported McCain over Obama by 21 points, slightly above the national average.[3] McCain also did well among white college graduates, whom he carried by 17 points, substantially above his nationwide performance.

McCain's support among Arizona's white working-class voters varied by region. Using the exit poll regions, which match fairly closely with the Phoenix and Tucson metro areas but include a third region (Rest of State) that roughly combines our South, North, and West regions, we find that McCain's white working-class advantage was greatest in the Rest of State region (51 points), far less in the Phoenix area (13 points), and even less in the Tucson area (8 points). Among white college graduates, McCain's support was highest (25 points) in the Phoenix area and least in the Tuscon area (only a 1 point advantage).

Geographic Voting Shifts in Arizona

Maps B-3 and B-4 show how voting patterns played out geographically in 2008 and 1988. Each county is color-coded by its margin for the victorious presidential candidate (dark blue for a Democratic victory of 10 points or more; light blue for a Democratic victory of under 10 points; bright red for a Republican victory of 10 points or more; light red for a Republican victory of under 10 points). In addition, our five Arizona regions are marked on each map by heavy black lines.

According to the 2008 map, only two regions had any blue in them: the Tucson metro area and the North region (except for tiny Santa Cruz County, adjacent to Tuscon in the Southeast region, which has a population of around 40,000). As shown in table B-4, these were the only regions that Obama carried in Arizona, by 6 and 10 percentage points, respectively. McCain carried the other three regions, including the Phoenix metro area (bright red) by 11 points. Since the Phoenix metro contributed 64 percent of the statewide vote, it was obviously central to the GOP's 2008 victory. McCain also carried

Table B-4. Democratic Margins in the 1988 and 2008 Presidential Elections for Arizona Regions

Percent

Region	Democratic margin		Change, 1988–2008
	1988	2008	
Phoenix	−30	−11	19
Tuscon	−2	6	8
North	0	10	10
West	−26	−25	1
Southeast	−10	−18	−7

Source: Authors' analysis of 1988 and 2008 Arizona election returns.

the Southeast region (bright red, except for Santa Cruz County) by 18 points and the West (bright red) by 25 points.

As shown in the map for 1988—when Republicans carried the state by 21 points—there were only two blue counties in Arizona, located on the far eastern border and very lightly populated. Thus, while Republicans did dominate the vote in 2008, their dominance was far less than it had been twenty years before.

Map B-5 shows where the political shifts in Arizona took place over the 1988–2008 period. Counties that are dark green had margin shifts toward the Democrats of 10 points or more, light-green counties had margin shifts toward the Democrats of 10 points or less, orange counties had margin shifts toward the Republicans of 10 points or more, and light-yellow counties had margin shifts toward the Republicans of 10 points or less.

The Southeast region, where four of five counties are yellow or orange, is the only region that moved toward the GOP over the time period (by 7 points). The West region split evenly between light-yellow and light-green counties (though the light-green counties are the two metro areas in the region, Yuma and Prescott) and had a modest 1 point move toward the Democrats. The North region, on the other hand, had a strong 10 point move toward the Democrats, led by the dark-green Flagstaff metro area. Much more significant than those shifts is what happened in the two big metro areas, Tuscon and Phoenix. Tucson (light green), which accounted for 17 percent of the Arizona vote, shifted toward the Democrats by 8 points. And the Phoenix metro area (accounting for 64 percent of the statewide vote), led by Maricopa County (dark green), shifted toward the Democrats by an impressive 19 points. Together, the two metro areas represent 81 percent of

Map B-1. Arizona Metropolitan Areas and Regions

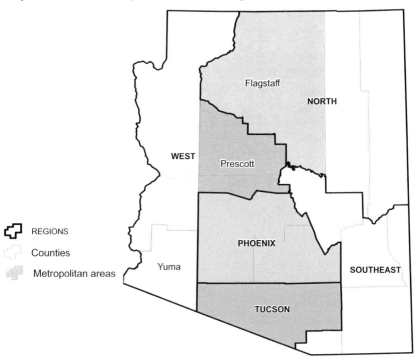

Map B-2. Arizona Population Growth by County, 2000–10

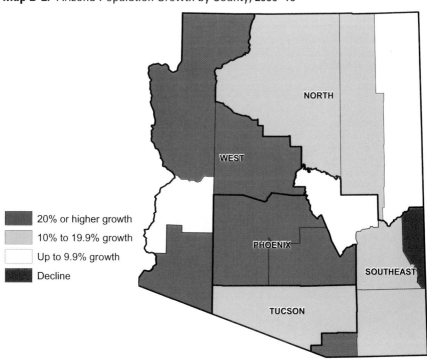

Source: Authors' calculations based on decennial census data.

Map B-3. Arizona County Presidential Voting, 2008

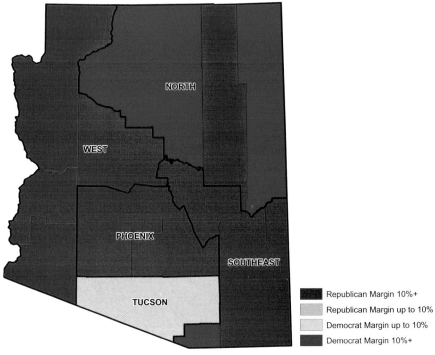

Source: Authors' calculations based on election data.

Map B-4. Arizona County Presidential Voting, 1988

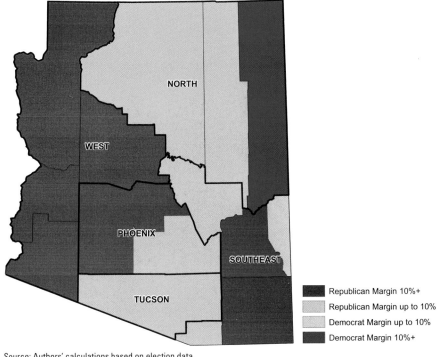

Source: Authors' calculations based on election data.

Map B-5. Arizona County Presidential Voting Change, 1988–2008

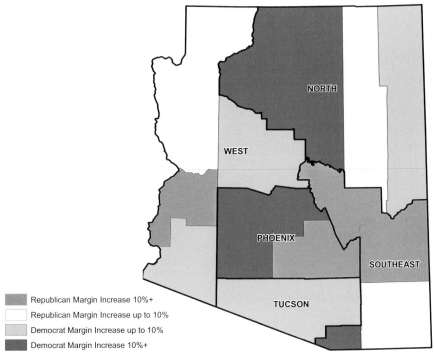

- Republican Margin Increase 10%+
- Republican Margin Increase up to 10%
- Democrat Margin Increase up to 10%
- Democrat Margin Increase 10%+

Source: Authors' calculations based on election data.

Map C-1. Colorado Metropolitan Areas and Regions

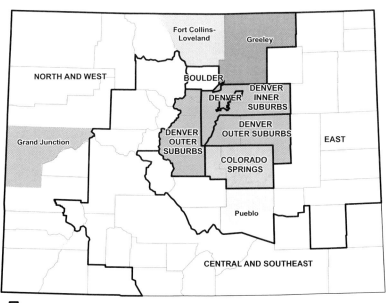

 REGIONS

Counties

Metropolitan areas

Map C-2. Colorado Population Growth by County, 2000–10

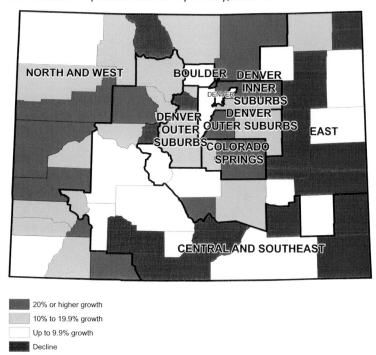

Legend:
- 20% or higher growth
- 10% to 19.9% growth
- Up to 9.9% growth
- Decline

Source: Authors' calculations based on decennial census data.

Map C-3. Colorado County Presidential Voting, 2008

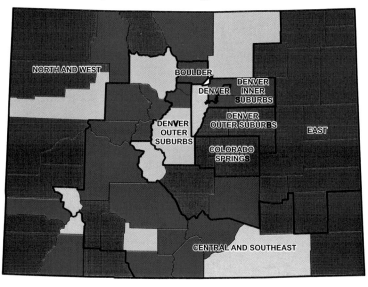

Legend:
- Republican Margin 10%+
- Republican Margin up to 10%
- Democrat Margin up to 10%
- Democrat Margin 10%+

Source: Authors' calculations based on election data.

Map C-4. Colorado County Presidential Voting, 1988

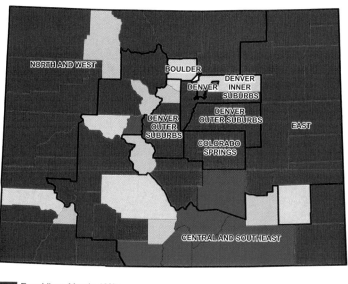

Republican Margin 10%+
Republican Margin up to 10%
Democrat Margin up to 10%
Democrat Margin 10%+

Source: Authors' calculations based on election data.

Map C-5. Colorado County Presidential Voting Change, 1988–2008

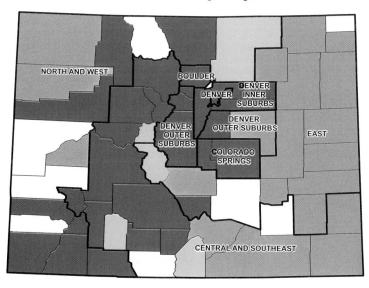

Republican Margin Increase 10%+
Republican Margin Increase up to 10%
Democrat Margin Increase up to 10%
Democrat Margin Increase 10%+

Source: Authors' calculations based on election data.

Map D-1. Idaho Metropolitan Areas and Regions

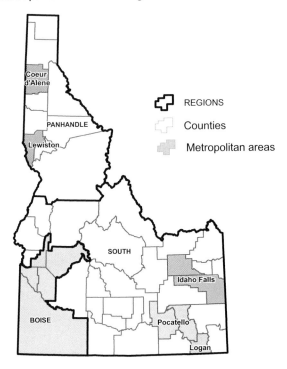

Map D-2. Idaho Population Growth by County, 2000–10

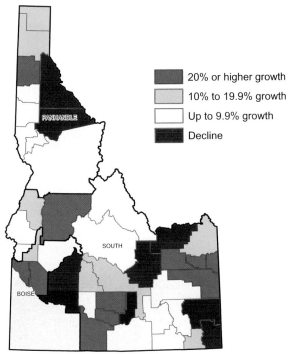

Source: Authors' calculations based on decennial census data.

Map D-3. Idaho County Presidential Voting, 2008

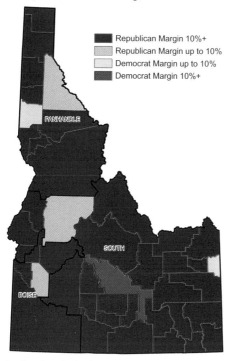

Republican Margin 10%+
Republican Margin up to 10%
Democrat Margin up to 10%
Democrat Margin 10%+

PANHANDLE

SOUTH

BOISE

Source: Authors' calculations based on election data.

Map D-4. Idaho County Presidential Voting, 1988

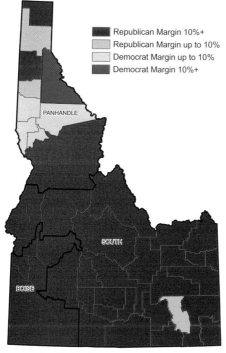

Republican Margin 10%+
Republican Margin up to 10%
Democrat Margin up to 10%
Democrat Margin 10%+

PANHANDLE

SOUTH

BOISE

Source: Authors' calculations based on election data.

Map D-5. Idaho County Presidential Voting Change, 1988–2008

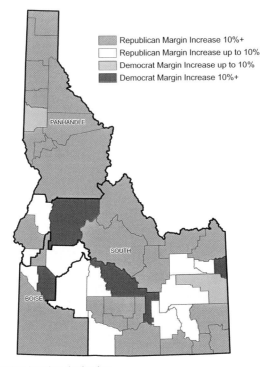

Republican Margin Increase 10%+
Republican Margin Increase up to 10%
Democrat Margin Increase up to 10%
Democrat Margin Increase 10%+

PANHANDLE

SOUTH

BOISE

Source: Authors' calculations based on election data.

Map E-1. Nevada Metropolitan Areas and Regions

RENO

Carson City   RURAL HEARTLAND

REGIONS

Counties

Metropolitan areas

LAS VEGAS

Map E-2. Nevada Population Growth by County, 2000–10

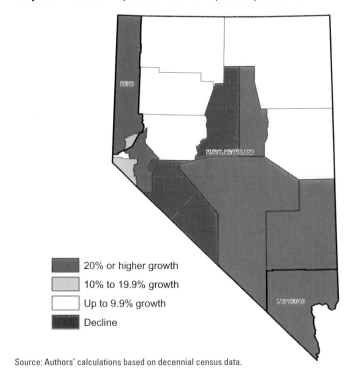

- 20% or higher growth
- 10% to 19.9% growth
- Up to 9.9% growth
- Decline

RENO

RURAL HEARTLAND

LAS VEGAS

Source: Authors' calculations based on decennial census data.

Map E-3. Nevada County Presidential Voting, 2008

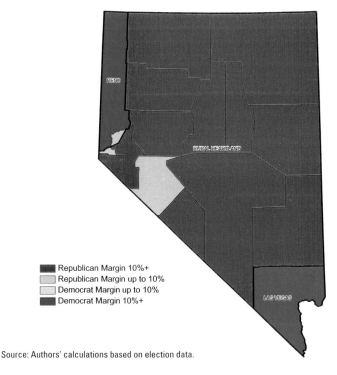

- Republican Margin 10%+
- Republican Margin up to 10%
- Democrat Margin up to 10%
- Democrat Margin 10%+

RENO

RURAL HEARTLAND

LAS VEGAS

Source: Authors' calculations based on election data.

Map E-4. Nevada County Presidential Voting, 1988

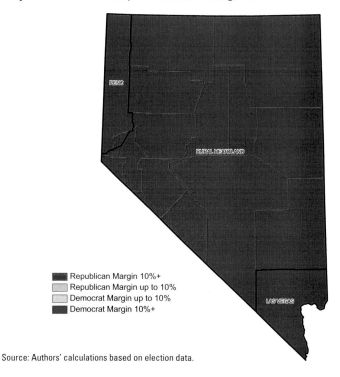

Republican Margin 10%+
Republican Margin up to 10%
Democrat Margin up to 10%
Democrat Margin 10%+

Source: Authors' calculations based on election data.

Map E-5. Nevada County Presidential Voting Change, 1988–2008

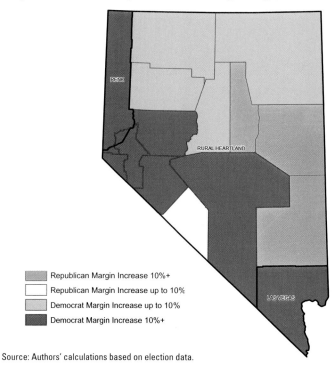

Republican Margin Increase 10%+
Republican Margin Increase up to 10%
Democrat Margin Increase up to 10%
Democrat Margin Increase 10%+

Source: Authors' calculations based on election data.

Map F-1. New Mexico Metropolitan Areas and Regions

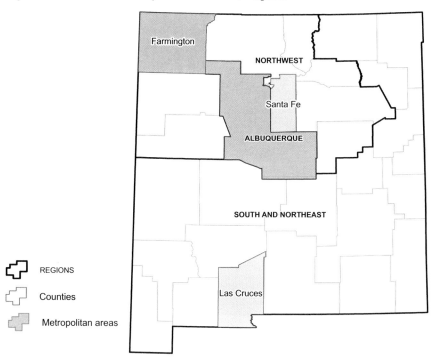

Map F-2. New Mexico Population Growth by County, 2000–10

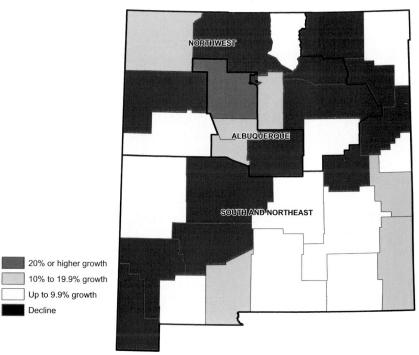

Source: Authors' calculations based on decennial census data.

Map F-3. New Mexico County Presidential Voting, 2008

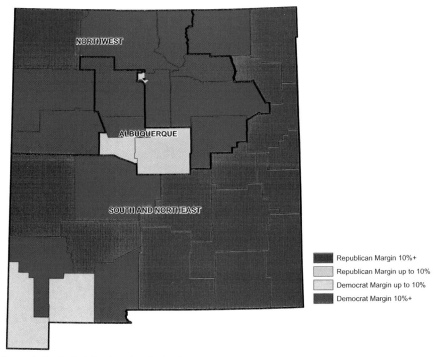

Republican Margin 10%+
Republican Margin up to 10%
Democrat Margin up to 10%
Democrat Margin 10%+

Source: Authors' calculations based on election data.

Map F-4. New Mexico County Presidential Voting, 1988

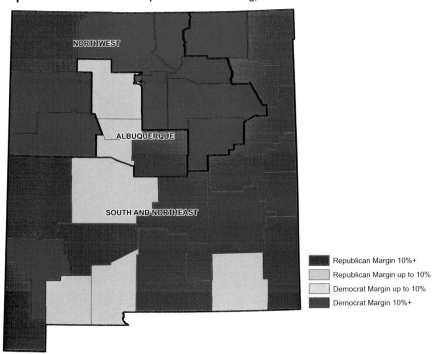

Republican Margin 10%+
Republican Margin up to 10%
Democrat Margin up to 10%
Democrat Margin 10%+

Source: Authors' calculations based on election data.

Map F-5. New Mexico County Presidential Voting Change, 1988–2008

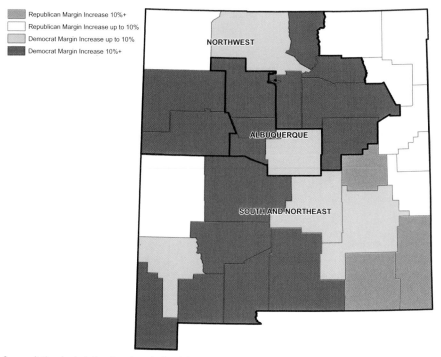

Republican Margin Increase 10%+
Republican Margin Increase up to 10%
Democrat Margin Increase up to 10%
Democrat Margin Increase 10%+

NORTHWEST

ALBUQUERQUE

SOUTH AND NORTHEAST

Source: Authors' calculations based on election data.

Map G-1. Utah Metropolitan Areas and Regions

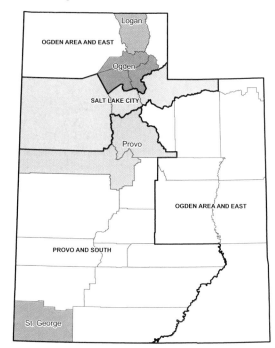

Logan

OGDEN AREA AND EAST

Ogden

SALT LAKE CITY

Provo

OGDEN AREA AND EAST

PROVO AND SOUTH

St. George

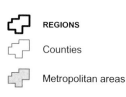

REGIONS

Counties

Metropolitan areas

Map G-2. Utah Population Growth by County, 2000–10

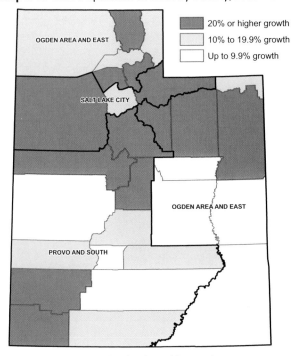

Legend:
- 20% or higher growth
- 10% to 19.9% growth
- Up to 9.9% growth

OGDEN AREA AND EAST

SALT LAKE CITY

OGDEN AREA AND EAST

PROVO AND SOUTH

Source: Authors' calculations based on decennial census data.

Map G-3. Utah County Presidential Voting, 2008

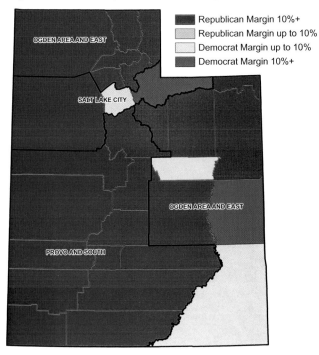

Legend:
- Republican Margin 10%+
- Republican Margin up to 10%
- Democrat Margin up to 10%
- Democrat Margin 10%+

OGDEN AREA AND EAST

SALT LAKE CITY

OGDEN AREA AND EAST

PROVO AND SOUTH

Source: Authors' calculations based on election data.

Map G-4. Utah County Presidential Voting, 1988

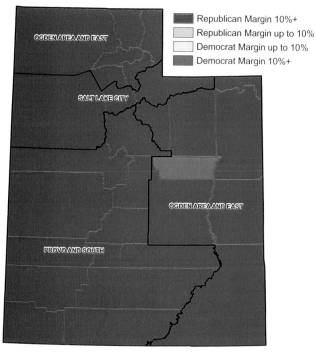

Republican Margin 10%+
Republican Margin up to 10%
Democrat Margin up to 10%
Democrat Margin 10%+

OGDEN AREA AND EAST

SALT LAKE CITY

OGDEN AREA AND EAST

PROVO AND SOUTH

Source: Authors' calculations based on election data.

Map G-5. Utah County Presidential Voting Change, 1988–2008

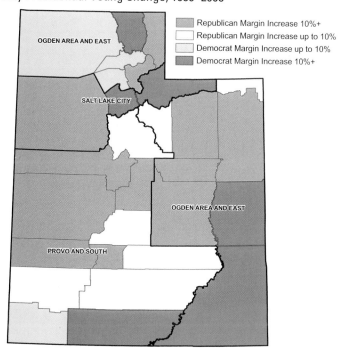

Republican Margin Increase 10%+
Republican Margin Increase up to 10%
Democrat Margin Increase up to 10%
Democrat Margin Increase 10%+

OGDEN AREA AND EAST

SALT LAKE CITY

OGDEN AREA AND EAST

PROVO AND SOUTH

Source: Authors' calculations based on election data.

the statewide vote shifting strongly to very strongly toward the Democrats over the time period.

It is interesting to compare the political shifts in map B-5 to the population growth map (map B-2). The second-slowest-growing region, the Southeast (12 percent growth since 2000), containing the only declining (red) county, is also the only region that has moved toward the GOP since 1988. The fastest-growing region, the very populous Phoenix metro (29 percent growth since 2000), is also the region that has moved the most sharply toward the Democrats.

Better news for the GOP is that the pro-Republican West region is the second-fastest-growing region (25 percent since 2000) and has exhibited only a modest shift toward the Democrats since 1988. However, the West provides only 9 percent of the statewide vote, while the pro-Democratic Tucson metro area, which is also growing fairly fast (16 percent), contributes 17 percent of the Arizona vote and has had a sharper shift toward the Democrats.

Toward the 2012 Election and Beyond

Arizona's population growth patterns appear, on net, to reinforce the general Democratic trend in the state. The continuation of these and other trends, especially in the two big metro areas, could well put the state's red status in doubt over the long term. But the 2010 election was nevertheless a good one for Arizona Republicans, as it generally was in the country as a whole. Republican senator John McCain and Republican governor Jan Brewer were easily reelected. The GOP also won the U.S. House vote in the state by 53–42 percent and took back two of the three congressional seats (the 1st and 5th Districts) that they lost in the 2006–08 elections.

Looking toward 2012, the pickings are likely to be more difficult for the GOP in Arizona. The political environment is likely to be less GOP-friendly in 2012 than in 2010, when Republicans countrywide did so well. The relative turnout of pro-Democratic groups will likely be higher, and the various demographic changes that are making Arizona more Democrat-friendly over time will have had an entire four years to accumulate. More Hispanics, more members of the Millennial generation, and fewer working-class whites could mean a more challenging election for the GOP in 2012 and in subsequent years.

One critical question for 2012 is whether the declining white working class will continue to show its strong support for the Republicans. Any slippage would cut substantially into the GOP's statewide lead. Another group to watch is white college-graduate voters—especially in the Phoenix and Tucson metro areas, where they loom relatively large. These voters are already sympathetic to the Democrats in the Tuscon area; if they move toward the Democrats in the Phoenix area, they could make the 2012 election a hotly contested one.

Also very important is whether the growing Hispanic population continues its relatively high level of support for the GOP. The party's relatively modest 15-point deficit among this group in 2008 made a significant contribution to the GOP's election victory by keeping down the Democratic vote. If that deficit widens substantially in 2012, it could have a big impact, particularly in the Phoenix metro, where 40 percent of eligible voters are Hispanics and their share of voters is growing most rapidly.

The key regions are, obviously, the fast-growing Phoenix and Tucson metro areas; the Phoenix area gets special emphasis because it is growing the fastest and already has the largest share of the Arizona vote (64 percent). If Republican margins continue to decrease in Phoenix and Democratic margins increase in Tucson, that will inevitably make future elections a great deal closer. Also interesting to watch is whether the Flagstaff metro area in the North region continues to move sharply toward the Democrats and whether the two metros in the West, Prescott and Yuma, will continue their modest pro-Democratic trend and possibly weaken the GOP hold on that region.

Colorado

Colorado's demographic history is one of boom or bust, but typically the boom periods have prevailed. It currently has nine electoral college delegates. It did not gain a delegate as a result of the 2010 census, but it enjoyed increases after each of the previous three censuses. The tech boom of the 1990s drew people to Colorado, bringing new vitality to the greater Denver region, and Colorado ranked third in growth among states for that decade. Due in part to the bursting tech bubble and the recent recession, the high level of growth tailed off somewhat, but the state still ranked ninth in population growth for 2000–10.

Regions of Colorado

Colorado's regional scheme for this analysis is depicted in map C-1, with relative size and growth patterns for regions shown in map C-2 and table C-1. These regions are defined as follows:

   — *Denver:* Denver County, coterminous with the city of Denver

   —*Denver Inner Suburbs:* Adams, Arapahoe, and Jefferson counties

   —*Denver Outer Suburbs:* Douglas, Ebert, Park, Gilpin, Clear Creek, and Broomfield counties[4]

Together these first three regions constitute the Denver–Aurora metropolitan area, centered on the city of Denver, which, with a population of 600,000, is also the state's largest county. The inner suburban counties have a collective population of 1.5 million; the outer suburban counties have a combined population just shy of 400,000. Led by rapidly growing Douglas County, Denver's outer suburbs are the most rapidly growing region of the state. Overall, metropolitan Denver accounts for over half (51 percent) of the state's population, with 31 percent of Colorado residents living in Denver's inner suburbs, 8 percent in the outer suburbs, and 12 percent residing in the city of Denver.

—*Boulder:* Boulder County is coincident with the Boulder metropolitan area, the state's third-largest metropolitan area, and is home to the University of Colorado. It accounts for 6 percent of the state's population. Its more controlled growth has been more modest than that of its metropolitan neighbors.

—*Colorado Springs:* The Colorado Springs metropolitan area, with a population of 645,000 the state's second largest, comprises El Paso and Teller counties. The metro area, which accounts for 13 percent of the state's population, has grown by 20 percent since 2000.

—*East:* This region comprises sixteen counties to the east and south of the Denver–Aurora and Colorado Springs metropolitan areas. One small metropolitan area, the Pueblo metropolitan area, consisting of Pueblo County, lies within this spacious if not highly populated region. This region, which contains less than 7 percent of Colorado's population, is growing by a modest 7.6 percent.

—*Southeast and Central:* This region consists of nineteen counties in southern and central Colorado, all small in size and showing at best modest population growth. The region, which does not contain any metropolitan areas, accounts for 5 percent of the state's population.

—*North and West:* This sprawling region consists of sixteen counties in the western and northern part of Colorado and includes the Fort Collins–Loveland metropolitan area—which lies just above Boulder and is the state's fourth-largest metropolitan area—as well as the Greeley metropolitan area to the east[5] and the Grand Junction metropolitan area, which abuts the western boundary of the state. These metropolitan areas are growing at a moderate to rapid pace, with Fort Collins and Greeley located on the northern end of Colorado's Front Range megapolitan area. This briskly growing region contains nearly one-fifth of the state's population.

Looking between and within these regions, it is Colorado's metropolitan area populations, including the suburbs of Denver, that showed the most

Table C-1. 2010 Population and 2000–10 Growth Rate for Colorado Regions

| Region | 2010 population | | Growth rate (percent) |
	Number	Percent of state	
Denver city	600,158	11.9	8.4
Denver inner suburbs	1,548,149	30.8	13.6
Denver outer suburbs	395,175	7.9	50.1
Boulder	294,567	5.9	9.2
Colorado Springs	645,613	12.8	20.1
East	329,790	6.6	7.6
Southeast and Central	243,510	4.8	7.1
North and West	972,234	19.3	24.4
Colorado total	5,029,196	100.0	16.9

Source: Authors' analysis of data from the 2000 and 2010 U.S. decennial censuses.

rapid growth from 2000 to 2010 and within which demographic segments are changing most rapidly.

Colorado's Eligible Voters

We focus first on Colorado's eligible voter population—citizens ages 18 and older—based on results from the 2010 American Community Survey and describe changes since the 2000 census (see tables A-2A and A2-B). More than one-quarter of Colorado's electorate is made up of white, working-age college graduates, a share that is well above their share in the other Mountain West states. Moreover, since 2000, this group along with minorities has been the fastest growing of Colorado's key demographic segments. As discussed later, white college graduates tend to have been on the fence in their past voting preferences, while the white working-class segment was more Republican oriented.

In Colorado as in most other states, the working-age, white working class makes up the largest share, 39 percent, of the key demographic segments. Yet its growth since 2000 has been much smaller than that of the other key segments, leading to a 6-point decline in its share of eligible voters. Colorado groups that grew most rapidly included those with a college education, male managers and professionals, unmarried women, Hispanics, and persons over age 45 (their growth being attributable to the aging of baby boomers). Nearly two-thirds of Colorado's electorate was born out of state, especially in non-Western parts of the United States. The greatest growth since 2000 has occurred among migrants born in California, the rest of the West, and outside the country.

These eligible voter profiles and growth tendencies have played out quite differently across regions (see tables C-2A and C-2B). White, working-age college graduates account for a substantial share of eligible voters in Denver's outer suburbs and in Boulder. It is only in those two regions, as well as the city of Denver, that the share of white college graduates is as high as or higher than that of the white working class. In Colorado's remaining regions, the white, working-age working class constitutes at least 38 percent of eligible voters.

In Denver's outer suburbs and Boulder, minorities make up the smallest segments of eligible voters. The highest minority share by far, 35 percent, is seen in the city of Denver. Almost three-fifths of these are Hispanics, more than a quarter are blacks, and the remainder consists of Asians and other groups. Indeed, the city of Denver is the most diverse of all regions in terms of racial and ethnic groups and other key demographic segments.

Table C-2B shows changes in shares across Colorado regions for our key demographic segments and other demographic groups in 2000–10. All regions showed declines in the share of the white working-class population, but the declines were most pronounced in Denver's inner and outer suburbs, the Boulder metro area, and the North and West regions. All of these regions showed substantial gains in their minority share, especially the Denver inner suburbs, although all but one region in the state (Southeast and Central) showed some gains. For white, working-age college graduates, the greatest gain in share occurred in the city of Denver. In Colorado as a whole as well as in almost every region (with the exception of the Southeast and Central region), the share of eligible voters among both white college graduates and minorities was increasing.

The aging of the baby boomers has increased the share of the 45- to 64-year-old electorate in each of the regions of Colorado. In only a few regions—Denver, Denver's inner suburbs, and Colorado Springs—was there a gain in the share of the young voter population. That could reflect the recent migration of younger families to these areas or the coming of age of large late-teen populations. All regions except the Southeast and Central region showed a decrease in the share of eligible voters who are married women and an increase in unmarried women. Those changes were most pronounced in the outer Denver suburbs and in the East region.

Overall, these shifts indicate that there is substantial demographic change in the fast-gaining parts of Denver's outer suburbs, the Colorado Springs metropolitan area, and the surging North and West regions. The strongest

Table C-2A. 2010 Share of Eligible Voters by Demographic Segment and Attribute for Colorado Regions

Percent

Demographic segment/ attribute	Denver						South-east and	North and	
	City	Inner sub-urbs	Outer sub-urbs	Boulder	Colorado Springs	East	Central	West	Total state
Segment									
All minorities	35	25	11	13	22	25	22	15	22
Whites, age 65+	10	13	11	13	12	17	13	15	13
Whites, working-age college graduate	31	23	42	39	23	15	27	23	27
Whites, working-age non–college graduate	24	39	37	35	43	43	38	47	39
Age									
18–29	27	21	15	30	25	18	20	23	22
30–44	29	27	30	24	26	22	27	24	26
45–64	30	37	43	33	35	39	36	36	36
65+	14	15	12	14	14	20	17	17	15
Race/ethnicity									
White	65	75	89	87	78	75	78	85	78
Black	10	4	1	1	5	3	1	1	4
Hispanic	20	15	6	8	11	21	19	11	14
All other	5	5	4	5	6	2	3	3	4
Gender/marital status									
Male	50	49	49	49	50	50	53	50	50
Female, married	18	27	33	24	28	26	26	27	26
Female, not married	32	24	17	27	22	24	20	23	24
Education									
High school graduate or less	31	35	21	19	29	44	32	33	32
Some college	27	34	28	33	39	35	34	37	34
College graduate	42	31	51	48	31	21	34	30	35
Male occupation									
Managerial/professional	43	36	55	57	40	31	33	35	40
All other	57	64	45	43	60	69	67	65	60
Place of birth									
Same state	37	38	26	24	23	50	38	38	35
California	6	7	8	9	9	5	5	7	7
Other Western state	7	8	8	6	8	8	7	11	8
Rest of United States	43	41	54	56	55	35	47	42	45
Abroad	7	7	5	4	4	2	3	3	5

Source: Authors' analysis of data from the 2010 American Community Survey.

Table C-2B. 2000–10 Change in Share of Eligible Voters by Demographic Segment and Attribute for Colorado Regions

Percent

Demographic segment/ attribute	Denver						South-east and	North and	Total
	City	Inner sub-urbs	Outer sub-urbs	Boulder	Colorado Springs	East	Central	West	state
Segment									
All minorities	1.7	6.0	2.6	3.2	2.5	2.1	−0.1	2.4	2.9
Whites, age 65+	−2.3	1.0	3.3	2.7	0.6	1.4	2.7	1.3	1.0
Whites, working-age college graduate	3.9	1.3	1.4	0.6	0.7	1.7	2.0	2.0	2.0
Whites, working-age non–college graduate	−3.4	−8.4	−7.3	−6.5	−3.9	−5.1	−4.6	−5.7	−5.9
Age									
18–29	2.4	0.2	−2.1	−1.1	0.8	−0.4	−2.3	−1.4	−0.3
30–44	−3.8	−7.1	−9.9	−6.5	−8.0	−8.9	−5.4	−6.1	−6.9
45–64	3.4	4.8	8.4	4.7	6.1	7.8	5.1	5.8	5.7
65+	−2.0	2.1	3.6	2.9	1.1	1.6	2.6	1.7	1.5
Race/ethnicity									
White	−1.7	−6.0	−2.6	−3.2	−2.5	−2.1	0.1	−2.4	−2.9
Black	−0.9	0.7	0.0	0.2	−0.6	0.4	0.3	0.1	0.0
Hispanic	1.8	4.2	1.8	1.6	2.0	2.5	−0.4	2.1	2.2
All other	0.8	1.1	0.8	1.3	1.1	−0.8	0.0	0.2	0.7
Gender/marital status									
Male	0.5	0.2	−0.9	−1.2	0.1	−1.0	1.6	0.1	0.0
Female, married	−2.4	−2.3	−1.7	−0.8	−2.3	−3.9	−1.3	−2.7	−2.1
Female, not married	1.9	2.1	2.6	2.0	2.2	4.9	−0.3	2.6	2.2
Education									
High school graduate or less	−5.5	−3.4	−1.6	−3.1	−5.0	−6.1	−6.1	−6.3	−4.8
Some college	−0.8	−0.3	−3.9	−0.4	1.9	2.0	1.8	1.9	0.3
College graduate	6.3	3.7	5.5	3.5	3.1	4.1	4.3	4.5	4.6
Male occupation									
Managerial/professional	2.8	−0.2	2.8	5.6	1.0	1.6	0.1	2.9	1.9
All other	−2.8	0.2	−2.8	−5.6	−1.0	−1.6	−0.1	−2.9	−1.9
Place of birth									
Same state	1.3	3.2	0.8	1.6	3.5	−1.1	−1.6	0.9	1.3
California	1.1	1.4	0.5	0.6	1.6	0.9	−0.8	0.2	0.9
Other Western state	−0.3	0.3	0.3	−0.3	0.4	1.2	−0.7	1.0	0.4
Rest of United States	−3.8	−6.8	−3.1	−2.7	−5.6	−1.6	2.8	−2.8	−3.8
Abroad	1.7	1.9	1.6	0.8	0.1	0.5	0.3	0.6	1.1

Source: Authors' analysis of data from the 2010 American Community Survey and the 2000 U.S. decennial census.

growth in key demographic segments, both across the state and in these regions, is seen among white college graduates and minorities while the shares of the white working class are declining. That means that the "outer" regions, while far more Republican than the city of Denver or its inner suburbs, are now gaining segments that are less predictably oriented toward the GOP. That is a change with potentially large implications.

Demographic Voting Trends in Colorado

Now we turn to how Coloradans have been voting in recent elections, which is intimately bound up with the changes that have been taking place. The results and analysis not only illuminate how Colorado arrived at its current political coloration but provide some hints to how Colorado's politics might change in the future as demographic and geographic shifts continue.

Table C-3 displays some basic exit poll data from the 2008 presidential election. In 2008, Colorado voted Democratic in the presidential election for the first time since 1992, giving Barack Obama a 9-point victory (54–45 percent). Democrats also added a Senate seat (following Mark Udall's 11-point victory over Bob Schaffer),[6] giving them both of Colorado's Senate seats, and an additional House seat, increasing their advantage in that body to 5-2.

The basic building blocks of Obama's victory can be discerned from the data in the table. Not only did he carry white voters (81 percent of voters, a 5-point decrease from the 2004 election) by 50 percent to 48 percent,[7] he also received very strong support from minority voters, including 85 percent among blacks (4 percent of voters) and 61 percent among Hispanics (13 percent of voters), a 5-point increase over 2004. Obama lost male voters overall by a narrow 1-point margin but carried female voters by 15 points. Among whites, the gender gap was smaller: he lost white men by 2 points and carried white women by 6 points.

Also among whites, Obama carried white college graduates by 56–42 percent, while losing the white working class by 57–42.[8] Obama carried young (18- to 29-year-old) voters by a 2-point margin, a very modest showing compared with his margins for the nation and in most states among this group. He also carried every age group except for seniors, doing best among 50- to 64-year-olds, whom he carried 60–38 percent.

It is instructive to dig a little deeper into the exit poll data to compare the white working-class vote with the white college-graduate vote. As mentioned, Colorado white working-class voters supported McCain over Obama by

Table C-3. Colorado Voting in the 2008 Presidential Election for Selected
Demographic Groups

Percent

Group	Democratic	Republican	Democratic-Republican
White	50	48	2
Black	85	15	70
Hispanic	61	38	23
Men	49	50	−1
Women	56	41	15
White men	48	50	−2
White women	52	46	6
High school dropout	67	29	38
High school graduate	47	52	−5
Some college	47	52	−5
College graduate	52	47	5
Postgraduate	63	34	29
White non-college	42	57	−15
White college	56	42	14
18–29	50	48	2
30–39	54	45	9
40–49	50	49	1
50–64	60	38	22
65+	44	53	−9
All	53	46	7

Source: Authors' analysis of data from the 2008 National Election Pool Colorado state exit poll.

15 points. That was actually slightly less than Obama's nationwide deficit of 18 points among these voters. But among white college graduates, Obama's 14-point advantage was far better than his nationwide results (a 4-point deficit). His strong performance among white college-graduate voters assumes additional importance when compared with Democrat Al Gore's 20-point loss among this group in 2000. Clearly there was a significant warming trend toward Democrats among Colorado's white college graduates.

Obama's deficits among white working-class voters were by no means uniform across Colorado; in fact, there were some dramatic variations. Here we have to use the exit poll regions: Denver–Boulder; Arapahoe–Jefferson (roughly equivalent to the Denver inner suburbs); Central (roughly equivalent to our Central and Southeast region); East; and West (the last two regions are close to our East and North and West regions). Obama actually carried white working-class voters in the Denver–Boulder exit poll region by 10 points and in Arapahoe–Jefferson by 6 points. But in the other three exit poll regions—Central, East, and West—his deficits were respectively 33, 38, and 24 points. Among white college-graduate voters, the pattern was different. Obama carried these voters in every region except the East, where he lost them by 18 points. His strongest performance was in the Denver–Boulder exit poll region, where he carried white college-graduate voters by 51 points.

Geographic Voting Shifts in Colorado

How did the voting patterns that we found play out geographically? Maps C-3 and C-4 reveal this information for 2008 and 1988. Each county is color-coded by its margin for the victorious presidential candidate (dark blue for a Democratic victory of 10 points or more; light blue for a Democratic victory of under 10 points; bright red for a Republican victory of 10 points or more; light red for a Republican victory of under 10 points). In addition, our eight Colorado regions are shown on each map by heavy black lines.

It is striking how much of the 2008 map is colored not only red but bright red, indicating that McCain carried the county by 10 points or more. How, then, did Obama wind up with a relatively easy 9-point victory in the state? The answer lies in the distribution of voters. Denver, which is just one county on the map and a small one, had 272,000 voters in 2008—11 percent of the statewide total—and they went for Obama by 52 points (see table C-4), 12 points more than for John Kerry in 2004. The three counties of the Denver inner suburbs—Adams, Arapahoe, and Jefferson—cast 722,000 votes (30 percent of the statewide total) and gave Obama a 13-point margin, 16 points better than Kerry's performance in the previous election. Just northwest of Jefferson County is Boulder, which accounted for 7 percent of the statewide vote and went for Obama by 46 points. In this relatively small area—Denver, the Denver inner suburbs, and Boulder—lies about half of the statewide vote, which was strongly to overwhelmingly Democratic in 2008.

Obama also did well in the Southeast and Central region, which accounted for 5 percent of the statewide vote, carrying it by 17 points. Combined with his performance in Denver, the Denver inner suburbs, and Boulder, that was enough to give Obama his healthy 9-point victory despite the GOP's domination of the rest of the state: McCain took the Denver outer suburbs by 13 points; the Colorado Springs metro area by 19 points; the North and

Table C-4. Democratic Margins in the 1988 and 2008 Presidential Elections for Colorado Regions

Percent

Region	Democratic margin		Change, 1988–2008
	1988	2008	
Denver city	24	52	29
Denver inner suburbs	−13	13	25
Denver outer suburbs	−32	−13	19
Boulder	8	46	38
Colorado Springs	−41	−19	22
East	2	−8	−10
Central and Southeast	−1	17	19
North and West	−16	−5	11

Source: Authors' analysis of 1988 and 2008 Colorado election returns.

West region, which includes the Fort Collins, Greeley, and Grand Junction metro areas, by 5 points; and the East region by 8 points (only the Pueblo metro area went Democratic in the latter region). But even in these areas, where McCain performed relatively well, there were some remarkable swings toward the Democrats between the 2004 and 2008 elections: 15 points in the Denver outer suburbs, 16 points in the Colorado Springs metro area, and 13 points in the North and West region, including pro-Democratic shifts of 16 and 18 points, respectively, in the Fort Collins and Greeley metro areas.

One of the most obvious visual differences in the map for 1988—when Republicans carried the state by 8 points—is that Democratic strength in the Southeast and Central region is concentrated in the southeast part of that region rather than evenly distributed throughout as it was in 2008. But because the whole region is very lightly populated, the significance of that difference is less than meets the eye. Far more consequential is that in the heavily populated center of the map, Arapahoe and Jefferson counties in the Denver inner suburbs were bright red (heavily Republican) in 1988 but dark blue (heavily Democratic) in 2008 and that Boulder was light blue (weakly Democratic) in 1988 but dark blue in 2008. In addition, Larimer County (Fort Collins), adjacent to Boulder—which is the fourth-largest metro area in the state and cast 7 percent of the statewide vote—was bright red in 1988 but had changed to light blue by 2008.

Map C-5 shows where political shifts took place over the 1988–2008 period. Counties that are dark green had margin shifts toward the Democrats of 10 points or more, light-green counties had margin shifts toward the Democrats of 10 points or less, orange counties had margin shifts toward the Republicans of 10 points or more, and light-yellow counties had margin shifts toward the Republicans of 10 points or less. The most striking thing is how much of the map is orange, indicating a margin shift of 10 points or more toward the Republicans, despite the fact that the state as a whole moved strongly toward the Democrats over the time period (by 17 points). The orange parts of the map include almost all of the East region. Reflecting this pattern, the East region of Colorado, as shown in table C-4, moved toward the GOP by 10 points over this period. But the East represents only 5 percent of the Colorado vote.

All other regions of Colorado moved toward the Democrats over the same time period. For example, in the North and West region, which accounts for 20 percent of the statewide vote, Republican gains in the far west of the state, including in the Grand Junction metro area (Mesa County), were more than counterbalanced by Democratic gains in the southwest corner and, importantly, by strong gains in the Fort Collins metro area (15 points) and a modest gain in the conservative Greeley metro area (4 points), the third- and fourth-largest metro areas in the state respectively. The net result was a healthy 11-point gain for the Democrats over the time period (table C-4).

Gains were larger (19 points) in the Southeast and Central region (6 percent of the vote), where Republican gains in the southeast corner where outweighed by Democratic gains in the central part of the region; in the Colorado Springs metro area (22 points), where Democrats made significant progress in heavily Republican El Paso County; and in the Denver outer suburbs (19 points), where Democrats' significant progress (24 points) in populous, fast-growing Douglas County was far more important than the ground that they lost in neighboring, thinly populated Elbert County.

But the biggest gains for the Democrats in the 1988–2008 period came in the Denver inner suburbs (25 points, with an especially sharp 35-point gain in Arapahoe County), Denver itself (29 points), and Boulder (38 points). As mentioned earlier, these three areas by themselves accounted for about half of the statewide vote.

Further insight into these patterns can be gained by comparing the political shifts in map C-5 to the population growth map (map C-2). One clear pattern is that a good chunk of the counties that gave the GOP margin gains between 1988 and 2008 are also counties that are losing population (colored red in map C-2). On the other hand, almost every county that shifted toward the Democrats is also a growing county. That would appear to be very good news for the Democrats. But there are mitigating factors that support continued GOP strength in the state and could provide the basis for a GOP comeback. To begin, other counties that gave the Republicans margin gains—and there are a fair number—are growing, some quite sharply. In addition, while some of the most important Democratic-shifting counties, like Jefferson, are growing, they are in the slowest growth category (yellow). And Douglas County in the Denver outer suburbs, while it has moved toward the Democrats since 1988, remains strongly Republican (by 17 points in 2008) and is growing phenomenally fast (by 62 percent since 2000). The same could be said of El Paso County in the Colorado Springs metro area: despite moving toward the Democrats, it is still strongly Republican (by 19 points) and growing fast (by 20 percent since 2000).

Toward the 2012 Election and Beyond

Colorado's demographic and geographic trends provide a useful interpretive framework for thinking about the 2012 election and beyond. Since 1988, these trends have been, on net, very good for the Democrats. But that does not mean that all trends benefiting the Democrats will continue indefinitely or, when they do continue, that they will benefit the Democrats to the same extent as in the past. The 2010 election illustrates this uncertainty. Chiefly because of the poor economy, the political environment turned against the Democrats and created an extraordinarily favorable climate for Republican candidates in 2010. While Democrats did manage to hold Michael Bennet's Senate seat and retain the governorship with John Hickenlooper, they nevertheless lost the U.S. House vote in the state by 50-42 and seats in the 3rd and 4th congressional districts.

The 2012 election is also likely to present stern challenges for the Democrats. While Obama will benefit from the ongoing demographic shifts described here—more minority and white college-graduate voters, fewer white working-class voters—his coalition will come under strong pressure from the GOP challenger on several fronts. First, consider that Obama received only 64 percent support from minorities in 2012. That relatively low figure was driven by Obama's 61 percent support among Colorado's Hispanic voters, who made up about two-thirds of the state's minority vote. Clearly, if Hispanic support for Obama falls any lower in 2012 than it did in the 2008 election, that would be a great boon for the GOP. On the other hand, there is certainly room for Obama to increase his support among these voters, which would strengthen his overall position.

White college graduates, the other part of his growth coalition, will be critical in 2012. When Kerry lost the state in 2004, he ran a 2-point deficit among this group, so Obama's 14-point advantage in 2008 was a huge shift. The GOP candidate will seek to shift this group back toward its earlier GOP sympathies or at least to whittle down significantly Obama's 2008 advantage among the group. Then there is the group most sympathetic to the GOP: the white working class. McCain carried these voters by 15 points in 2008, and given the current economic situation, there is certainly room for a sharper swing toward the Republicans in 2012. If the GOP advantage among these voters approaches the 30 points that the party attained nationwide in the 2010 election, it would have an excellent chance of taking the state.

And there are geographic challenges for the Democrats as well. While Democratic fortunes have been bolstered considerably by favorable trends in the growing parts of the state, including its fastest-growing areas, will those trends hold in 2012? Some of these growing areas, such as the Denver outer suburbs and the Colorado Springs metro area, are more Democrat-friendly than they used to be but remain fairly conservative, so the potential for a shift back toward the GOP is very real. And serious Republican gains in these fast-growing parts of Colorado would put a great deal of pressure on Democratic performance in relatively liberal areas such as Denver County, Boulder, and particularly the Denver inner suburbs. It is too early, therefore, to pronounce Colorado a blue state, despite favorable trends for the Democrats and election results like those in 2008. For the time being, color it purple and expect a vigorous contest between the parties in future elections.

Idaho

Idaho continues to be one of the rapidly growing Western states that attract spillover migration from California, the rest of the West, and other parts of the United States. Spurred by its booming high-tech industry of recent decades, Idaho increased its population by more than one-fifth between 2000 and 2010 and was the fourth-fastest-growing state in the country. Yet the 2010 census did not provide for an additional congressional seat, so it continues with 4 electoral college votes in the 2012 election. Idaho has been one of the most Republican-leaning states in the recent history of presidential elections. Only once since 1952 did the state vote for a Democratic candidate—Lyndon Johnson in 1964—and John McCain's margin over Barack Obama in 2008 was 62 percent to 36 percent. Yet as in most of the Mountain West, its demographics are changing, bringing in more minorities and urban

Table D-1. 2010 Population and 2000–10 Growth Rate for Idaho Regions

Region	2010 population		Growth rate (percent)
	Number	Percent of state	
Boise	616,561	39.3	32.6
Panhandle	317,751	20.3	14.0
South	633,270	40.4	15.1
Idaho total	1,567,582	100.0	21.1

Source: Authors' analysis of data from the 2000 and 2010 U.S. decennial censuses.

residents from the West Coast, who could have some impact on politics in parts of the state.

Regions of Idaho

The analysis presented here is based on the following regions, designated in map D-1, and on the population and growth statistics shown in map D-2 and table D-1.

—*Boise:* The Boise metropolitan area comprises five counties that have a combined population of 616,000. The area, which experienced rapid growth (33 percent) over the 2000–10 period, contains 39 percent of the state's population and includes the state's two largest counties, Ada and Canyon, which grew at rates of 30 percent and 44 percent, respectively.

—*Panhandle:* The Panhandle comprises ten counties in the northern part of the state. Its largest and fastest-growing county (27 percent growth), Kootenai, which is conterminous with the Coeur d'Arlene metropolitan area, contains a third of the region's population of 317,000. The region, which as a whole represents about one-fifth of the state's population, grew by a more modest 14 percent.

—*South:* The South region consists of the remaining 29 counties below the Panhandle and east of metropolitan Boise. It contains the third- and fourth-largest metropolitan areas in the state, Idaho Falls and Pocatello. The former, abutting West Yellowstone, Montana, and home to the Idaho National Laboratory, grew by a healthy 28 percent in 2000–10, while Pocatello grew by only 9 percent. The region contains Sun Valley and parts of the Logan, Utah, and Jackson Hole, Wyoming, metropolitan areas that spill over into Idaho. The South region, which contains 40 percent of the state's population, has grown by 15 percent since 2000. Overall the center of growth in this briskly gaining Mountain West state is Boise, although pockets of growth are associated with its smaller metropolitan areas

Idaho's Eligible Voters

A statewide perspective on Idaho's eligible voter population draws from statistics shown in tables A-2A and A-2B. It is clear from this across-states comparison that Idaho has the whitest eligible voter population of all six Mountain West states. Only 10 percent of Idaho's eligible voters are minorities, with Hispanics accounting for 6 percentage points. Among the white blocs, working-class whites dominate all others, at 55 percent of the total, and represent three times Idaho's white college-graduate share. Nonetheless, the white working-class share of the state's population declined by 5 percent in 2000–10 at the same time that the other key segments—minorities, white seniors, and white college graduates—showed gains. Thus the state is somewhat less "white" than in 2000

An examination of voting bloc shares across the three regions within the state (table D-2) shows that Boise has the highest share of minorities (12 percent) and white college graduates (21 percent) and the lowest shares of white seniors and white, working-class eligible voters of any of the three regions. The influx of many new immigrants and out-of-state migrants has increased Boise's minority share noticeably since 2000, making the region somewhat more diverse than the other two regions.

The South region broadly mirrors the state as a whole with respect to its shares of key voting blocs, although its white senior share is slightly larger than the statewide share. Like Boise, it increased its minority share and reduced its white working-class share, though to a lesser extent. The Panhandle region stands out as the greatest demographic outlier in that its minority share of the electorate, which is only 6 percent, has increased by less than 1 percent since 2000. While it has also showed a reduction in its white working-class share since 2000, its 2010 white working-class share of 58 percent was the largest in the three regions. In addition, its white senior share is a hefty 20 percent of the electorate, having risen nearly 2 points since 2000.

In sum, Idaho's largely white electorate is becoming somewhat more diverse in terms of its minority and white, college-graduate voting blocs, although the increase is concentrated mostly in the Boise metropolitan area.

Demographic Voting Trends in Idaho

We now turn to how Idahoans have been voting in recent elections. Table D-3 displays some basic exit poll data from the 2008 presidential election. In

Table D-2. 2010 Share of Eligible Voters and 2000–2010 Change in Share
by Demographic Segment and Attribute for Idaho Regions
Percent

Demographic segment/attribute	2010 share				2000–10 change in share			
	Boise	Pan-handle	South	Total state	Boise	Pan-handle	South	Total state
Segment								
All minorities	12	6	10	10	4.0	0.8	2.0	2.5
Whites, age 65+	14	20	18	17	0.7	1.7	1.3	1.1
Whites, working-age college graduate	21	16	16	18	1.6	1.8	1.7	1.9
Whites, working-age non–college graduate	52	58	57	55	−6.3	−4.4	−5.0	−5.5
Age								
18–29	22	21	24	22	−2.1	−0.1	−0.5	−1.0
30–44	29	22	24	25	−4.7	−5.4	−4.1	−4.4
45–64	34	37	34	34	5.5	3.5	3.0	3.9
65+	16	20	18	18	1.4	2.0	1.5	1.5
Race/ethnicity								
White	88	94	90	90	−4.0	−0.8	−2.0	−2.5
Black	0	0	0	0	0.0	0.0	0.0	0.0
Hispanic	8	2	7	6	3.2	0.8	2.3	2.4
All other	4	4	3	3	0.7	0.0	−0.4	0.1
Gender/marital status								
Male	49	50	49	50	−0.3	0.2	0.1	0.0
Female, married	28	29	31	29	−2.3	−2.4	−1.8	−2.2
Female, not married	22	22	20	21	2.6	2.2	1.7	2.2
Education								
High school graduate or less	36	41	43	40	−4.7	−6.2	−2.9	−4.5
Some college	38	38	37	38	1.2	2.6	−0.1	1.0
College graduate	27	21	20	23	3.6	3.6	3.0	3.6
Male occupation								
Managerial/professional	39	31	29	33	4.3	4.6	−1.9	1.9
All other	61	69	71	67	−4.3	−4.6	1.9	−1.9
Place of birth								
Same state	37	30	47	40	0.3	−1.1	−1.5	−1.0
California	15	15	10	13	2.3	1.4	1.9	2.0
Other Western state	21	29	22	23	−0.2	1.6	2.1	1.1
Rest of United States	24	24	18	22	−3.3	−1.5	−2.8	−2.5
Abroad	3	1	3	3	0.9	−0.4	0.4	0.4

Source: Authors' analysis of data from the 2010 American Community Survey and the 2000 U.S. decennial census.

Table D-3. Idaho Voting in the 2008 Presidential Election for Selected
Demographic Groups

Group	Democratic	Republican	Democratic-Republican
White	33	65	−32
Minority	66	31	35
Men	32	65	−33
Women	41	58	−17
White men	29	68	−39
White women	37	61	−24
High school dropout	45	55	−10
High school graduate	35	63	−28
Some college	34	65	−31
College graduate	41	55	−14
Postgraduate	46	50	−4
White non-college	30	69	−39
White college	40	56	−16
18–29	41	56	−15
30–39	38	59	−21
40–49	32	65	−33
50–64	32	66	−34
65+	36	63	−27
All	36	61	−25

Source: Authors' analysis of data from the 2008 National Election Pool Idaho state exit poll.

2008, Idaho voted overwhelmingly Republican, by 61–36 percent. McCain's victory was based on 65 percent to 33 percent support from white voters, who, according to the exit polls, made up 90 percent of all voters.[9] That more than made up for McCain's 35-point loss (31–66 percent) among minority voters, primarily Hispanic, who were just 10 percent of the electorate (although they had increased by 2 points since 2004).[10]

McCain carried male voters by 33 points and female voters by 17 points, resulting in quite a large gender gap; basically the same gap was seen between white men and white women, whom McCain carried by 39 and 24 points, respectively. He carried every education group. His best education group was high school graduates, which he carried by 28 points, followed by those with some college (+31 points). His worst was postgraduates (+4). He also carried all age groups, though his margin was smallest among young voters (+15). Idaho white working-class voters supported McCain over Obama by

39 points, far above the national average.[11] He did much less well among white college graduates, carrying them by 16 points, though that was still substantially above his nationwide performance.

McCain's support among white working-class voters varied by region. Using the exit poll regions, which match up fairly closely with the Boise and Panhandle areas but include two other regions, Southwest and Southeast, which we combine in our South region, we find that McCain's white working-class advantage is greatest in the Southwest/Southeast regions (48 points), less in the Panhandle (36 points), and less still in the Boise area (21 points), though still substantial. Among white college graduates, McCain's support was highest in the Southwest/Southeast regions, where he led by 30 points, and least in the Boise area (only a 6-point advantage).

Geographic Voting Shifts in Idaho

Maps D-3 and D-4 show how voting patterns played out geographically in 2008 and 1988. Each county is color-coded by its margin for the victorious presidential candidate (dark blue for a Democratic victory of 10 points or more; light blue for a Democratic victory of under 10 points; bright red for a Republican victory of 10 points or more; light red for a Republican victory of under 10 points). In addition, our three Idaho regions are shown on each map by heavy black lines.

Almost all of the 2008 map is red, and much of it is bright red. Only three counties are blue: Latah County (Moscow micropolitan area) in the Panhandle and Blaine and Teton counties in the South (the latter is part of the Jackson,Wyoming/Idaho micropolitan area). Together, these counties contain a population of only about 70,000, so it is hardly surprising that McCain carried all three Idaho regions (table D-4): the South, which he carried by 38 points, the Panhandle (+21 points), and the Boise metro area (+15).

The 1988 map is very similar to the 2008 map in terms of the relative amount of red and blue. Indeed, the GOP's statewide margin in the 1988 election (26 points) was virtually identical to that in 2008 (25 points). But there are still some interesting differences to be noted in the location of blue counties. In 1988, there were five blue counties, all in the Panhandle, and no blue counties in the South, whereas in 2008 there was just one blue county in the Panhandle and two in the South.

Map D-5 shows where political shifts in Idaho took place over the 1988–2008 period. Counties that are dark green had margin shifts toward the Democrats of 10 points or more, light-green counties had margin shifts

Table D-4. Democratic Margins in the 1988 and 2008 Presidential Election for Idaho Regions

Percent

Region	Democratic margin		Change, 1988–2008
	1988	2008	
Boise	−29	−15	14
Panhandle	−4	−21	−18
South	−35	−38	−3

Source: Authors' analysis of 1988 and 2008 Idaho election returns.

toward the Democrats of 10 points or less, orange counties had margin shifts toward the Republicans of 10 points or more, and light-yellow counties had margin shifts toward the Republicans of 10 points or less.

The Panhandle has only one green county, Latah, showing a shift to the Democrats. The other 1988 blue counties near it in the Panhandle are all orange on this map, indicating strong shifts to the GOP. Consistent with that pattern, this region shows the strongest pro-Republican trend over the period: 18 points. The South has mostly light-yellow and orange counties, but it also has four green counties: Teton, Bonneville (Idaho Falls metro area), Blaine, and Valley (near the Boise metro area). These changes netted a modest 3-point move to the GOP. The other green county on the map, Ada, in the Boise metro area, is the most important. Ada, the central county of the Boise metro, by itself accounts for 27 percent of the statewide vote. Ada experienced a strong 22-point pro-Democratic shift between 1988 and 2008, driving the Boise metro as a whole (40 percent of the statewide vote) 14 points toward the Democrats over the period.

It is interesting to compare the political shifts in map D-5 to the population growth map (map D-2). The good news for Democrats is that all of the Democratic-shifting counties are growing counties and four of the six are very rapidly growing counties (dark green on the population growth map): Teton (69 percent since 2000); Ada (30 percent); Bonneville (26 percent); and Valley (29 percent). Moreover, all the declining (red) counties are Republican trending. On the other hand, there are plenty of growing counties that are Republican trending, and they dominate the South and Panhandle regions and damp down the effect of fast-growing, Democratic-trending Ada in the Boise metro area. Thus, growth patterns have been having a decidedly mixed effect on Idaho politics.

Toward the 2012 Election and Beyond

The 2010 election was a very good one for the GOP in Idaho, with easy reelection victories for Republican senator Mike Crapo and Republican governor Butch Otter. It also took back the congressional seat (for the 1st District) that it lost in the 2008 election. The electoral situation could be somewhat more difficult for the GOP in Idaho in 2012, though it is highly unlikely that Republican control of the state would be truly threatened. The political environment is likely to be less GOP friendly in 2012 than in 2010, and various Democrat-friendly demographic changes will have had four full years to accumulate: more minorities, more college-educated whites (who are significantly less pro-Republican than their working-class counterparts), and fewer working-class whites could make the Democrats more competitive than they were in either 2008 or 2010.

One critical question for 2012 and beyond is whether the declining white working class will continue its strong support for the Republicans. Other trends to watch are whether white college-graduate voters, whose share of voters is actually increasing (especially in the Boise metro), start to move toward the Democrats in a substantial way and whether the growing minority population continues its high level of support for the Democrats. The key region to watch over the long term is the relatively populous and fast-growing Boise metro area. If Republican margins continue to decrease in this area, that could make the state more competitive over time. Also interesting to watch is whether the Panhandle continues its sharp trend toward the GOP. It is this trend that has kept Idaho in a rough political equilibrium, despite the pro-Democratic trend in the Boise metro area.

Nevada

Nevada remains the fastest-growing state in the country despite experiencing a historic slump in recent years as a consequence of the housing melt-down.[12] The Silver State grew 66 percent in the 1990s and another 35 percent in 2000–10. Historically it has been a major magnet for tourists, retirees, in-migrating residents from other states, especially California, and immigrants from abroad. And while its number of electoral college votes is small—only 6 votes, based on the 2010 census, up from 5 after the 2000 census and up from the minimum of 3 after the 1980 census—the state is hotly contested politically. Republican George W. Bush won the 2000 and 2004 elections by small margins (by 2 and 4 percentage points, respectively), but Democrat Barack Obama won by 12 points in 2008.

Table E-1. 2010 Population and 2000–10 Growth Rate for Nevada Regions

Region	2010 population		Growth rate (percent)
	Number	Percent of state	
Las Vegas	1,951,269	72.3	41.8
Reno	425,417	15.8	24.1
Rural Heartland	323,865	12.0	15.8
Nevada total	2,700,551	100.0	35.1

Source: Authors' analysis of data from the 2000 and 2010 U.S. decennial censuses.

Regions of Nevada

The analysis presented here is based on the following regions, designated in map E-1, and on the population and growth statistics shown in map E-2 and table E-1.

—*Las Vegas:* Clark County, which is coterminous with the Las Vegas–Paradise metropolitan area, has a population of 1.9 million. It is the fastest-growing major metropolitan area in the United States, with 86 percent growth in the 1990s and another 42 percent in 2000–10. Las Vegas contains almost three-quarters (72 percent) of Nevada's population, thus dominating the state's electorate.

—*Reno:* Washoe and Storey counties are coincident with the Reno–Sparks metropolitan area. At 425,000, the population of this region is less than a quarter of that of Las Vegas; it constitutes 16 percent of the state's population. The region has grown at a robust rate of 24 percent since 2000.

—*Rural Heartland:* This region consists of the remaining fourteen counties in Nevada. One of them, Carson City County, represents the third, much smaller metropolitan area in the state. Most of the additional counties are either declining in population or growing modestly, with two exceptions: Nye County, which lies adjacent to Las Vegas, and Lyon County, which lies adjacent to the Reno and Carson City metro areas. The Rural Heartland contains 12 percent of Nevada's population; it registered overall growth of 16 percent in 2000–10.

Even considering the recent slowdown, Nevada's rapid growth since 2000, especially in Las Vegas and to a lesser degree in Reno, suggests that a good deal of turnover has taken place in the electorate over the last several election cycles.

Nevada's Eligible Voters

A statewide perspective on Nevada's eligible voter population draws from statistics shown in tables A-2A and A-2B. The ratio of white, working-class eligible voters to white, college-graduate eligible voters—the former outnumber the latter by more than 3 to 1—is higher in Nevada than in all other Mountain West states. More than three in ten of its eligible voters are minorities, including 15 percent Hispanic, 8 percent black, and 10 percent Asian and other. Much of this "rainbow" includes spillover populations of Hispanics, blacks, and Asians from California as well as immigrants to the state, who are predominantly Mexicans and others from Latin America. In fact, only about 14 percent of Nevada's eligible voters were born in the state; more than one-fifth were born in California, 12 percent were foreign born, and 40 percent were born in a non-Western state. Nevada has the most non-native electorate of all the states. Nevada's electorate is less well educated than that of the Mountain West's most educated state, Colorado: 42 percent of Nevadans have at most a high school education while 32 percent of Coloradans do, and only 20 percent hold a bachelor's degree (35 percent of Coloradans do). That is consistent with Nevada's industrial makeup, which includes a high proportion of low-skill service industries.

The state's demographic profile shows a high number of working-class whites, but eligible voter gains among minorities in 2000–10 are changing its profile. The minority share of the state's voters increased by 10 percentage points, from 24 percent in 2000 to 34 percent in 2010. Hispanics accounted for half of that gain, and in 2010 they accounted for 15 percent of the state's eligible voters. White seniors and college graduates maintained nearly the same statewide share of eligible voters (14 and 12 percent, respectively). It is the white working-class share that took the greatest plunge, from 50 percent in 2000 to a still substantial 40 percent in 2010. These trends are especially strong in the Las Vegas region (see table E-2), where minorities (40 percent) have now overtaken working-class whites (36 percent) as a share of the electorate. White seniors and college graduates each now constitute a 12 percent share in the region.

That contrasts with the Rural Heartland, where working-class whites outnumber minorities by 3 to 1 and white college graduates by 5 to 1. White seniors and Hispanic-dominated minorities gained in share, while the shares of both the white working class and white college graduates declined. This region remains the whitest of the state's three regions. We see a noticeably

Table E-2. 2010 Share of Eligible Voters and 2000–10 Change in Share by Demographic Segment and Attribute for Nevada Regions

Percent

Demographic segment/ attribute	2010 share				2000–10 change in share			
	Las Vegas	Reno	Rural Heart- land	State total	Las Vegas	Reno	Rural Heart- land	Total state
Segment								
All minorities	40	23	17	34	12.2	6.2	2.7	10.3
Whites, age 65+	12	15	20	14	−0.9	0.8	3.7	−0.1
Whites, working-age college graduate	12	18	10	12	0.1	0.5	−1.3	−0.1
Whites, working-age non–college graduate	36	45	53	40	−11.4	−7.4	−5.2	−10.1
Age								
18–29	22	23	17	21	1.5	2.4	0.5	1.6
30–44	27	24	22	26	−5.1	−8.3	−9.1	−6.1
45–64	34	37	39	35	2.7	4.1	3.7	3.0
65+	17	17	23	18	0.9	1.8	4.9	1.6
Race/ethnicity								
White	60	77	83	66	−12.2	−6.2	−2.7	−10.3
Black	11	2	1	8	2.1	0.2	−0.2	1.7
Hispanic	17	12	10	15	6.2	4.2	2.8	5.5
All other	12	8	6	10	3.9	1.8	0.1	3.1
Gender/marital status								
Male	50	50	51	50	0.0	−0.5	0.1	−0.1
Female, married	23	24	27	24	−3.4	−1.9	−3.3	−3.2
Female, not married	27	25	22	26	3.4	2.4	3.2	3.3
Education								
High school graduate or less	44	35	49	43	−5.2	−5.2	−0.6	−4.5
Some college	36	40	36	37	1.4	2.5	−0.3	1.3
College graduate	20	25	16	20	3.8	2.7	0.9	3.2
Male occupation								
Managerial/professional	28	34	25	29	4.0	3.8	−1.2	3.1
All other	72	66	75	71	−4.0	−3.8	1.2	−3.1
Place of birth								
Same state	11	21	18	14	2.0	4.5	1.9	2.2
California	21	30	29	23	4.3	−0.4	2.3	2.9
Other Western state	10	11	17	11	−2.0	−1.0	−1.3	−1.9
Rest of United States	44	30	31	40	−8.4	−4.4	−3.1	−6.6
Abroad	14	8	5	12	4.2	1.3	0.2	3.3

Source: Authors' analysis of data from the 2010 American Community Survey and the 2000 U.S. decennial census.

Table E-3. Nevada Voting in the 2008 Presidential Election for Selected Demographic Groups

Percent

Group	Democratic	Republican	Democratic-Republican
White	45	53	−8
Black	94	5	89
Hispanic	76	22	54
Men	51	47	4
Women	59	38	21
White men	40	57	−17
White women	49	48	1
High school dropout	70	26	44
High school graduate	60	40	20
Some college	56	42	14
College graduate	50	48	2
Postgraduate	56	42	14
White non-college	43	54	−11
White college	47	51	−4
18–29	67	31	36
30–39	63	35	28
40–49	54	44	10
50–64	52	46	6
65+	42	55	−13
All	55	43	12

Source: Authors' analysis of data from 2008 National Election Pool Nevada state exit poll.

higher share of white college graduates in the Reno region than in Las Vegas or the Rural Heartland, with a modest half-percentage-point gain in share since 2000. But the greatest gain in share in Reno (up 6 points), just as in Las Vegas (up 12 points), is shown for minorities, many of California origin. Clearly the most dynamic part of the state in terms of overall population growth and potential shifts in key voting blocs lies in the Las Vegas metropolitan area. Any such shifts and the preferences of the state's many new voters will have a great impact on Nevada's electoral choices in the next election and beyond.

Demographic Voting Trends in Nevada

We now turn to how Nevadans have been voting in recent elections. Table E-3 displays some basic exit poll data from the 2008 presidential election.

In 2008, Nevada voted Democratic in the presidential election for the first time since 1996, giving Barack Obama a 12-point victory (55–43 percent). The basic building blocks of Obama's victory can be discerned from the data in the table. While he lost white voters (69 percent of voters, an 8-point decrease from the 2004 election), by 45 to 53 percent, [13] that deficit was more than counterbalanced by very strong support from minority voters, including 94 percent among blacks (10 percent of voters, a 1-point increase over 2004) and 76 percent among Hispanics (16 percent of voters, a 6-point increase over 2004).

White voters have been steadily shrinking as a proportion of Nevada's voters. According to exit polls, they declined from 88 to 77 percent between 1988 and 2008, while minority voters overall increased from 12 to 31 percent and Hispanic voters tripled from 5 to 16 percent. Hispanic voters have also increased their support for the Democrats over the time period, going from a 9-point deficit to a 54-point advantage. Obama won male voters overall by a narrow 4-point margin but carried female voters by 21 points. Among whites, Obama lost men by 17 points but carried women by a point.

His strongest age group was 18- to 29-year-olds, whom he carried by 36 points (67-31 percent). He also carried 30- to 39-year-olds by 28 points. The only age group that he failed to carry was seniors, losing them by 13 points. Breaking down white voters, Obama lost the white working class by 11 points, while running only a 4-point deficit among white college graduates.

In the 1988 election, Bush senior ran 29 points ahead of Dukakis among Nevada's white working-class voters, so Obama's 11-point deficit in 2008 represents a considerable swing to the Democrats among those voters. So does Obama's 4-point deficit among white college graduates, since Dukakis lost those voters by 24 points in 1988. Moreover, according to the exit polls white working-class voters have been shrinking as a proportion of voters, declining by 24 points since 1988, while the share of white college graduates has increased by 4 points.

Obama's support among white working-class voters in Nevada varied substantially by region. Using the exit poll regions, which match up almost exactly with our Nevada regions (the exit poll Reno region does not include Storey county, which we include in our Reno region since it is part of the Reno metro area), we find that Obama carried white working-class voters in the Reno region by 7 points and lost them by a modest 8 points in the Las Vegas region. But in the vast Rural Heartland, Obama's deficit was an astronomical 32 points among these voters—close to the deficit that Democrats suffered in that region in 1988. In Las Vegas and Reno, however, Obama's 2008 performance represents large Democratic gains of 18 and 31 points, respectively, in white working-class support.

Support of white college graduates for Obama also varied by region of Nevada. In the Las Vegas region, he carried these voters by 4 points; in the Reno area, he lost them by 8 points; and in the Rural Heartland, he lost them by an overwhelming 36 points. The figure for the Las Vegas region represents a very substantial 28-point shift toward the Democrats among white college graduates since 1988.

Geographic Voting Shifts in Nevada

Maps E-3 and E-4 show how voting patterns played out geographically in 2008 and 1988. Each county is color-coded by its margin for the victorious presidential candidate (dark blue for a Democratic victory of 10 points or more; light blue for a Democratic victory of under 10 points; bright red for a Republican victory of 10 points or more; light red for a Republican victory of under 10 points). In addition, our three Nevada regions are shown on each map by heavy black lines.

The 2008 map is almost all red and much of it bright red, indicating McCain carried the county by 10 points or more. That is because McCain carried every county in the vast rural heartland of Nevada, frequently by gaudy margins. In fact, as shown in table E-4, he carried the entire region by 19 percentage points. But the other two regions tell quite a different story. Obama carried the Reno region, which accounted for 19 percent of the vote in 2008, by 12 points, including Washoe County by 13 points (hence its dark blue color). And the Las Vegas region (Clark County), with 67 percent of the vote, went for Obama by 19 points (also dark blue). Together, these two geographically small regions cast 86 percent of Nevada's vote and made the state an easy Obama victory despite the sea of red that covers most of the map. The map for 1988, when Republicans carried the state by 21 points, is quite different. In that election there was no county, not even Clark or Washoe, that did not give the GOP at least a 10-point margin. Hence the map's uniform bright red color.

Map E-5 shows where political shifts in Nevada took place over the 1988–2008 period. Counties that are dark green had margin shifts toward the Democrats of 10 points or more, light-green counties had margin shifts toward the Democrats of 10 points or less, orange counties had margin shifts

Table E-4. Democratic Margins in the 1988 and 2008 Presidential Elections for Nevada Regions

Percent

Region	Democratic margin		Change, 1988–2008
	1988	2008	
Las Vegas	−16	19	35
Reno	−22	12	35
Rural Heartland	−34	−19	15

Source: Authors' analysis of 1988 and 2008 Nevada election returns.

toward the Republicans of 10 points or more, and light-yellow counties had margin shifts toward the Republicans of 10 points or less.

The Rural Heartland counties are a mixed story. On one hand, there is a surprising amount of dark green, including Nye County, the mushroom-shaped county adjacent to Clark County, and a cluster of other counties in southwestern Nevada. In addition, a good chunk of northern Nevada is light green, indicating a pro-Democratic shift of under 10 points. On the other hand, a cluster of eastern Nevada counties above Clark County are orange and another county, Esmeralda, is light yellow. These changes, however, resulted in a fairly substantial 15-point move toward the Democrats over the time period. The Reno and Las Vegas regions tell a less ambiguous story, with both regions shifting toward the Democrats by a massive 35 points over the time period. Given that these regions contribute 86 percent of the state's vote, these shifts are clearly of great significance.

It is interesting to compare the political shifts in map E-5 to the population growth map (map E-2). The only declining (red) and relatively slow growth (yellow) counties in Nevada are located in the Rural Heartland, where the GOP has remained relatively strong and the shift toward the Democrats has been relatively modest. Overall, this region's growth rate is the lowest of the three (16 percent since 2000). But Las Vegas, where Democratic support is currently the highest and where there has been a massive pro-Democratic shift, shows by far the highest growth rate of the three regions (42 percent). And Reno, where the shift has been equally big, is also growing strongly (24 percent). Given these population growth patterns, it seems doubtful that the GOP can remain competitive in the state without pushing back the pro-Democratic trends in the state's two big metropolitan areas. The Rural Heartland's population is simply too small and growing too slowly to provide an adequate bulwark against a Democratic advance.

Toward the 2012 Election and Beyond

The demographic and geographic trends in Nevada have generally been very favorable to the Democrats, as exemplified by the results of the 2008 election. But there is no guarantee that the pro-Democratic shifts will continue in the future. In 2010, despite Democrat Harry Reid's surprisingly comfortable hold on his Senate seat, Republicans won the U.S. House popular vote by 51–45 percent, picked up a House seat, and kept the governorship, with Brian Sandoval.

The 2012 election is also likely to present serious challenges for the Democrats. While Obama will benefit from the ongoing demographic shifts described here—more minority voters, fewer white working-class voters—his coalition will come under strong pressure from the GOP challenger on several fronts. First, McCain carried white working-class voters by 11 points in 2008. Given the economic situation, a sharper swing toward Republicans in 2012 seems a distinct possibility. With a strong enough surge in support among this group, the GOP could carry the state. Geographically, the key challenge for the Democrats is holding their large advantage in the Las Vegas metropolitan area. This area dominates the state, so a significant move back toward the GOP in this area could flip the state back to the Republicans. These possibilities suggest that it is too early to pronounce Nevada a blue state on the basis of Obama's easy victory in 2008. Instead, we color it purple and expect tough, close elections for many years to come.

New Mexico

After Idaho, New Mexico is the next-smallest of the Mountain West states discussed in this volume, having 5 electoral college votes; however, it has proved to be significant in national politics. It was in New Mexico that Al Gore beat George W. Bush by only 365 votes in 2000 and that Bush beat John Kerry by a margin of 1 percent in 2004. Barack Obama's 2008 margin of 15 points was far more comfortable, but history shows that results can change. Although New Mexico is growing more slowly than the other Mountain West states, it is still growing faster than the United States as a whole and it continues to attract migrants from other parts of the United States as well as from abroad.

Regions of New Mexico

The regions for New Mexico are displayed in map F-1, with supporting information about their population size and growth in map F-2 and table F-1.

—*Albuquerque:* The Albuquerque metropolitan area, which has a population of 858,000, comprises Bernalillo (location of the city of Albuquerque), Sandoval, Valencia, and Torrance counties. It represents 43 percent of the state's population, and with 22 percent growth in 2000–10, it is by far the most rapidly growing region of the state. Suburban Sandoval county is, at 45 percent growth, the growth leader in this metro area.

—*Northwest:* This region consists of nine counties in the northwestern part of the state, including Santa Fe County, which is coincident with the Santa Fe metropolitan area, and San Juan County, which is coincident with the Farmington metropolitan area. The small Santa Fe and Farmington metropolitan areas are the fastest-growing areas (at 11 percent and 14 percent growth respectively since 2000) within the region, which includes five small counties that are declining in population. Overall the Northwest region, which includes about one-fourth of the state's population, registered a modest 6.4 percent growth rate in 2000–10.

—*South and Northeast:* This region, which consists of twenty counties in the southern and northeastern part of the state, including Doña Ana County, is coincident with the Las Cruces metropolitan area. The latter, with just under 20 percent growth in 2000–10, is the fastest-growing county in the region, which includes ten counties declining in population. The South and Northeast region makes up about a third of the state's population; it has grown a modest 8.6 percent since 2000.

Demographic shifts within the state are likely to have their greatest political impact in the relatively rapidly growing Albuquerque metropolitan area and in the adjacent Santa Fe metropolitan area in the Northwest region, metropolitan areas that have been trending Democratic in a state that has been heavily contested in past presidential races.

New Mexico's Eligible Voters

It can be argued that New Mexico is the most multiethnic of all states on the U.S. mainland. Its eligible voter population is 48 percent white. Among its minority population, which reflects its long history of Spanish influence and its Native American heritage, the largely native-born Hispanic population constitutes 39 percentage points of eligible voters and American Indians nearly 10 points. The latter are heavily concentrated in the Northwest region. The state's much smaller Asian and black populations are concentrated in the Albuquerque metro area. (See eligible voter statistics in tables A-2A and A-2B.)

Despite the overriding importance of minorities in New Mexico, nearly a quarter of its eligible voters are working-class whites, almost twice the share

Table F-1. 2010 Population and 2000–10 Growth Rate for New Mexico Regions

Region	2010 population		Growth rate (percent)
	Number	Percent of state	
Albuquerque	887,077	43.1	21.6
Northwest	503,013	24.4	6.4
South and Northeast	669,089	32.5	8.6
New Mexico total	2,059,179	100.0	13.2

Source: Authors' analysis of data from the 2000 and 2010 U.S. decennial censuses.

(13 percent) of white college graduates. The small number of white college graduates reflects the state's generally low education levels and high poverty, and there is a lack of workers in skilled services. Over the 2000–10 period, the state showed a 3.6-point decline in the share of eligible voters who were white working class, but there was a 3.9-point gain in the share of minorities, led by Hispanics. Thus minorities have been increasing their share of New Mexico's electorate, while that of the white working class has been declining.

The above shifts are apparent to some degree in each region (see table F-2), with declines in the share of white, working-class eligible voters in each of the three regions, especially Albuquerque and the South and Northeast. The South and Northeast region also showed the greatest gains in the share of Hispanic-dominated minority eligible voters. Albuquerque can be seen as a swing region in presidential elections as it lies between the more Democratic-leaning Northwest and the more Republican-leaning South and Northeast region. So the shift away from working-class whites, coupled with the relatively strong growth among minorities and a relatively high share of white college graduates (Albuquerque is the most highly educated of the state's three regions) may help push Albuquerque in a more Democratic direction.

The Northwest region has the largest share of minorities, especially native Americans. Only 40 percent of its electorate is white. The fact that it contains upscale communities like Santa Fe and Taos intermingled with Native American pueblos gives it a varied mix of key demographic segments, including the white working class (19 percent) and white college graduates (12 percent). Like the state as a whole, it has shown declines in its share of the white working class and gains in minorities, which may make this already Democratic-leaning region even more so. Similar trends are also at work in the South and Northeast region, especially the decline in the white working class. But because this region's white working-class share is the highest in the

Table F-2. 2010 Share of Eligible Voters and 2000–10 Change in Share by Demographic Segment and Attribute for New Mexico Regions

Percent

Demographic segment/ attribute	2010 share				2000–10 change in share			
	Albu- querque	North- west	South and North- east	State total	Albu- querque	North- west	South and North- east	Total state
Segment								
All minorities	50	60	47	52	5.2	0.4	5.2	3.9
Whites, age 65+	11	9	14	12	0.1	2.1	–0.1	0.6
Whites, working-age college graduate	16	12	9	13	–0.8	–1.0	–0.9	–0.8
Whites, working-age non–college graduate	23	19	30	24	–4.5	–1.5	–4.1	–3.6
Age								
18–29	22	20	23	22	0.8	–0.9	1.3	0.5
30–44	24	23	22	23	–7.2	–7.7	–6.4	–7.0
45–64	36	39	34	36	5.1	5.1	4.1	4.7
65+	17	18	21	19	1.3	3.5	1.0	1.7
Race/ethnicity								
White	50	40	53	48	–5.2	–0.4	–5.2	–3.9
Black	3	0	2	2	0.2	0.0	0.5	0.3
Hispanic	39	34	41	39	4.2	–1.5	4.8	3.0
All other	9	26	3	11	0.8	1.9	–0.2	0.6
Gender/marital status								
Male	48	48	50	49	0.4	0.8	0.9	0.7
Female, married	24	22	26	24	–3.2	–5.0	–3.8	–3.9
Female, not married	28	30	25	27	2.8	4.2	2.9	3.2
Education								
High school graduate or less	36	45	45	41	–5.6	–4.0	–6.9	–5.8
Some college	36	32	37	35	3.8	3.2	5.6	4.3
College graduate	28	23	17	23	1.8	0.8	1.2	1.5
Male occupation								
Managerial/professional	40	33	28	34	3.5	–1.4	–0.1	1.3
All other	60	67	72	66	–3.5	1.4	0.1	–1.3
Place of birth								
Same state	46	57	42	47	2.7	2.2	1.7	2.1
California	7	6	6	6	1.0	1.2	1.9	1.3
Other Western state	9	11	7	9	0.4	–2.1	0.9	–0.1
Rest of United States	34	24	38	33	–5.3	–1.8	–4.8	–4.1
Abroad	5	3	6	5	1.2	0.6	0.3	0.8

Source: Authors' analysis of data from the 2010 American Community Survey and the 2000 decennial census.

Table F-3. New Mexico Voting in the 2008 Presidential Election
for Selected Demographic Groups

Percent

Group	Democratic	Republican	Democratic-Republican
White	42	56	−14
Black	86	11	75
Hispanic	69	30	39
Other	79	20	59
Men	54	45	9
Women	59	39	20
White men	43	55	−12
White women	41	57	−16
High school dropout	73	26	47
High school graduate	58	41	17
Some college	58	40	18
College graduate	56	43	13
Postgraduate	55	43	12
White non-college	36	62	−26
White college	49	49	0
18–29	71	27	44
30–39	51	48	3
40–49	50	49	1
50–64	57	42	15
65+	53	46	7
All	57	42	15

Source: Authors' analysis of data from the 2008 National Election Pool state exit poll.

state (30 percent) and its white college-graduate segment the lowest (9 percent), it is likely to retain its relative pro-Republican orientation.

Demographic Voting Trends in New Mexico

We now turn to how New Mexicans have been voting in recent elections. Table F-3 displays some basic exit poll data from the 2008 presidential election. In 2008, New Mexico voted Democratic in the presidential election by a fairly wide margin (57-42). The Democrats also picked up a Senate seat and two House seats in that election.[14]

Obama's 15-point margin stands in stark contrast to the tiny margins received by Bush in 2004 (.79 percent) and by Gore in 2000 (.06 percent).

Obama did lose white voters in New Mexico (half of all voters)[15] by 56–42 percent but carried Hispanic voters (41 percent of voters) by 69–30 percent (his 39-point margin was 27 points larger than Kerry's in 2004) and carried primarily Native American "other race" voters (7 percent of the electorate) by an even more overwhelming 79–20 percent. That pattern of support produced his easy victory.

White voters have been shrinking significantly as a proportion of New Mexico's voters over time. According to exit polls, they declined from 61 to 50 percent between 1988 and 2008, while minority voters increased from 39 to 50 percent, driven by a 13-point increase in Hispanics (blacks actually declined slightly as a percent of voters over the time period). Obama carried male voters by 9 points and female voters by 20 points. Interestingly, a reverse gender gap is observed in comparing white men and white women: Obama lost white men by 12 points but white women by 16 points. Obama carried all education groups, with an especially large advantage among high school dropouts (47 points). He also carried all age groups, though he did the best by far among young voters: he carried 18- to 29-year-olds by 44 points (71–27 percent). New Mexico's white working-class voters supported McCain over Obama by 26 points, significantly above McCain's nationwide margin of 18 points. But among white college graduates, Obama and McCain tied, 49–49 percent—a better showing for Obama than his nationwide 4-point deficit.

In the 1988 election, Bush senior ran 39 points ahead of Dukakis among New Mexico's white working-class voters, so Obama's 26-point deficit in 2008 actually represents some improvement for Democrats among those voters. So does Obama's 49–49 percent tie among white college graduates, since Dukakis lost those voters by 14 points in 1988. Even more significant, according to the exit polls, conservatively inclined white working-class voters have been shrinking as a proportion of voters, declining by 17 points, while the share of white college graduates has increased by 5 points.

Obama's support among New Mexico's white working-class voters varies strongly by region. Using the exit poll regions, which match up very closely with our New Mexico regions, we find that Obama's white working-class deficit in the Albuquerque metro area was 31 points and that it was even greater in the South and East region (38 points). In the Northwest region, however, it was just 4 points. White college-graduate support showed even more variation: Obama lost white college-graduate voters by 14 points in the Albuquerque metro area and by 34 points in the South and East region,

Table F-4. Democratic Margins in 1988 and 2008 Presidential Elections
for New Mexico Regions

Percent

Region	Democratic margin		Change, 1988–2008
	1988	2008	
Albuquerque	−8	18	26
Northwest	13	33	20
South and Northeast	−12	−2	10

Source: Authors' analysis of 1988 and 2008 New Mexico election returns.

but he carried this group by an overwhelming 42 points in the Northwest
region. The last result represents an amazing 56-point swing toward the
Democrats since 1988.

Geographic Voting Shifts in New Mexico

Maps F-3 and F-4 show how voting patterns played out geographically in
2008 and 1988. Each county is color-coded by its margin for the victorious
presidential candidate (dark blue for a Democratic victory of 10 points or
more; light blue for a Democratic victory of under 10 points; bright red for a
Republican victory of 10 points or more; light red for a Republican victory of
under 10 points). In addition, our three New Mexico regions are shown on
each map by heavy black lines.

The 2008 map reveals a fair amount of bright red, indicating that McCain
carried the county by 10 points or more. But almost all of that is in the large
South and Northeast region, the only region that McCain managed to carry
(though by a meager 2 points; see table F-4). This region contributes about
a third of New Mexico's vote, a share that is down 7 points since the 1988
election. But the other two regions tell quite a different story. Obama carried
the Northwest region, which accounts for 22 percent of the vote and includes
the Santa Fe and Farmington metro areas, by 33 points. And he carried the
Albuquerque metro, which contributes 46 percent of the statewide vote, by
18 points (up 5 points since the 1988 election).

There is substantially more blue in the 2008 map than the 1988 map, consistent with the pro-Democratic shift over the time period (20 points). But
the most significant difference does not stand out visually, so we flag it here:
the shift of populous (but small in land area) Bernalillo County in the Albuquerque metro area from light red in 1988 to dark blue in 2008. Since that

county alone accounts for about a third of the New Mexico vote, that is an extremely important shift.

Map F-5 shows where the political shifts in New Mexico took place over the 1988–2008 period. Counties that are dark green had margin shifts toward the Democrats of 10 points or more, light-green counties had margin shifts toward the Democrats of 10 points or less, orange counties had margin shifts toward the Republicans of 10 points or more, and light-yellow counties had margin shifts toward the Republicans of 10 points or less.

The far eastern part of the South and Northeast region is all orange or light yellow, indicating shifts toward the GOP. Most of the rest of the region is at least light green, reflecting shifts toward the Democrats. These changes netted a 10-point shift toward the Democrats since 1988. The Northwest region has only one GOP-shifting area, the light-yellow Farmington metro area in the northwest corner of the map. That was more than counterbalanced by pro-Democratic shifts in the rest of the region, including in the dark-green Santa Fe metro area (9 percent of the statewide vote), 26 points more Democratic since 1988, and in dark-green Taos (a 28-point shift toward the Democrats). The net result in the Northwest was a 20-point shift toward the Democrats over the time period. The biggest shift, however, was in the Albuquerque metro area. As the map shows, the area is entirely green, with three of the four counties dark green. The latter include populous Bernalillo County, which experienced a massive 30-point Democratic shift that fueled the 26-point shift in the Albuquerque metro area as a whole over the time period.

It is interesting to compare the political shifts in map F-5 to the population growth map (map F-2). The South and Northeast region is made up of almost all declining (red) and relatively slow growth (yellow) counties. The most important exception is the Las Cruces metro area, which is light green, reflecting its growth rate of just under 20 percent, the fastest growth rate in the region. Interestingly, Las Cruces is also the one part of the vast South and Northeast region that has shifted more than 20 points toward the Democrats since 1988 (22 points). The other exceptions are two lightly populated counties—Lea and Roosevelt—in the southeast corner of the region that have grown by 17 and 10 percent respectively since 2000 but have shifted toward the Republicans by 13 and 2 points respectively since 1988.

The Democratic-shifting Northwest region shows a similar pattern of declining or slow-growth counties, but again there are a few exceptions. One is the Santa Fe metro area, colored light green and growing at 11 percent. Santa Fe is also the part of the Northwest region (along with Taos) that has shifted most sharply to the Democrats since 1988. The other exception is the Farmington metro area, colored yellow and growing at 14 percent, which has shifted toward the Republicans, though by only a modest 3 points, since 1988.

The Albuquerque metro area contains only one county that has grown at a rate of less than 10 percent since 2000. As a result, its overall growth rate (21.6 percent) is far higher than that of the other two New Mexico regions (6 percent for the Northwest and 8.6 percent for the South and Northeast). That means that the area that has shifted most sharply toward the Democrats since 1988 is also the area that is now growing fastest. These population growth patterns, combined with the pattern of pro-Democratic shifts in the state, would not appear to favor the GOP. Republicans will therefore be hard-pressed to remain competitive in the state over the long term without substantially pushing back some of the pro-Democratic trends, especially in the Albuquerque metro area.

Toward the 2012 Election and Beyond

Despite the many trends that favor the Democrats, it would be wrong to count the GOP out in New Mexico. In 2010, Republicans picked up the governorship with Susana Martinez and also gained a U.S. House seat. The 2012 election is also likely to be challenging for the Democrats. While Obama will benefit from the ongoing demographic shifts described here—chiefly the increase in minority voters and the decline in white working-class voters— his coalition could be vulnerable in several ways. First, consider the minority vote, especially Hispanics. While Obama received support from 69 percent of Hispanic voters in 2008, Kerry did quite a bit worse in 2004, carrying only 56 percent. A slide back to Kerry's level in 2012 would greatly aid GOP efforts to carry the state, as would a fade in Hispanic turnout. Similarly, the preferences of white college graduates, the other part of Obama's growth coalition, will be critical in 2012. If the Republicans can move these voters away from an even split while holding on to the GOP's overwhelming support among the white working class, they will be in a good position to take the state.

Geographically, Obama's New Mexico coalition is a classic "coalition of the ascendant" centered in the relatively fast-growing and populous Albuquerque metro area. If Republicans can significantly compress Obama's margin in this area in 2012 while running up their margin in the conservative-leaning South and Northeast region, they certainly have a shot at taking back the state despite Obama's wide victory margin in 2008. It would be premature, therefore, to pronounce New Mexico a blue state based on the 2008 election results and favorable long-term trends for the Democrats. The color purple is more appropriate for the state, as is the expectation of vigorously contested elections down the road.

Utah

The Beehive State is part of the phalanx of fast-growing Mountain West states, ranking third nationally over the 2000–10 period with a growth rate of 24 percent. It continues to draw migrants from California and other Western states as well as an increasing number of new immigrants. It also registers the highest fertility rate (average number of lifetime births per woman) of the fifty states. Utah's attraction has a lot to do with its high-tech industries, natural amenities, and for much of the last decade, affordable housing (relative to California's). As a result of its growth, as recorded in the 2010 census, it earned an extra electoral college vote, bringing its new total to 6 votes.

Utah shares with Idaho a strong Republican leaning. The last Democratic presidential candidate to win the state was Lyndon Johnson in 1964. In 2008, John McCain bested Barack Obama by 63 percent to 34 percent. But its gains in new out-of-state populations could change that margin in the future, even if its status as a red state seems unlikely to change.

Regions of Utah

The analysis presented here is based on the following regions, designated in map G-1, and on the population and growth statistics shown in map G-2 and table G-1.

—*Salt Lake City:* The Salt Lake City metropolitan area, with a population of 1.12 million, comprises three counties and accounts for 41 percent of the state's population. With a 16 percent growth rate, it is the least fast growing of the three regions, though the outer counties included in the metro area, westernmost Toole County and easternmost Summit County, grew by 43 percent and 22 percent respectively.

—*Ogden and East:* This region, to the north and east of the Salt Lake City metropolitan area, contains fourteen counties. It also includes the Ogden metropolitan area, which with a population of 547,000 is the state's second-largest metro, and the smaller Logan metropolitan area, home of Utah State University. Both of these metropolitan areas, located just north of Salt Lake City, grew by 23 percent. Wasatch County, which abuts the Salt Lake City metropolitan area to the east, is the state's fastest-growing county, at 55 percent. The region, which accounts for 30 percent of the state's population, has grown 23 percent since 2000.

Table G-1. 2010 Population and 2000–10 Growth Rate for Utah Regions

Region	2010 population		Growth rate (percent)
	Number	Percent of state	
Salt Lake City	1,124,197	40.7	16.0
Ogden and East	844,213	30.5	22.6
Provo and South	795,475	28.8	38.2
Utah total	2,763,885	100.0	23.8

Source: Authors' analysis of data from the 2000 and 2010 U.S. decennial censuses.

—*Provo and South:* This region comprises twelve counties in the south and west quadrant of Utah, including the Provo metropolitan area. It is the fastest growing of the three regions, with a 2000–10 growth rate of 38 percent, and it accounts for 29 percent of the state's population. The Provo metropolitan area, which has a population of 526,000, is the third largest in the state, but it is growing at a more rapid rate (40 percent) than either Salt Lake City (16 percent) or Ogden (24 percent). Growing even more rapidly is the smaller St. George metropolitan area, bordering Nevada on the state's southwest corner, which had a 2000–10 growth rate of 53 percent.

In sum, Utah remains a rapidly growing state, especially in the suburbs of Salt Lake City, the Provo metropolitan area, and the southwest corner bordering Nevada. The extent to which its growth may change the political orientation of the state depends on the makeup of new eligible voters in each of these fast-growing areas.

Utah's Eligible Voters

Statewide statistics on Utah's eligible voter population are shown in tables A-2A and A-2B. Utah's eligible voter profile looks most like that of Idaho among the other five states in the Mountain West region with respect to racial/ethnic makeup. With only 12 percent of its electorate identifying as minorities, Utah is only slightly less white than Idaho. Its largely white electorate differs in other respects, however. Because of the state's younger age structure, the share of white seniors, which is 17 percent in Idaho, is only 13 percent in Utah. In addition, the state's higher education attainment shows up in the 21 percent share of the electorate claimed by white college graduates—a share that is higher in Utah than in all of the Mountain West states except Colorado. Yet, as in Idaho, working-class whites constitute a hefty share (54 percent) of eligible voters. The 2000–10 shifts in the state's key voting blocs—positive for minorities and negative for working-class whites—mirror those of Idaho in relative magnitude.

Of Utah's three regions, it is clear that metropolitan Salt Lake City has the most diverse electorate and the greatest increase in diversity (table G-2). Fully 16 percent of Salt Lake City's eligible voters are minorities (9 percentage points of which are Hispanic) while the corresponding figures are 11 percent in Ogden and East and 8 percent in Provo and South. In addition, the 2000–10 gains in minority share were much larger for Salt Lake City. The Salt Lake City metro area also stands out in that it has a lower share of working-class whites than either of the other two regions. Nonetheless, all three regions have relatively high shares of white college graduates—similar to that of the state as a whole—reflecting Utah's high educational attainment.

On most measures, the Ogden and East region lies between the Salt Lake City region and the Provo and South region. The Provo and South region not only is the whitest but also has the highest share of working-class whites and young adults. More than a third of the region's electorate is aged 18 to 29; in the other two regions, the share is 26 to 27 percent. Yet as indicated above, this region accounts for nearly 30 percent of the state's population, and it is the fastest growing of the three. The fact that its electorate is demographically distinct from the other two—less diverse and more working class—may impact future voting trends in the state.

Demographic Voting Trends in Utah

We now turn to how Utah has been voting in recent elections. Table G-3 displays some basic exit poll data from the 2008 presidential election. In 2008, Utah voted overwhelmingly Republican, by 63–34 percent. According to the exit polls, McCain's victory was based on 66 percent to 31 percent support from white voters, who constituted 90 percent of all voters.[16] That more than made up for McCain's 23-point loss (36–59 percent) among minority voters—primarily Hispanic—who were just 10 percent of the electorate (up a point since 2004).[17]

McCain carried male and female voters by identical 29-point margins, so there was no gender gap whatsoever. The same lack of a gender gap can be seen when comparing white men and white women, whom McCain carried by 35 and 33 points, respectively. McCain also carried every education group but high school dropouts (a very small group of voters—less than 2 percent). His best education group was college graduates (those with a four-year degree only), whom he carried by 39 points. He also carried all age groups,

Table G-2. 2010 Share of Eligible Voters and 2000–10 Change in Share by Demographic Segment and Attribute for Utah Regions

Percent

Demographic segment/ attribute	2010 share				2000–10 change in share			
	Salt Lake City	Ogden and East	Provo and South	Total	Salt Lake City	Ogden	Provo	Total
Segment								
All minorities	16	11	8	12	4.1	1.9	2.9	2.9
Whites, age 65+	12	13	14	13	0.3	0.3	0.5	0.4
Whites, working-age college graduate	21	20	20	21	1.6	3.4	3.0	2.6
Whites, working-age non–college graduate	51	55	57	54	−6.1	−5.7	−6.4	−5.8
Age								
18–29	27	26	34	29	−2.2	−3.3	−4.4	−2.9
30–44	28	28	26	28	−2.6	−2.5	0.9	−1.7
45–64	31	31	26	30	4.2	5.2	2.9	4.0
65+	13	14	15	14	0.6	0.6	0.5	0.6
Race/ethnicity								
White	84	89	92	88	−4.1	−1.9	−2.9	−2.9
Black	1	1	0	1	0.3	−0.1	0.0	0.1
Hispanic	9	7	4	7	2.9	1.9	1.8	2.2
All other	6	4	3	4	0.9	0.2	1.0	0.6
Gender/marital status								
Male	50	50	49	49	0.0	0.1	0.7	0.2
Female, married	27	32	31	30	−2.7	−0.8	−1.1	−1.5
Female, not married	23	18	20	20	2.7	0.8	0.4	1.4
Education								
High school graduate or less	35	34	29	33	−2.9	−5.7	−3.9	−4.2
Some college	38	40	46	41	−0.1	0.3	−1.2	−0.1
College graduate	27	26	26	26	3.0	5.4	5.1	4.3
Male occupation								
Managerial/professional	36	35	39	36	1.2	2.7	3.3	2.3
All other	64	65	61	64	−1.2	−2.7	−3.3	−2.3
Place of birth								
Same State	58	59	54	57	0.1	−0.2	−3.0	−0.9
California	8	8	12	9	0.0	1.1	0.9	0.7
Other Western state	12	13	16	14	0.0	−1.9	1.4	−0.2
Rest of United States	16	17	15	16	−1.6	0.6	0.2	−0.4
Abroad	6	3	3	4	1.5	0.3	0.5	0.7

Source: Authors' analysis of data from the 2010 American Community Survey and the 2000 U.S. decennial census.

Table G-3. Utah Voting in the 2008 Presidential Election for Selected Demographic Groups

Group	Democratic	Republican	Democratic-Republican
White	31	66	−35
Minority	59	36	23
Men	34	63	−29
Women	34	63	−29
White men	31	66	−35
White women	32	65	−33
High school dropout	78	22	56
High school graduate	41	57	−16
Some college	34	62	−28
College graduate	29	68	−39
Postgraduate	30	68	−38
White non-college	34	63	−29
White college	28	69	−41
18–29	33	62	−29
30–39	46	51	−5
40–49	32	66	−34
50–64	28	68	−40
65+	30	70	−40
All	34	63	−29

Source: Authors' analysis of data from the 2008 National Election Pool Utah state exit poll.

including young voters. His margin was largest among those 50 to 64 years of age (40 points) and 65+.

Utah white working-class voters supported McCain over Obama by 29 points, far above the national average.[18] He did even better among white college graduates, carrying them by 41 points—far, far above his nationwide performance and in startling contrast to his performance among white college graduates in other states, who tended to be more liberal than their white working-class counterparts. McCain's support among Utah's white working-class voters varied dramatically by region. Using the exit poll regions, whose Salt Lake, Ogden and East, and Provo and West regions match up roughly with our Salt Lake, Ogden and East, and Provo and South regions, we find that McCain's white working-class advantage was overwhelming in the Ogden and East (58 percentage points) and Provo and West (+68 points) regions but far less in the Salt Lake area (only +15). A similar pattern can be seen for white college graduates. McCain's support among this group was overwhelming in the Ogden and East (+29) and Provo and West (+60) regions but far, far less in the Salt Lake City area—in fact, Obama, not McCain, carried white college graduates there, albeit by a modest 4-point margin.

Geographic Voting Shifts in Utah

Maps G-3 and G-4 show how voting patterns played out geographically in 2008 and 1988. Each county is color-coded by its margin for the victorious presidential candidate (dark blue for a Democratic victory of 10 points or more; light blue for a Democratic victory of under 10 points; bright red for a Republican victory of 10 points or more; light red for a Republican victory of under 10 points). In addition, our three Utah regions are shown on each map by heavy black lines.

Almost all of the 2008 map is red, and the overwhelmingly majority of that is bright red. Only three counties are blue—Grand, on the eastern border of the Ogden and East region, and Salt Lake and Summit in the Salt Lake City metro area—and they account for 42 percent of the statewide vote. Of these three counties, Salt Lake is by far the most important, accounting by itself for 38 percent of the Utah vote.

However, since Obama's margin in Salt Lake County was exceedingly modest (under 1 percent) and since he lost the other county (Tooele) in the metro area by 30 points, McCain was still able to carry the Salt Lake City metro area as a whole by a point. And McCain really cleaned up in the sea of red constituting the other two regions of the state: he carried Ogden and East by 40 points and Provo and South by an astonishing 57 points. It is worth noting that the Provo metro area had the largest margin for McCain of any metro area in the United States with a quarter-million or more in population. The 1988 map shows some important differences. There is only one blue county, lightly populated Carbon (under 20,000 in population). Every other county in the state is bright red, indicating strong GOP support, including Salt Lake and the other counties in the Salt Lake City metro area.

Map G-5 shows where the political shifts in Utah took place over the 1988–2008 period. Counties that are dark green had margin shifts toward the Democrats of 10 points or more, light-green counties had margin shifts toward the Democrats of 10 points or less, orange counties had margin shifts toward the Republicans of 10 points or more, and light-yellow counties had margin shifts toward the Republicans of 10 points or less.

The Salt Lake City metro area has two dark-green counties, including Salt Lake, which moved toward the Democrats by 20 points. The other county,

Table G-4. Democratic Margins in the 1988 and 2008 Presidential Elections
for Utah Regions
Percent

Region	Democratic margin		Change, 1988–2008
	1988	2008	
Salt Lake City	–20	–1	19
Provo and South	–55	–57	–3
Ogden and East	–40	–40	0

Source: Authors' analysis of 1988 and 2008 Utah election returns.

Tooele, is orange, indicating a sharp move in the other direction. The net
results of these trends in the Salt Lake City metro was a substantial 19-point
move toward the Democrats over the time period (table G-4). The Ogden
and East region has a mix of Democratic- and Republican-shifting counties.
While the number of Republican-shifting counties in the region is larger
than the number of Democratic-shifting ones, the latter include Davis, the
central county of the Ogden metro area. Thanks chiefly to the Davis shift, the
net result of the trends was stability—no change in the region over the time
period. In the Provo and South region, the three green, Democratic-shifting
counties are clearly outnumbered by orange and light-yellow Republican-
shifting counties, including Utah, the central county of the Provo metro area.
The net result of these trends in this region was a 3-point shift toward the
GOP over the time period.

It is interesting to compare the political shifts in map G-5 to the population growth map (map G-2). The good news for Democrats is that all of
the Democratic-shifting counties are growing counties, including some with
fairly high growth rates, like Summit (growth rate of 22 percent) and, most
important, Salt Lake (15 percent) in the Salt Lake city metro area. Overall,
this strongly Democratic-shifting metro area, by far the largest in the state,
has grown 16 percent since 2000.

But that is where the good news for the Democrats stops. The two other
regions, which are deeply conservative, have not been moving toward the
Democrats. And it is here that the highest growth rates are to be found—
note the many GOP-shifting counties in the highest growth category. Overall, the Ogden and East region has grown by 23 percent since 2000, and the
Provo and South region—the most conservative in the state—has grown by a
mind-boggling 38 percent. Thus, the solid growth in the Salt Lake City metro

area has had its liberalizing effects damped down by the rapid population growth in the rest of the state, which is far more conservative. The net result is a modest change over time, generally in a pro-Democratic direction but from a very conservative base.

Toward the 2012 Election and Beyond

The GOP predictably had a very good election in 2010. It easily retained its U.S. Senate seat (with new candidate Mike Lee) and reelected its incumbent governor Gary Herbert. However, the political environment in 2012 is likely to be less GOP friendly, and various demographic changes that are typically Democrat friendly will have had an entire four years to accumulate: more minorities, more college-educated whites, and fewer working-class whites. However, "typical" does not really apply to Utah, at least in terms of the working-class white/white college-graduate dynamic—or rather, it applies only to the Salt Lake City metro area; the rest of the state is quite a different story.

Therefore the critical question for Utah going forward is whether the regions outside the Salt Lake City region will continue to be relatively unaffected by demographic change. If so, the decisive GOP advantage in the state is likely to remain overwhelming in 2012 and beyond. If not, that advantage could start to weaken, though it has a long way to go before the state is likely even to approach becoming competitive.

On the other hand, a close watch should be kept on the Salt Lake City metro area, where the most rapid demographic change is found and significant shifts in political culture are taking place. It is trends in this metro area that create at least the possibility of change in Utah, and if change does come, it will be led by shifts in this area.

Notes

1. Brookings Metropolitan Policy Program, *Mountain Megas: America's Newest Metropolitan Places and a Federal Partnership to Make Them Prosper* (2008).

2. The Current Population Survey has the white share of voters somewhat higher, at 79.5 percent.

3. No exit poll data for Arizona are available for the 1988 election, so no comparisons can be made to performance in that election.

4. Growth figures for this region are slightly inflated by the inclusion of Broomfield County, which did not exist in 2000, in the region.

5. Data limitations—the division of Colorado into "PUMAs" (Public Use Microdata Areas) in the American Community Survey—would have it difficult for us to include these metro areas in any other region but the North and West. But it is also true that the Fort Collins and Greeley metro areas are typically put in a "west region" for Colorado by

exit and other pollsters, due to traditional similarities in political culture and behavior between these areas and the rest of the western region of Colorado.

6. The basic demographic pattern of Udall's support was very similar to that of Obama.

7. According to exit poll data. Another data source, the Current Population Survey (CPS) Voter Supplement, showed a smaller decrease of 3 points for Colorado white voters between 2004 and 2008. In general, exit poll and CPS data show similar compositional trends in the electorate, though there are typically small differences in magnitude, especially at the state level.

8. Comparing compositional levels of white working-class and white college-graduate voters in Colorado is trickier than comparing support levels. Both the exit polls and CPS agree that, compared to nationwide figures, there was a relatively high proportion of white college-graduate voters in Colorado in 2008 and a relatively low proportion of white working-class voters. But the exit polls say that white college-graduate voters actually outnumbered white working-class voters, 49 percent to 32 percent, while the CPS says that white working-class voters are still the larger group, by 47 percent to 39 percent.

9. The CPS has the white share of voters slightly higher, at 92 percent.

10. The CPS has the increase in minority share higher, at 5 points.

11. No exit poll data for Idaho are available for the 1988 election and no exit poll data by education are available for the 2004 election, so comparisons on this characteristic cannot be made to either the 1988 or 2004 elections.

12. William H. Frey, "Housing Bust Shatters State Migration Patterns," Brookings WebEd, December 2007(www.brookings.edu/opinions/2007/1228_migration_frey.aspx).

13. Both exit poll and CPS data agree on this figure.

14. Tom Udall's share of the vote in his Senate victory was somewhat larger than Obama's, but allowing for that, the demographic pattern of his support was basically the same as Obama's.

15. Here the exit polls and the CPS disagree; the CPS has the share of white voters at 56 percent.

16. The CPS has the white share of voters substantially higher, at 95 percent.

17. Here the CPS and exit polls agree.

18. No exit poll data for Utah are available from the 1988 election and no exit poll data by education are available for the 2004 election, so comparisons on this characteristic cannot be made to either the 1988 or 2004 elections.

two

Metropolitan Voting Patterns in the Mountain West:

THE NEW AND OLD POLITICAL HEARTLANDS

ROBERT E. LANG AND THOMAS W. SANCHEZ

In a 2008 analysis of regional growth patterns, Robert Lang, Andrea Sarzynski, and Mark Muro of the Brookings Institution dubbed the booming Mountain West the "New Heartland."[1] The analysis focused on the large metro areas, or "Mountain Megas," in Arizona, Colorado, Nevada, New Mexico, and Utah. This chapter also focuses on electoral politics in the Mountain West's big metropolitan areas, where increasing scale and demographic diversity are shifting the electoral dynamic of statewide races. The net result is that the Mountain West is not just growing but also is evolving into a far more centrist swing region that will likely play a significant role in determining the outcome of future presidential elections.

While population growth rates in this region have slowed since 2008, due largely to the Great Recession, three Mountain West states each gained an electoral vote in the 2010 census reapportionment. By contrast, the old Midwestern heartland states of Illinois, Indiana, Michigan, Ohio, and Wisconsin saw three states lose votes—and in the case of Ohio, two electoral votes were lost. Ohio has been referred to as the "mother of presidents," a label that has two meanings. The state has produced an inordinate number of presidents (eight), and it has been a critical swing state that helps determine who becomes president. As recently as 2004, when George W. Bush defeated John Kerry, Ohio proved to be the pivotal state. Lang and others found that in 2004, Ohio's rural and micropolitan vote handed electoral victory to Bush by counterweighing Kerry's slim electoral edge in the state's metropolitan areas.[2]

69

In just one decade, a shift in representative power between the Old and New Heartland occurred that is equivalent to the voting power of a state such as Connecticut or Oklahoma. Tellingly, Peoria, Arizona, now contains more people than Peoria, Illinois, giving the old vaudevillian line "Will it play in Peoria?" a new Sun Belt meaning. While the Old Heartland remains a critical swing region, the New Heartland states of Nevada, Colorado, and New Mexico—with more electoral votes (20) than Ohio (18)—could easily become the place that decides the next presidential election. Anticipated demographic changes, including more population growth in the West than in the East, along with class dynamics, cynicism, and party identification, are shifting this dynamic.[3]

This chapter looks at the character of recent statewide voting in the Mountain West. The region is sufficiently dissimilar from the Midwest that its dynamic as a swing region may prove fundamentally different from that in the Old Heartland. Counterintuitively, the Mountain West is among the most urban places in the United States.[4] The West's wide open spaces give the impression that the region is predominantly rural, but the actual number of people living in rural areas is rather small relative to the number in the large metropolitan areas. In 1997, Lang, Popper, and Popper showed that in 1990 a significant share of the Mountain West still met the census's nineteenth-century definition of "frontier" based on population density at the county level.[5] The weight of the West's urban areas overwhelms rural districts, and thus—unlike in, say, Ohio—it would be harder for a candidate to eke out a win there simply by sweeping rural areas. More important, growth in metropolitan areas has outpaced growth in rural areas in the West, and therefore the share of rural growth—small as it was—is in fact contracting across much of the Mountain West.

Meanwhile, U.S. politics as a whole is being transformed by both population growth and diversification.[6] In just the past two decades, the United States gained over 60 million new residents, the equivalent of adding either a France or a United Kingdom to the nation's existing population. Interestingly, about half of the gain was due to the growth of the Hispanic population, which, at over 30 million people, exceeds the current population of Venezuela. The projections are for the country to continue growing and diversifying. Passel and Cohn project that the United States will gain an additional 100 million residents by the mid-twenty-first century, at which point its demographic composition is likely to be majority minority.[7] To put that in perspective, consider that the United States is on track to add more new residents by 2050 than any other country except India and Pakistan.[8]

Unlike the Midwest, the Mountain West—especially the urban West—is rapidly diversifying. Census data show that states such as Nevada, Arizona, and even Colorado and Utah have seen their demographic composition dramatically transformed in just the last few decades and that some are now at the edge of majority-minority status (in New Mexico, whites are already in the minority). The following data analysis also shows that most of the region's diversification has occurred in its fast-growing and increasingly large-scale metropolitan areas. In the most recent elections, Republicans in particular have had a difficult time attracting minority voters, and for the most part they are not adapting to the nation's changing demographic reality.[9]

In fact, minority voters in the West as a whole may have prevented the Republicans from gaining control of the U.S. Senate in the 2010 midterm election. The Tea Party movement, so dominant in the 2010 cycle, failed to defeat key Democratic Senate targets in California (Barbara Boxer), Washington (Patty Murray), Colorado (Michael Bennet), and Nevada (Harry Reid). In all cases, the urban and minority vote offset a wave of white rural voters. By contrast, the latter demographic was able to deliver for the Republicans in the Midwest, where Senate seats changed parties in Illinois, Indiana, and Wisconsin. It can be argued that if a long-serving and once popular incumbent senator such as Democrat Russ Feingold of Wisconsin had been fortunate enough to be running for reelection in the New Heartland, he would have retained his seat.

In sum, the New Heartland is growing ever more urban and diverse. In 2008, Lang, Sanchez, and Berube, using the outcome of recent elections as a guide, demonstrated that this trend would tend to favor Democrats.[10] In 2000, Democratic candidate Al Gore came within five electoral votes of defeating Republican George W. Bush for the presidency. Gore lost two small states with four electoral votes to Bush—New Hampshire and Nevada. If there is a similarly close race in 2012, it is now more likely that a state like Nevada (currently six electoral votes) or Colorado will swing to the Democrats. That prediction is based on the fact that in the historically significant conservative wave election of 2010—when the GOP gained sixty-three House seats, the best post–World War II seat gain by either party in a midterm election—both states reelected their incumbent Democratic senators. The difference is minority voters, especially Hispanics. These voters are to the New Heartland of the twenty-first century what white ethnic voters from southern and eastern Europe were to the Old Heartland in the twentieth century. They are now the potential deciding voters in any toss-up presidential election.

Table 2-1. Population of the Five Metro Areas Analyzed, 2000 and 2010

Metro area	County	Population 2000	Population 2010	Change 2010–00	Percent change
Phoenix		3,251,876	4,192,887	941,011	28.9
	Maricopa	3,072,149	3,817,117	744,968	24.2
	Pinal	179,727	375,770	196,043	109.1
Denver		2,196,053	2,543,482	347,429	15.8
	Adams	363,857	441,603	77,746	21.4
	Arapahoe	487,967	572,003	84,036	17.2
	Broomfield	38,297	55,889	17,592	45.9
	Clear Creek	9,322	9,088	-234	-2.5
	Denver	554,636	600,158	45,522	8.2
	Douglas	175,766	285,465	109,699	62.4
	Elbert	19,872	23,086	3,214	16.2
	Gilpin	4,757	5,441	684	14.4
	Jefferson	527,056	534,543	7,487	1.4
	Park	14,523	16,206	1,683	11.6
Las Vegas		1,375,765	1,951,269	575,504	41.8
	Clark	1,375,765	1,951,269	575,504	41.8
Albuquerque		729,649	887,077	157,428	21.6
	Bernalillo	556,678	662,564	105,886	19.0
	Sandoval	89,908	131,561	41,653	46.3
	Torrance	16,911	16,383	-528	-3.1
	Valencia	66,152	76,569	10,417	15.7
Salt Lake		968,858	1,124,197	155,339	16.0
	Salt Lake	898,387	1,029,655	131,268	14.6
	Summit	29,736	36,324	6,588	22.2
	Tooele	40,735	58,218	17,483	42.9
Total		8,522,201	10,698,912	2,176,711	25.5

Source: U.S. Census Bureau, "American Factfinder" (http://factfinder2.census.gov/faces/nav/jsf/pages/index. xhtml).

Metro Analysis

To highlight the trends in Mountain West electoral politics, our analysis focuses on the five most populous metro areas within Arizona, Colorado, Nevada, New Mexico, and Utah. These are the Phoenix, Denver, Las Vegas, Albuquerque, and Salt Lake City metropolitan areas, which comprise twenty counties in total. These areas totaled 8.5 million in population in 2000, a figure that had grown to nearly 11 million by 2010 (see table 2-1). That growth

Table 2-2. Metro Area Share of State Population, 2000 and 2010

Metro area	Percent of state population 2000	2010	Percent change
Phoenix	63.4	65.6	2.2
Denver	51.1	50.6	−0.5
Las Vegas	68.8	72.3	3.4
Albuquerque	40.1	43.1	3.0
Salt Lake	43.4	40.7	−2.7
Total	55.0	56.5	1.4

Source: U.S. Census Bureau, "American Factfinder" (http://factfinder2.census.gov/faces/nav/jsf/pages/index. xhtml).

has also translated into a larger share of their state's population for these metro areas (see table 2-2).

Until just recently, the Mountain West experienced some of the fastest population growth in the country. Nevada, Arizona, and Utah ranked first, second, and third in state growth rates between 2000 and 2007. None of the nine U.S. Census Bureau–defined regional divisions grew faster than the Mountain division, including these five Mountain West states plus Montana, Wyoming, and Idaho, in the first part of this decade. The Mountain division also is projected to continue growing the fastest of all the country's divisions through 2030. While the region experienced periods of rapid growth and leveling off going back to the eighteenth century, today's sustained rapid growth projections signal that a new growth dynamic is at work in the region.[11]

In terms of election outcomes, we not only assess how these metro areas performed individually but also compare their outcomes to those of the non-metro areas of the state and the state as a whole. If the voting behavior of these metros does in fact differ from that of surrounding areas, we argue that metro areas themselves are gaining as significant forces in national politics and that their significance will increase as they grow in size (in terms of both geography and population) and change in composition. In 2006, Lang and Sanchez conducted similar analyses, using counties as the primary geographic and political unit, in which county demographics in relation to the urban core were significant predictors of voting behavior in national contests.[12] This analysis instead shifts the scale from counties that make up metro areas to whole metros by comparing U.S. presidential, House, and Senate election results for the Phoenix, Denver, Las Vegas, Albuquerque, and Salt Lake metros from 2000 and 2010 (2000 to 2008 for the presidential results). That not only allows us

Table 2-3. Comparison of Change in Metro Area Population and in Minority Population with Changes in Other Areas, 2000–10

Percent

Metro area	Metro area		Rest of state		Whole state	
	General population	Minority population	General population	Minority population	General population	Minority population
Phoenix	28.9	55.8	17.1	29.5	24.6	45.2
Denver	15.8	37.5	18.1	37.1	16.9	37.3
Las Vegas	41.8	85.6	20.4	50.6	35.1	78.1
Albuquerque	21.6	35.1	7.6	13.8	13.2	21.9
Salt Lake	16.0	56.3	29.7	75.3	23.8	64.8
Total	25.5	54.7	18.5	31.2	22.4	44.7

Source: U.S. Census Bureau, "American Factfinder" (http://factfinder2.census.gov/faces/nav/jsf/pages/index.xhtml).

to show how metros reflect the voting behavior of their own states but also illustrates how change over time has been occurring in the region. Table 2-3 illustrates the demographic dynamics discussed earlier and compares the five metros with areas in the rest of their own state and with the whole state for the ten-year change in total population and the ten-year change in minority population.[13] Both absolute population growth and the (mostly) in-migration of minorities are significant factors in regional demographic change.

As shown in table 2-3, each of the five metro areas has experienced substantial population growth, particularly among racial minorities, outpacing growth in nonmetro areas and in the state as a whole. The Las Vegas metro area experienced the most rapid population growth and nearly doubled its share of racial minorities (42 percent and 86 percent respectively). Overall, the Denver and Salt Lake City metro areas and the states of New Mexico and Colorado experienced the slowest rates of population change; however, their minority populations grew at significant rates. New Mexico is the most rural of the states. Its racial diversity extends to rural areas, and it has the lowest rates of nonmetro population growth and minority population increases. The state has a centuries-long pattern of Hispanic urban and rural settlement. Consider, for example, that New Mexico's capital was established before Boston.

Metro Election Results

Along with the dramatic demographic and population changes experienced by these Western metros and their states, there have been some notable

Table 2-4. Comparison of Share of Votes for Democratic and for Republican Candidates in U.S. Presidential Elections in Metro Areas with Shares in Other Areas, 2000 and 2008

Percent

Metro area	Metro area				Rest of state				Whole state			
	2000		2008		2000		2008		2000		2008	
	Dem	Rep	Dem	Rep	Dem	Rep	Dem	Rep	Dem	Rep	Dem	Rep
Phoenix	43.1	53.1	43.5	54.2	47.1	47.6	47.5	51.9	44.7	51.0	44.9	53.4
Denver	47.0	47.1	57.1	40.3	38.1	54.2	50.1	49.3	42.4	50.8	53.7	44.7
Las Vegas	51.3	44.7	58.3	39.4	37.0	57.6	48.6	49.4	46.0	49.5	55.1	42.7
Albuquerque	48.0	47.4	58.4	40.0	47.8	48.2	55.6	43.3	47.9	47.8	56.9	41.8
Salt Lake	35.0	55.9	47.5	48.1	19.8	75.1	24.5	72.6	26.3	66.8	34.2	62.2
Total	44.9	49.9	51.6	45.9	38.2	55.8	45.8	53.0	41.7	52.7	49.0	49.0

Source: *Atlas of U.S. Presidential Elections* (http://uselectionatlas.org/).

trends in national election voting behavior during the same time period. Two presidential elections, in 2000 and 2008, that roughly correspond to the demographic data time frame discussed here (2000 to 2010) are shown in tables 2-4 and 2-5.

Note that there was a shift in voting from Republican to Democratic in most of the big metropolitan areas between 2000 and 2008. The major exception was Phoenix, most likely because the Republican candidate for president that year, Arizona senator John McCain, is a resident of Phoenix. In some cases the shift was rather dramatic. Democrats came close to actually winning the Salt Lake City region in 2008 and actually did win in Salt Lake County. The data in tables 2-4 and 2-5 also show that the shift in voter preference was not limited to the biggest metropolitan areas. In fact, there are second-tier cities in most of these states that are becoming more Democratic. For instance, places such as Reno, Nevada; Tucson and Flagstaff, Arizona; and Boulder and Fort Collins, Colorado, are all college towns and their politics are in some cases actually leading their respective states toward more progressive politics. Even areas outside the metro areas seem to be trending toward the Democrats; they are in essence catching up with the more progressive voting in the big metropolitan areas.

Next we compare voting in the 2000 and 2010 U.S. House and Senate elections for each of the metro areas with voting in the rest of their states. In 2000, all five metros voted majority Republican in U.S. House races while only two

Table 2-5. Comparison of Change in Votes for Democratic and for Republican Candidates in U.S. Presidential Elections in Metro Areas with Changes in Other Areas, 2000–08

Percent

Metro area	Metro area		Rest of state		Whole state	
	Democrat	Republican	Democrat	Republican	Democrat	Republican
Phoenix	2.6	−4.5	5.8	−6.8	3.8	−5.4
Denver	4.9	−2.1	24.0	−16.3	14.9	−9.5
Las Vegas	6.3	−5.4	6.3	-4.9	6.8	−5.7
Albuquerque	5.5	−0.2	−3.2	3.3	0.6	1.7
Salt Lake	6.4	−7.6	−15.5	14.1	−6.1	4.8
Totals	4.5	−3.8	7.7	−5.4	6.1	−4.64

Source: Authors' calculations.

(Phoenix and Denver) did so in 2010. In addition, the overall gap between Democratic and Republican voting in the metros narrowed from 13 percent (41 percent Democratic to 54 percent Republican) in 2000 to 4 percent (46 percent Democratic to 50 percent Republican) in 2010. All five metros showed consistent Democratic voting gains from 2000 to 2010 (see table 2-6).

Voting behavior from 2000 to 2010 for the Phoenix, Denver, Las Vegas, Albuquerque, and Salt Lake metro areas was much more consistent than behavior for the balance of their states or the state as a whole. The average changes across metro and nonmetro areas for the five metros were very similar, showing proportional increases in Democratic voting and decreases in Republican voting. The rest of their own states and their states as a whole showed more variation, with Colorado showing larger gains in Democratic votes and Utah showing Republican gains (see table 2-7).

It is a bit difficult to make direct comparisons of 2000 and 2010 U.S. Senate votes across the five metro areas because there were no 2000 U.S. Senate elections in Colorado and no 2010 U.S. Senate elections in New Mexico; in addition, there was no 2000 Democratic challenger in Arizona (see table 2-8).[14] Despite the previously mentioned caveats, the trends in voting behavior from Republican to Democratic are similar to those in U.S. House elections, with these metros being fairly consistent and with the rest of their states showing more variability. Again, as in U.S. House elections for 2000 and 2010, Democratic voting increased and Republican voting decreased.

It is important to consider why presidential election results differ from those of congressional elections and how the political winds can be assessed

Table 2-6. Comparison of Share of Votes for Democratic and for Republican Candidates in U.S. House Elections in Metro Areas with Shares in Other Areas, 2000 and 2010

Percent

	Metro area				Rest of state				Whole state			
	2000		2010		2000		2010		2000		2010	
Metro area	Dem	Rep	Dem	Rep	Dem	Rep	Dem	Rep	Dem	Rep	Dem	Rep
Phoenix	36.8	60.0	39.4	55.5	40.1	55.7	45.9	48.9	38.1	58.3	41.9	53.0
Denver	42.9	50.3	47.8	48.2	19.1	68.3	43.1	52.0	30.5	59.7	45.4	50.1
Las Vegas	46.1	49.2	52.4	43.8	25.7	68.8	32.0	63.9	38.4	56.5	45.2	50.9
Albuquerque	45.4	49.3	50.9	49.1	55.4	44.5	52.2	47.8	51.0	46.6	51.6	48.4
Salt Lake	41.4	55.3	47.9	47.7	39.2	56.9	23.7	71.0	40.2	56.2	34.1	61.0
Total	41.3	54.0	45.8	50.2	33.3	60.0	41.1	54.6	37.5	56.86	43.6	52.2

Source: *Atlas of U.S. Presidential Elections* (http://uselectionatlas.org/).

by one or the other. Bafumi, Erikson, and Wlezien discuss the interaction and dynamics that exist between presidential elections and midterm (congressional) elections by stating:

> One mystery of U.S. politics is why the president's party regularly loses congressional seats at midterm. Although presidential coattails and their withdrawal provide a partial explanation, coattails cannot account for the fact that the presidential party typically performs worse than normal at midterm. . . . Polls early in the midterm year project a normal vote result in November. But as the campaign progresses, vote preferences almost always move toward the out party. This shift is not a negative referendum on the president, as midterms do not show a pattern of declining presidential popularity or increasing salience of presidential performance. The shift accords with "balance" theory, where the midterm campaign motivates some to vote against the party of the president in order to achieve policy moderation.[15]

Other explanations are that congressional races are more variable or reactionary and have a strong local focus. Comparing congressional and presidential races is like comparing dissaggregate data to aggregate data. There is more smoothing or averaging in the aggregate data than in disaggregate data, which shows more variability, especially for data with a spatial dimension. Lang and Sanchez (2006) shows the spatial variability of election results by

Table 2-7. Comparison of Change in Votes for Democratic and for Republican Candidates in U.S. House Elections in Metro Areas with Changes in Other Areas, 2000–10

Percent

Metro area	Metro area		Rest of state		Whole state	
	Democrat	Republican	Democrat	Republican	Democrat	Republican
Phoenix	2.6	−4.5	5.8	−6.8	3.8	−5.4
Denver	4.9	−2.1	24.0	−16.3	14.9	−9.5
Las Vegas	6.3	−5.4	6.3	−4.9	6.8	−5.7
Albuquerque	5.5	−0.2	−3.2	3.3	0.6	1.7
Salt Lake	6.4	−7.6	−15.5	14.1	−6.1	4.8
Total	4.5	−3.8	7.7	−5.4	6.1	−4.64

Source: Authors' calculations.

county and also for subdivisions of counties (for example, precincts).[16] The analysis discussed here provides a multilevel perspective on trends, and it is therefore both interesting and significant that the results show consistent trends toward increased Democratic shares of voting across presidential, House, and Senate results in these Western metro areas.

Summary

The results of this analysis suggest that from 2000 to 2010 the voting behavior of the selected five Western metros, Phoenix, Denver, Las Vegas, Albuquerque, and Salt Lake, was shifting from its Republican foundations. These findings appear to mesh with prior research that focused on sub–metro level voting behavior, particularly that of the suburbs compared with that of the urban core of metro areas. Lang, Sanchez, and Berube (2008) noted the urbanizing characteristics of the suburbs and voting behavior there in explaining observed changes in voting outcomes for presidential races between 2004 and 2008.[17] As they discuss, lower-density suburbs were once the domain of Republicans, but the outward spread of "urban voting" now appears to be taking hold in metro areas, especially as low-income, racial minorities integrate the suburbs. This represents a breakdown of the distinctive opinions and political persuasions of city and suburbs discussed by Gainsborough, who noted that this distinction was greater in older metropolitan areas

Table 2-8. Comparison of Share of Votes for Democratic and for Republican Candidates in U.S. Senate Elections in Metro Areas with Shares in Other Areas, 2000 and 2010

Percent

Metro area	Metro area				Rest of state				Whole state			
	2000		2010		2000		2010		2000		2010	
	Dem	Rep	Dem	Rep	Dem	Rep	Dem	Rep	Dem	Rep	Dem	Rep
Phoenix	0.0	81.0	32.4	61.0	0.0	76.6	38.0	55.0	0.0	79.3	34.6	58.7
Denver	...	...	51.7	43.0	...	...	44.4	49.9	...	...	48.1	46.4
Las Vegas	44.8	50.7	54.4	41.3	31.1	62.4	42.8	50.5	39.7	55.1	50.3	44.5
Albuquerque	60.8	39.1	Na	...	62.4	37.6	...	...	61.7	38.3	...	...
Salt Lake	42.3	54.8	46.6	49.4	23.4	73.7	22.4	70.7	31.5	65.6	32.8	61.6
Total	25.6	64.1	44.0	50.4	24.7	65.3	38.6	55.0	25.2	64.63	41.6	52.5

Source: *Atlas of U.S. Presidential Elections* (http://uselectionatlas.org/).

with more mature urban cores that have experienced decline and disinvestment.[18] Metro areas in the West, however, do not fall into that category, and the socioeconomic differences between cities and suburbs there are less entrenched and less distinctive.

So are metro areas emerging as political blocs similar to counties? Dreier, Mollenkopf, and Swanstrom (2004) alludes to this while explaining the relationship between the metropolitan landscape and regionalism.[19] In their view, one element of regionalism is understanding and empathy for urban challenges. As an appreciation for the regional nature of urban challenges increases, characteristics and opinions about "urban" issues also become expressed on a regional scale.

Metros are technically defined as areas with economic and social cohesion, but they may also include a political dimension as well, which is the manifestation of combined economic and social characteristics and experience. Does this run counter to Bill Bishop's (2008) hypothesis that "the big sort" produces political segregation and polarization?[20] Not necessarily. Even within metro areas—or even communities, as Bishop points out—sorting and clustering still occurs, but the evidence that we present here suggests that the overall mix of attitudes is still susceptible to trends in a particular political direction.

The Mountain West is transitioning from a once solid and reliably Republican region into a more contested space. The timing of this shift is fortunate for the Democrats, as the region is both trending their way and gaining electoral strength. But it is also important not to overread the data from the last several cycles. The West is by no means a lock for the Democrats. While the current politics of the national Republican Party—which borders on xenophobia—may alienate the growing number of Hispanic voters in the Mountain States, the Republicans can still pivot and find a Hispanic candidate for vice president. There are two good candidates within the region: Nevada's governor, Brian Sandoval, and New Mexico's governor, Susana Martinez. Senator Marco Rubio from Florida, a frequently mentioned candidate, has the added benefit in the West of having spent a big part of his childhood in Las Vegas. In effect, the Republicans could at least partly neutralize their current problems with Hispanic voters by selecting a Hispanic candidate for vice president.

Notes

1. Robert E. Lang, A. Sarzynski, and Mark Muro, "The Megapolitan West" (Metropolitan Policy Program, Brookings, August 2008).

2. Robert E. Lang, D. Dhavale, and K. Haworth, "Micro Politics: The 2004 Presidential Vote in Small-Town America," *Census Note* 4, no. 3 (Alexandria, Va.: Metropolitan Institute at Virginia Tech, November 2004).

3. See R. Morrill, L. Knopp, and M. Brown, "Anomalies in Red and Blue II: Towards an Understanding of the Roles of Setting, Values, and Demography in the 2004 and 2008 U.S. Presidential Elections," *Political Geography* 30, no. 3 (2011): 153–68; D. Brady, B. Sosnaud, and S. M. Frenk, "The Shifting and Diverging White Working Class in U.S. Presidential Elections, 1972–2004," *Social Science Research* 38, no. 1 (2009): 118–33; E. A. Williams and others, "The Effects of Crisis, Cynicism about Change, and Value Congruence on Perceptions of Authentic Leadership and Attributed Charisma in the 2008 Presidential Election," *Leadership Quarterly* (2011, forthcoming).

4. Lang, Sarzynski, and Muro, "The Megapolitan West."

5. Robert E. Lang, D. E. Popper, and F. J. Popper, "Is There Still a Frontier? The 1890 Census and the Modern West," *Journal of Rural Studies* 13, no. 4 (1997): 377–86.

6. M. H. Lopez, *Dissecting the 2008 Electorate: Most Diverse in U.S. History* (Washington: Pew Hispanic Center, 2009).

7. Jeffrey S. Passel and D'Vera Cohn, "U.S. Population Projections: 2005–2050" (Washington: Pew Research Center, 2009).

8. Robert E. Lang, M. Alfonzo, and C. Dawkins, "America 2109," *Planning* (May 2009): 10–15.

9. Robert E. Lang, "Demographics Shifting, but GOP Isn't," *Politico,* November 20, 2008, p. 19.

10. Robert E. Lang, Thomas W. Sanchez, and Alan Berube, "The New Suburban Politics: A County-Based Analysis of Metropolitan Voting Trends Since 2000," in *The Future*

of *Red, Blue, and Purple America: Election Demographics, 2008 and Beyond,* edited by Ruy Teixeira (Brookings, 2008).

11. U.S. Census Bureau, "Interim Projections of the Population by Sex for the United States, Regions, and Divisions: April 1, 2000 to July 1, 2030."

12. Robert E. Lang and Thomas W. Sanchez, "Suburban Blues, Election Report" (Metropolitan Institute, Virginia Tech, 2006).

13. This is based on census definitions of minorities as persons reporting themselves to be other than non-Hispanic, single-race white.

14. Republican John Kyl received 79 percent of the vote with the Independent, Green, and Libertarian candidates receiving a total of 19 percent of the vote.

15. J. Bafumi, R. S. Erikson, and C. Wlezien, "Forecasting the House Seats from Generic Congressional Polls: The 2010 Midterm Election," *PS: Political Science and Politics* 43 (October 2010): 633–36.

16. Lang and Sanchez, "Suburban Blues, Election Report."

17. Lang, Sanchez, and Berube, "The New Suburban Politics."

18. J. F. Gainsborough, *Fenced Off: The Suburbanization of American Politics* (Georgetown University Press, 2001).

19. P. Dreier, J. Mollenkopf, and Todd Swanstrom, *Place Matters: Metropolitics for the Twenty-First Century,* Studies in Government and Public Policy (University Press of Kansas, 2001).

20. B. Bishop and R. G. Cushing, *The Big Sort: Why the Clustering of Like-Minded America Is Tearing Us Apart* (Boston: Mariner Books, 2009).

three

Hispanics, Race, and the Changing Political Landscape of the United States and the Mountain West

WILLIAM H. FREY

One of the key shifts in the nation's political demographics that will make the Mountain West a key swing region in future presidential elections is the growth of minority populations, especially Hispanics, as a share of the region's electorate. As discussed below, minorities were responsible for winning ten states for Barack Obama in 2008, Nevada and New Mexico being prime examples, and the increases in the numbers of Hispanics, African Americans, and Asians in all of the Mountain West states will give them an even larger political voice in a region that has been long thought of as predominantly white.

This chapter begins with a detailed overview of how racial-ethnic groups played a key role across the nation in electing Barack Obama president in 2008. It examines the extraordinary minority turnout and voting changes between 2004 and 2008. It points up the particular importance of the changing racial demographics of the fast-growing "purple states," which are well represented in the Mountain West. It then takes up the more specific question of where minorities made a key difference in winning the election for Obama.

The chapter then turns to the post-2008 period and the six Mountain West states in this study—Arizona, Colorado, Idaho, Nevada, New Mexico, and Utah. It looks at the racial-ethnic makeup of each state's electorate, focusing specifically on how Hispanics, the largest and greatest-gaining minority in the region, differ from whites on a host of political and national and local issues that will affect the next presidential election, drawing from the Brookings Mountain West survey conducted especially for this volume (see chapter 5). The chapter concludes with some observations about what the results suggest for the 2012 election.

The Role of Race in the 2008 Presidential Election

Three years after the fact, the near-landslide election of President Barack Obama is now taken pretty much for granted. The luster of the historic victory of an African American as president seems to have worn off as a result of the Great Recession and the nation's increasingly divided politics, exacerbated by the rise of the then-unknown Tea Party movement.

Yet we should not lose sight of the fact that the Obama's election was a landmark event in American politics. A major reason why it occurred was the changing demographics of the American electorate—especially the rise in the numbers of young Hispanic, African American, and Asian voters, coupled with their enthusiastic support of the candidate. The numbers underlying this shift are recounted below in a comparison of minorities' size and turnout in the 2008 and the 2004 elections.[1]

Minority Demographics, Turnout, and Voting

The relationship between demographics and voting is not at all straightforward. But a change in the underlying demographic structure of the population can certainly impact the voting population and eventually election outcomes. It is clear that in 2008 the white population as a share of total population was smaller than in 2004 (65 percent in 2008, down from 68 percent in 2004) and that the Hispanic population share grew (from 14 percent to nearly 16 percent). The latter group, along with African Americans and Asians, will form a greater part of the voting base, especially in states with large minority populations.

Still, one must bear in mind that there is a sizable "translation gap" among minorities between the minority population and the minority population that is eligible to vote (figure 3-1). In 2008, 77 of every 100 whites in the population were eligible voters; the rest were either too young to vote or noncitizens. However, only 42 of every 100 Hispanics in the population were eligible voters because a much higher share of Hispanics are under 18 years of age and a significant share are noncitizens. That is also the case for Asians and somewhat less the case for blacks. Therefore, when one translates the racial composition of the population into the racial composition of eligible

Figure 3-1. Eligible Voters as a Share of Total Population, 2008

Percent

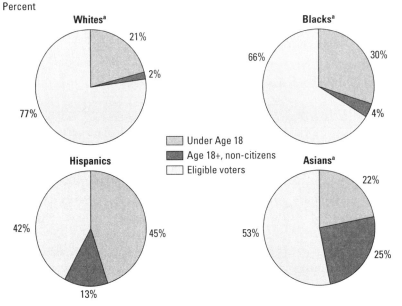

Source: Author's analysis of U.S. Census Bureau Current Population Survey "Voting and Registration Supplement," November 2008 (www.icpsr.umich.edu/icpsrweb/RCMD/studies/25643/version/1).

a. Non-Hispanic.

voters, a larger share of whites (73 percent of eligible voters versus 65 percent of the population) and a smaller share of minorities are eligible to vote.

Besides demographic shifts, another reason that minority voter representation increased in 2008 was an increase in the turnout rates (voters per eligible voters) for Hispanics, African Americans, and Asians (table 3-1, top panel).[2] Twenty-six states had a higher Hispanic turnout in 2008 than in 2004, with notable increases for Georgia, North Carolina, and Florida. Thirty states had higher black turnout in 2008 than 2004, with big gains for Nevada and Georgia. There was actually a slight decline in the turnout rate for whites from 2004 to 2008.

As a result of those developments, there was higher growth in the number of actual minority voters than in the number of eligible minority voters and lower growth in the number of actual white voters than in the number of eligible white voters. In all, 2 million more blacks voted in 2008 than in 2004 as well as almost 2 million more Hispanics and close to 1 million more Asians. What does that mean? If we look at the racial composition of the

Table 3-1. Turnout Rates and Democratic Margins, 2004 and 2008 Presidential Elections

Measure	Whites	Blacks	Hispanics	Asians
Turnout rate				
2004	67	60	47	45
2008	66	65	50	48
Democratic margin				
2004	−17	77	20	12
2008	−12	91	36	27

Source: Author's analysis of U.S. Census Bureau Current Population Survey "Voting and Registration Supplement," November 2004 (www.icpsr.umich.edu/icpsrweb/RCMD/studies/04272/version/2) and November 2008 (www.icpsr.umich.edu/icpsrweb/RCMD/studies/25643/version/1).

voting population, almost 1 in 4 voters was a minority in 2008[3] (figure 3-2) and Hispanics accounted for 7.4 percent of all voters, up from 6 percent in 2004. The actual figures, of course, differ across states.

Displayed in figure 3-3 are states with the highest Hispanic share of their total population; also displayed is the Hispanic share of their voter population. Clearly, some states do a better job of translating their Hispanic population into their voting population. They tend to be states like California, Florida, and New York, where Hispanics have been around for a long time and fewer of them are recent immigrants. On the other hand, in states like Arizona, Nevada, and Colorado, Hispanic representation in the population is much higher that it is among voters. Nonetheless, Hispanics made up a nontrivial share of voters in each of these states.

Because of both demographic shifts and increased turnout, minorities constituted a higher share of voters in 2008 than in 2004. Moreover, among those who voted, minorities—African Americans, Hispanics and Asians—showed a higher margin of voting for Obama than for John Kerry, the Democratic presidential candidate in 2004. As indicated in table 3-1 (bottom panel), the Democratic margin (percent voting for the Democratic candidate minus the percent voting for the Republican candidate) was higher in 2008 than in 2004 for each group: 91 percent versus 77 percent for blacks, 36 percent versus 20 percent for Hispanics, and 27 percent versus 12 percent for Asians. These voting gains for the Democrat, Obama, were magnified because of the larger minority voter base.

At the same time, it should be noted that the negative Democratic margin for whites (indicating a Republican voting preference) was smaller in 2008

Figure 3-2. Racial-Ethnic Composition of Population, Eligible Voters, and Voters, 2004 and 2008

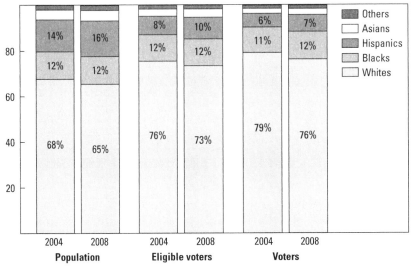

Source: Author's analysis of U.S. Census Bureau Current Population Survey "Voting and Registration Supplement," November 2004 (www.icpsr.umich.edu/icpsrweb/RCMD/studies/04272/version/2) and November 2008 (www.icpsr.umich.edu/icpsrweb/RCMD/studies/25643/version/1).

than in 2004. That led to Obama victories in some states where more enthusiastic minority voters pushed him over the "tipping point." Examples are discussed below.

Fast-Growing and Slow-Growing Purple States

Of course, in U.S. presidential elections winning in the Electoral College is the goal, so the most important states to focus on are those that are most "in play." Large parts of the country have long histories of voting Republican ("red states") or Democratic ("blue states") Those that are not locked in due to historical patterns or recent trends can be thought of as "purple states," and those are the ones in which the shifts in minority demographics and voting patterns can make the biggest difference

In the 2008 election, twenty purple states could be identified: purple Democratic states, which Obama carried, and purple Republican states, which Republican John McCain carried (see map 3-1) Purple states are defined here as those where one of the two major candidates won by a

Figure 3-3. Hispanic Share of State Population and Voters, 2008[a]

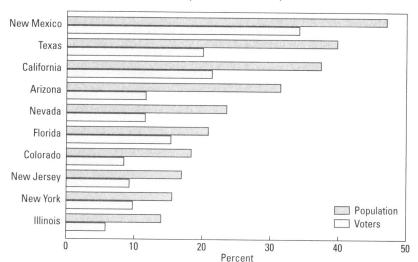

Source: Author's analysis of U.S. Census Bureau Current Population Survey "Voting and Registration Supplement," November 2008 (www.icpsr.umich.edu/icpsrweb/RCMD/studies/25643/version/1).
    a. States with largest Hispanic share of the population.

Map 3-1. Blue, Red, and Purple States, 2008

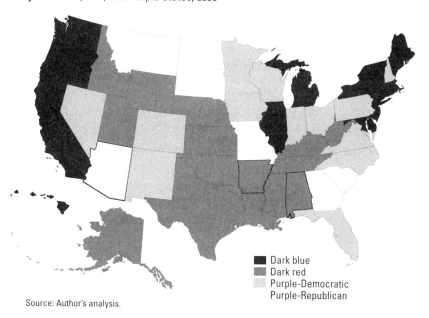

Source: Author's analysis.

10-point margin or less. Three additional states that have been close in recent elections—Nevada, New Mexico, and Wisconsin—are also considered purple in this analysis. The remaining states on the map are classified as "solid blue" or "solid red," depending on whether they were carried by Obama or McCain.

I also classified purple states as either "fast growing" or "slow growing" based on their 2004–08 population growth; they are depicted in map 3-2 and map 3-3. The ten fast-growing purple states are located largely in the Mountain West and in the Southeast; Obama won in six of the ten. Among the ten slow-growing purple states, located largely in the Northeast and Midwest, seven went for Obama. The racial contrast among voters in these two state groupings is stark (see figure 3-4). While more than a quarter of voters (27.5 percent) in fast-growing purple states are minorities, only 11.5 percent in slow-growing purple states are. Moreover, the minority population is growing much more rapidly in the fast-growing purple states.

To show how the changing racial composition of voters and voting patterns of minorities and whites affected the 2008 results, I focus here on selected states in different regions of the country:

Nevada and New Mexico. These two fast-growing purple states in the Mountain West flipped from voting Republican (for Bush) in 2004 to Democratic (for Obama) in 2008. Table 3-2 provides a comparison of the racial-ethnic profiles of their voting populations for 2004 and 2008. Over that period, Nevada increased both its Hispanic and black shares while the white share of its voters dropped from 80 to 73 percent. New Mexico showed a greater representation of minorities in each year than Nevada. Both states now have a sizable Hispanic voter presence.

Moreover, in both states, minorities, especially Hispanics, showed significantly higher support for the Democratic candidate in 2008 (see table 3-3). That had an impact on both states' Democratic victories in 2008, particularly in New Mexico, with its large Hispanic population. In Nevada, blacks also showed notable Democratic gains, but just as important was the shrinking of Republican support among Nevada's sizable white population.

Florida and Virginia. These two Southern fast-growing purple states also flipped from Republican to Democratic in the 2008 election. The minority share of Florida's voters increased from 24 percent to 29 percent, with Hispanics forming a larger share of voters than African Americans (table 3-2). In Virginia, blacks made up the dominant portion of minority voters.

Map 3-2. Fast-Growing Purple States, 2008

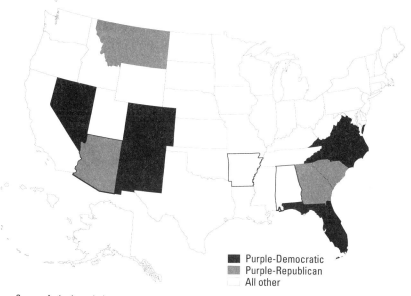

Source: Author's analysis.

Map 3-3. Slow-Growing Purple States, 2008

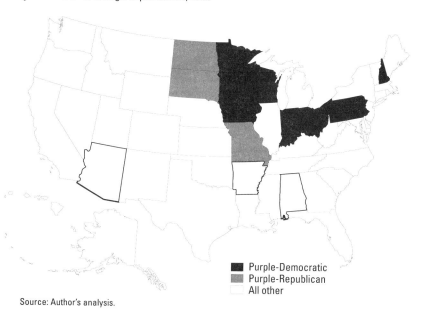

Source: Author's analysis.

Figure 3-4. Voter Profiles by State Category, 2008

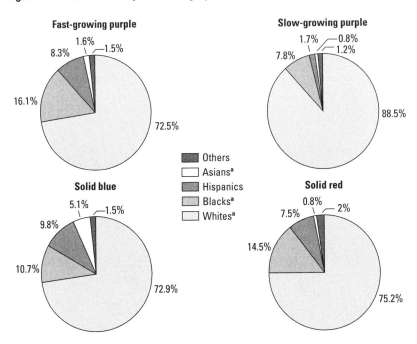

Source: Author's analysis of U.S. Census Bureau Current Population Survey "Voting and Registration Supplement," November 2008 (www.icpsr.umich.edu/icpsrweb/RCMD/studies/25643/version/1).
a. Non-Hispanic.

Buoyed by high turnout rates, blacks, Hispanics and Asians each increased their shares—so that minorities as a whole constituted more than a quarter (26 percent) of the state's voters in 2008, up from 19 percent in 2004.

In addition to changing voter racial profiles, minority voting patterns became more favorable to Democrats in 2008 in both states (table 3-3). In Florida, the Democratic margin for African Americans increased considerably and Hispanic margins flipped from Republican to Democratic. In Virginia, the black Democratic margin also increased, but just as important was the shrinking Republican margin among Virginia's whites. The latter was associated with a shift in allegiance in the rapidly growing and changing Northern Virginia suburbs of Washington, D.C. Thus increased minority vote shares, greater Democratic margins among minorities, and shrinking Republican margins among whites had much to do with the "red to blue" shifts in the 2008 results for Florida and Virginia.

Table 3-2. Racial-Ethnic Composition of Voters, 2004 and 2008, Selected States, by Region

Percent

Region/state	Year	Whites[a]	Blacks[a]	Hispanics	Asians[a]
Mountain West					
Nevada	2004	80	6	8	3
	2008	73	10	12	4
New Mexico	2004	56	3	33	0
	2008	55	2	34	2
South					
Florida	2004	76	11	11	1
	2008	71	12	15	1
Virginia	2004	81	15	2	1
	2008	74	19	2	4
Northeast and Midwest					
Ohio	2004	86	11	2	0
	2008	85	12	1	1
Pennsylvania	2004	89	8	2	1
	2008	87	9	3	1

Source: Author's analysis of U.S. Census Bureau Current Population Survey "Voting and Registration Supplement," November 2004 (www.icpsr.umich.edu/icpsrweb/RCMD/studies/04272/version/2) and November 2008 (www.icpsr.umich.edu/icpsrweb/RCMD/studies/25643/version/1).

a. Non-Hispanic.

Ohio and Pennsylvania. Ohio and Pennsylvania are slow-growing purple states. Ohio flipped from Republican to Democratic in the 2008 election, and Pennsylvania voted Democratic in both 2004 and 2008. The voting populations in both remain predominantly white, along with small minority populations dominated by blacks (table 3-2). In both states there were notable increases in black Democratic margins in 2008 (table 3-3), which contributed to Obama's wins, but the wins were also made possible by significant declines in white Republican margins. More so than in fast-growing states, the Democratic success in these two slow-growing states depended on minority support *and* on reduced GOP support among their large, Republican-leaning white electorates.

Where Did Minorities Elect Obama?

Where and how did minorities affect Obama's victory? In 2004 John Kerry took twenty states, in eleven of which (including the District of Columbia) whites voted for Democrats; because whites voted for Republicans in the

Table 3-3. Democratic Margins by Race-Ethnicity, 2004 and 2008, Selected States, by Region

Region/state	Year	Total	Whites[a]	Blacks[a]	Hispanics
Mountain West					
Nevada	2004	−3	−12	73	21
	2008	12	−8	89	54
New Mexico	2004	−1	−13	n.a.	12
	2008	15	−14	n.a.	39
South					
Florida	2004	−5	−15	73	−12
	2008	3	−14	92	15
Virginia	2004	−8	−36	75	na
	2008	6	−21	84	31
Northeast and Midwest					
Ohio	2004	−2	−12	68	na
	2008	5	−6	95	na
Pennsylvania	2004	2	−9	68	44
	2008	10	−3	90	44

Source: Author's analysis of National Election Pool exit poll data, collected by Edison Media Research and Mitofsky International for a consortium of news organizations, for 2008 (www.cnn.com/ELECTION/2008/results/polls.main/) and 2004 (www.cnn.com/ELECTION/2004/pages/results/states/US/P/00/epolls.0.html).
a. Non-Hispanic.

other nine, minorities carried those states for Kerry. In 2008, Obama carried twenty-nine states. Whites voted Democratic in nineteen of those states; in the remaining ten, Obama's victories depended on minorities. Yet the ten states where minorities made the difference for Obama were largely different from the nine where minorities made the difference for Kerry. That can be seen by comparing map 3-4, which shows the blue states that Kerry carried in 2004, with map 3-5, which shows the blue states that Obama carried in 2008. Each map depicts the states where whites made the difference for the Democratic candidate and those where minorities made the difference for the Democrat.

The three states where minorities made the difference for both Kerry and Obama were Pennsylvania, Maryland, and New Jersey. The seven new states where minorities made the difference for Obama (and that voted Republican in 2004) included the fast-growing purple states of Nevada, New Mexico, Virginia, North Carolina, and Florida as well as the slow-growing purple states of Indiana and Ohio.

Map 3-4. 2004 Blue States Won by Whites and Minorities

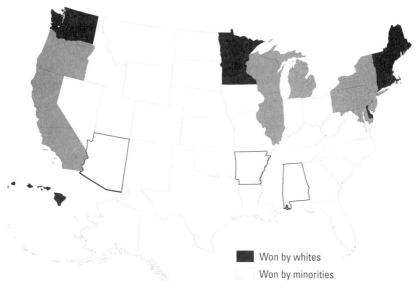

Won by whites

Won by minorities

Source: Author's analysis.

Map 3-5. 2008 Blue States Won by Whites and Minorities

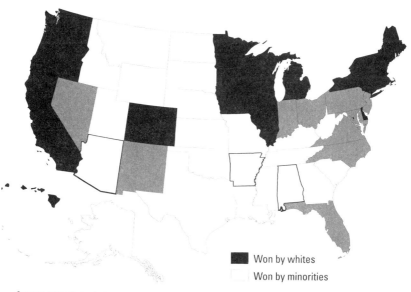

Won by whites

Won by minorities

Source: Author's analysis.

So, did minorities really win the election for Obama? As shown above, they were responsible for his wins in several fast-growing purple states in the Mountain West and Southeast. In addition, they made a difference in key slow-growing purple states like Ohio, Pennsylvania, and Indiana, where the white Republican margin shrank enough to allow the strong Democratic-leaning minorities to tip each state.

Thus, minority support for Obama contributed to his success, but not in just fast-growing purple states with rising Hispanic populations. It was also important in slow-growing purple states where shrinking white Republican margins combined with large minority Democratic margins among smaller minority (largely black) populations. The shrinking Republican margins among whites came about because of low white turnout and enthusiasm for the Republican candidate, John McCain. These circumstances set the stage for minorities to make a substantial contribution toward the election of Barack Obama.

Post-2008 Racial-Ethnic Profiles in the Mountain West

In the post-2008 period, the country appears to be much more divided along partisan lines as it was in the 2008 election. Hence there is reason to believe that the outcomes in Mountain West states will be just as important in determining the 2012 presidential election as they were in 2008 and perhaps more so. The demographics in this fast-growing region continue to shift in ways that make the views of racial-ethnic minorities, especially Hispanics, important for major politicians in both parties to consider.

Mountain West Racial-Ethnic Profiles

The racial-ethnic profiles of the Mountain West states highlight the importance of Hispanics in the region (see figure 3-5).[4] The Mountain West population is less than two-thirds white, as is that of the United States. However, Hispanics are much more heavily represented there, making up nearly a quarter of the region's population. Of course, as observed above for the nation as a whole, there is a significant "translation gap" between the share of Hispanics in the region's general population and their share of the region's eligible voters. Because of that gap, Hispanics represent a smaller but still sizable 16 percent of the region's voters.

The racial-ethnic profiles do differ across the six Mountain West states, which span the range from New Mexico, the region's only "minority white" state, to Idaho, where nearly 87 percent of residents are white (figure 3-6). In

Figure 3-5. Population and Eligible Voters by Race/Ethnicity, United States and Mountain West, 2010

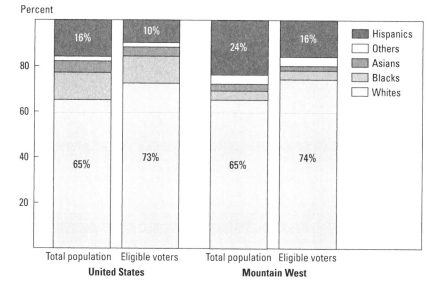

Source: Author's analysis of U.S. Census Bureau Current Population Survey "Annual Social and Economic (ASEC) Supplement Survey," 2010 (www.icpsr.umich.edu/icpsrweb/RCMD/studies/29652/version/1).

each of these states, Hispanics are the dominant minority group and make up a sizable share of the population of four of them (Arizona, Nevada, and Colorado as well as New Mexico). Yet even in the "white" states of Utah and Idaho, one in ten residents is Hispanic.

The "translation gap" somewhat reduces minority and Hispanic influences in each of these states (see figure 3-7). Still, Hispanics make up one-third of eligible voters in New Mexico, more than a fifth in Arizona, 14 percent in Nevada, and 12 percent in Colorado. As discussed, when white support for Republicans is diminished, even a small minority or Hispanic share can make a difference.

Surveying Hispanic and White Opinions

Much as they turned out to be the wild card in determining 2008 election outcomes in Nevada and New Mexico, Hispanic voters could play an even bigger role in the Mountain West states in 2012, not only in these states but in Arizona and Colorado as well. They could even lead the political parties to direct their messages more toward Hispanics in Utah and Idaho. In

Figure 3-6. Total Population by Race/Ethnicity, Mountain West States, 2010

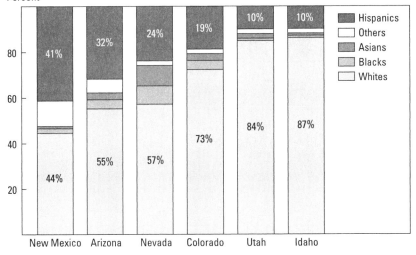

Source: Author's analysis of U.S. Census Bureau Current Population Survey "Annual Social and Economic (ASEC) Supplement Survey," 2010 (www.icpsr.umich.edu/icpsrweb/RCMD/studies/29652/version/1).

light of that, it is useful to examine just how greatly Hispanic opinions differ from those of whites in the Mountain West region. The Brookings Mountain West survey affords a unique opportunity to make this assessment. Conducted in August-September 2010, it represents a one-of-a-kind assessment of Hispanic and white adults in the Mountain West region and in four individual states with large Hispanic populations: New Mexico, Arizona, Nevada, and Colorado.[5]

Right Direction/Wrong Track. A standard survey question used to gauge how different groups view the direction in which the country is headed asks, *Generally speaking, do you think things in the country are going in the right direction, or do you feel things have gotten pretty seriously off on the wrong track?*

It is clear from figure 3-8 that overall, both whites and Hispanics in the Mountain West thought that the country was going down the wrong track, but whites were more extreme in this view. Seven in ten whites felt that way, while only 20 percent thought that the country was on the right course.[6] In contrast, only 56 percent of Hispanics felt that the country was on the wrong track, while 3 in 10 said that it was going in the right direction. The more optimistic view of Hispanics, even in a difficult economy, may reflect the

Figure 3-7. Eligible Voters by Race/Ethnicity, Mountain West States, 2010

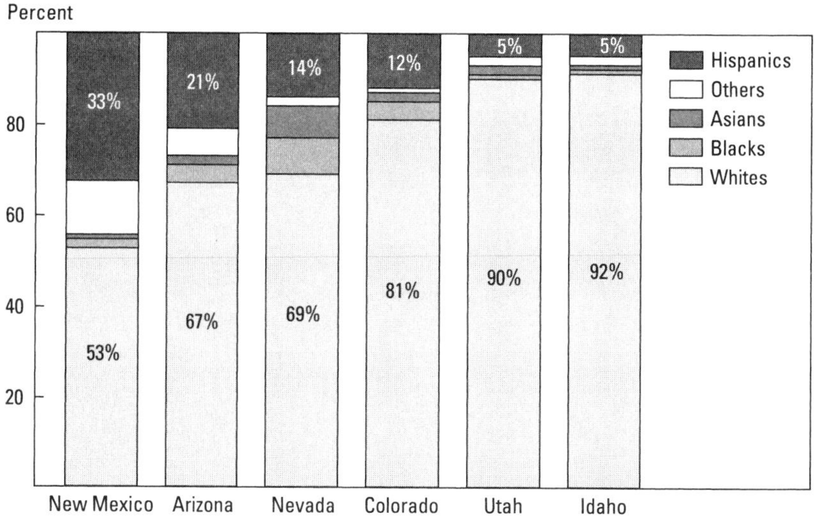

Percent

Source: Author's analysis of U.S. Census Bureau Current Population Survey "Annual Social and Economic (ASEC) Supplement Survey," 2010 (www.icpsr.umich.edu/icpsrweb/RCMD/studies/29652/version/1).

"new American" status of many of them, who are comparing their experience in the United States with that in their country of origin.

An examination of the same question for Hispanics and whites in the four individual states shows substantial variation (see table 3-4, which presents these results as the difference between the percent indicating "right direction" minus that indicating "wrong track"). Whites appear to be most negative in Nevada and Arizona—two states where the mortgage meltdown played havoc with the economy. Hispanics, too, were quite negative in Arizona, although as in other states, not nearly as negative as whites. In fact, in Colorado, where white negativity was least extreme, just as many Hispanics said that the country was going in the right direction as said that it was not.

The same question was asked with respect to where the state (rather than country) was headed. While once again both whites and Hispanics were more negative than positive, Hispanics were more likely to be pessimistic. Sixty-two percent thought that their state was headed down the wrong track, while only 52 percent of whites agreed. An examination of individual state results suggests that the region's opinions were shaped heavily by Arizona. Perhaps because of the state's controversial illegal immigrant legislation (discussed below), whites and Hispanics held extremely different views about the

Figure 3-8. Responses to Survey Question on Country's Direction by Mountain West State Adults[a]

Percent

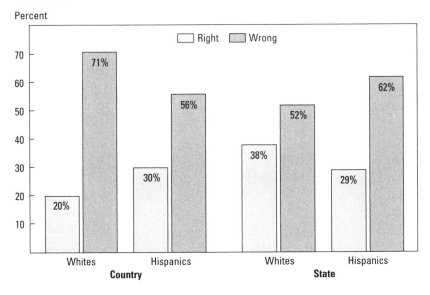

Source: Author's analysis of Brookings Mountain West survey, August-September 2010.
a. Respondents were asked whether the country was going in the right direction or was on the wrong track; the same question was asked about the respondent's state.

state's direction—very negative for Hispanics and only modestly negative for whites (table 3-4). It was the only Mountain West state, of the four examined, where Hispanics were more pessimistic than whites about the state's future direction. Overall, while both whites and Hispanics in the Mountain West tended to show some concern about the future direction of the country and their state, Hispanics were generally less negative, with the exception of those in Arizona.

Views of Leaders and Parties. Nearly two years after the 2008 election, Mountain West whites and Hispanics held differing and sometimes surprising views of political leaders and their parties. The results of the ranking of individuals and organizations are summarized in table 3-5. Among the several politicians and groups examined, the largest white-Hispanic discrepancy was apparent in views of President Barack Obama. Fifty-three percent of Hispanics had a favorable view of Obama while 35 percent had an unfavorable view. White opinions were almost the reverse, suggesting underlying Democratic leanings for Hispanics, along with an affinity for a minority president.

Table 3-4. Percent of Whites and Hispanics Indicating Right Direction minus Percent Indicating Wrong Track for National and State Governments, Selected States

Government	Arizona	Colorado	Nevada	New Mexico
National				
Whites	−59	−43	−60	−46
Hispanics	−36	0	−24	−25
State				
Whites	−14	−13	−63	−32
Hispanics	−57	2	−48	−28

Source: Author's analysis of Brookings Mountain West survey, August-September 2010.

Table 3-5. White and Hispanic Opinions of Public Figures and Party Members, Mountain West States

	Opinion		Favorable minus
Figure/member	Favorable	Unfavorable	unfavorable
Barack Obama			
Whites	34	55	−21
Hispanics	53	35	18
George W. Bush			
Whites	41	44	−3
Hispanics	32	51	−19
Sarah Palin			
Whites	35	47	−12
Hispanics	24	52	−28
Democrats in Congress			
Whites	25	57	−32
Hispanics	40	37	3
Republicans in Congress			
Whites	32	42	−10
Hispanics	30	47	−17
Tea Party members			
Whites	36	34	2
Hispanics	28	31	−3

Source: Author's analysis of Brookings Mountain West survey, August-September 2010.

One might expect a similar white-Hispanic difference in the opposite direction for former Republican president George W. Bush. In fact, Hispanic opinions of Bush were almost the mirror image of their views of Obama. Whites, on the other hand, were fairly tepid in their support of Bush, with slightly more disapproval (44 percent) than approval (41 percent). Both Hispanics and whites showed marked disapproval of Sarah Palin, the defeated Republican vice presidential candidate in 2008, who has since been strongly associated with the Tea Party. Tea Party members in general were not viewed very favorably by whites, as there were almost as many whites who disapproved of them as approved.

There was also a small surprise in views of Democratic and Republican members of Congress. As might be expected, Democrats were viewed quite unfavorably by whites. However, only a tepid 40 percent of Hispanics had favorable views of congressional Democrats. Similarly, only 32 percent of whites held favorable views of congressional Republicans, a percentage only slightly higher than that of Hispanics.

Clearly there were marked white-Hispanic differences in favorable views of President Obama. But those differences did not carry over as sharply in views of other leaders, and, in the case of members of Congress, there was almost uniform disapproval of both parties by whites and Hispanics.

Priority Issues

The ability to attract both white and Hispanic voters will also hinge on which issues these two groups see as high priorities. The survey assessed priority by asking respondents to rank a series of twelve different issues. Those ranking highest for whites and Hispanics are shown in table 3-6. Given the dismal economy, it is not surprising that both whites and Hispanics ranked "creating new jobs and economic growth" as their top priority. For Hispanics, this issue tied with "improving schools" as most important, though "improving schools" ranked second for whites. Below those issues there were sharp shifts. Hispanics were concerned with fighting crime and drugs in the community, protecting the environment and natural resources, and ensuring access to affordable health care. For whites, the last two issues were replaced, among the top five, with reducing federal government spending and reducing the flow of illegal immigrants to the United States. Whites also were concerned with crimes and drugs in the community, but that was seen as priority by only 43 percent of whites; in contrast, 59 percent of Hispanics saw the issue as a priority.

Table 3-6. Percent of Whites and Hispanics Ranking Selected Issues
as Extremely Important, Mountain West States

Group/rank	Percent	Issue
Whites		
1	57	Creating new jobs and economic growth
2	50	Improving schools
3	49	Reducing federal government spending
4	49	Reducing the flow of illegal immigrants to the United States
5	43	Fighting crime and drugs in our community
Hispanics		
1	63	Creating new jobs and economic growth
2	63	Improving schools
3	59	Fighting crime and drugs in our community
4	48	Protecting our environment and natural resources
5	47	Ensuring access to affordable health care

Source: Author's analysis of Brookings Mountain West survey, August-September 2010.

The issue of gaining access to health care ties into the health care law (Patient Protection and Affordable Care Act) passed by Congress and signed by President Obama in early 2010. This law remains controversial and is likely to affect voting in the 2012 election. The survey asked respondents a question about this law, specifically: "Based on what you have heard so far, do you support or oppose the new health care reform plan?"

As shown in figure 3-9, there was a sharp white-Hispanic division in support of this plan. Among whites, 61 percent opposed the plan, including 50 percent who strongly opposed the plan, while 32 percent supported it. Among Hispanics, 50 percent supported the plan, while 43 percent opposed it. This was one of the several issues that reflected greater Hispanic support for government-funded measures related to health, schools, and the environment that tend to be promoted by the Obama administration and Democratic candidates for office.

Illegal Immigration. As indicated in chapter 5 of this volume, Mountain West residents felt that illegal immigration impacted them more than residents in other regions. At the heart of this issue is the controversial Arizona immigration law (Arizona State Bill 1070), which engages local law enforcement in identifying illegal immigrants. The following question was asked specifically about this law:

Figure 3-9. Attitudes toward the Obama Health Care Plan, Whites and Hispanics

Percent

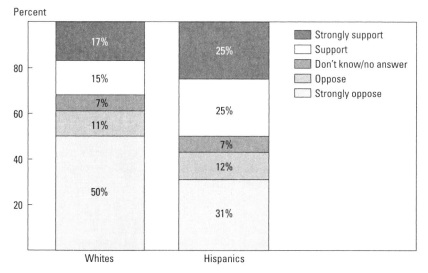

Source: Author's analysis of Brookings Mountain West survey, August-September 2010.

As you may know, the state of Arizona recently passed a law that gives the police the power to question anyone they suspect is in the country illegally, requires people to produce documents verifying their status if asked, and allows officers to detain anyone who cannot do so. Do you think this law goes too far in dealing with the issue of illegal immigration, doesn't go far enough, or is about right?

Regionwide, 46 percent of residents thought that the law was about right, with another 17 percent indicating that it did not go far enough.[7] Far less than half, 37 percent, said that it went too far. As shown in figure 3-10, the white-Hispanic divide on this question was especially stark. Among whites, half thought that it was about right and another 19 percent thought that it did not go far enough; only 30 percent thought that it went too far. Yet among Hispanics, fully 59 percent said that it went too far, 29 percent agreed that it was about right, and just 12 percent indicated that it did not go far enough.

These patterns differed somewhat among individual states, as shown in table 3-7. Not surprisingly, Arizona showed the greatest white-Hispanic extremes. Fully 67 percent of Arizona Hispanics thought that the law went too far while only 21 percent of whites did so. The smallest white-Hispanic

Figure 3-10. Attitudes toward the Arizona Immigration Law, Whites and Hispanics

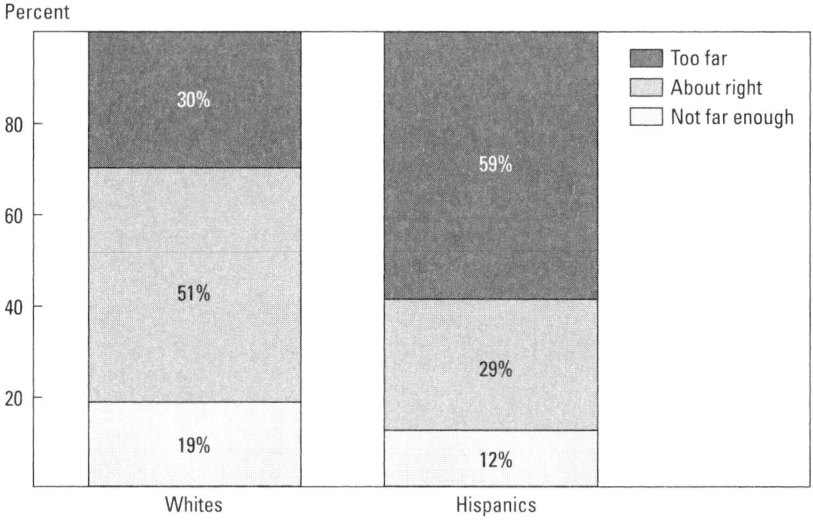

Percent

Source: Author's analysis of Brookings Mountain West survey, August-September 2010.

gap on this question was in neighboring New Mexico, where less than half (45 percent) of Hispanics and 34 percent of whites thought that Arizona's law went too far. New Mexico's Hispanic population is a larger share of the state total population, but it comprises fewer recent immigrants than Arizona's population does. While smaller than in Arizona, the white-Hispanic gap on this item was still fairly substantial in both Nevada and Colorado.

In another series of questions, residents were asked whether there should be more or less government involvement in stopping the flow of illegal immigrants across the border or in dealing with those already here. As shown in table 3-8, both whites and Hispanics would like to see more rather than less federal involvement in both areas. Over half of each group would like to see more involvement, though for whites the percentages were higher than 70 percent. When the question involved state rather than federal involvement, support shrank slightly, but responses still favored more state involvement. The concern with illegal immigration and desire for more government involvement seemed to be shared by whites and Hispanics in these states. Yet laws such as those enacted in Arizona tended to be viewed as overly severe and punitive by Hispanics, who were strongly opposed to them. These findings suggest that the substance of immigration solutions

Table 3-7. Percent of Whites and Hispanics Indicating that Arizona Immigration Law
Goes Too Far, Selected States

Group	Arizona	Colorado	Nevada	New Mexico	Mountain West
Whites	21	37	29	34	29
Hispanics	67	58	48	45	57

Source: Author's analysis of Brookings Mountain West survey, August-September 2010.

will be important to politicians who wish to receive the backing of Hispanics
as well as whites.

Minorities, the Mountain West, and the Next Election

What do these results imply for the 2012 presidential election? They certainly
show that minorities, Hispanics particularly, can and likely will make a difference in selected purple states, especially the expanding number of purple
states in the Mountain West. The rapid growth of minorities in Nevada,
Arizona, and Colorado and the already large share of them in New Mexico
could make a difference in the Mountain West states, which, as a group,
will represent thirty-one Electoral College votes, based on the 2010 census
apportionment. In 2008, Hispanics alone tipped the balance toward President Obama in Nevada and New Mexico. In 2012, they may make the difference in Colorado and may make Arizona—previously a solid Republican
bastion—more competitive.

The survey results presented here suggest that politicians must walk a fine
line on issues like health care and immigration if they want to appeal to both
whites and Hispanics. Republican-leaning whites in these states are wary of
the Obama health care law and strongly in favor of strict state and federal
measures designed to reduce illegal immigration. Both of these issues as well
as general views on Obama's presidency tend to split whites and Hispanics
in the Mountain West.

The 2008 election showed that energizing Hispanic and other minority
voters led to the high turnout that was key to their influence on election outcomes in critical purple states. Results of the 2012 presidential election will
likely be even more sensitive to high minority turnout because the Republican-leaning white majority, angered by the deteriorating economy, is likely
to be more energized than it was in November 2008.

In the long run, Hispanics and other minorities will increasingly influence
election results in these previously "white" Mountain West states, keeping

Table 3-8. Whites' and Hispanics' Desired Level of Federal and State Involvement in Illegal Migration, Mountain West States
Percent

Federal/state involvement	Level			More minus less
	More	Same/ don't know	Less	
Federal				
Stopping the flow of illegal immigrants across our border				
Whites	77	17	6	71
Hispanics	68	19	13	55
Dealing with the millions of illegal immigrants within our country				
Whites	72	19	9	63
Hispanics	58	22	20	38
State				
Dealing with the millions of illegal immigrants within our country				
Whites	66	22	12	54
Hispanics	52	26	22	30

Source: Author's analysis of Brookings Mountain West survey, August-September 2010.

them very much in play in national elections. As young minority residents advance to voting age and make up ever larger shares of eligible voters, candidates for national, state, and local offices will need to cater to their interests in government solutions for the economy, good schools, affordable health care, and the environment. With respect to the political effects of minorities' increased electoral clout, "demography is destiny." In the short run, however, politicians will have to strike a delicate balance between the interests of minority populations and those of the typically larger white, Republican-leaning population. Minorities' near-term influence will depend on particular candidates' interest in and commitment to energizing these groups, as was the case in November 2008.

Notes

1. The polling data presented here are from the National Election Pool exit poll, conducted by Edison Media Research and Mitofsky International for a consortium of news organizations, for 2008 (www.cnn.com/ELECTION/2008/results/polls.main/) and 2004 (www.cnn.com/ELECTION/2004/pages/results/states/US/P/00/epolls.0.html). The data

on voters, eligible voters, and voter turnout are drawn from of the U.S. Census Bureau Current Population Survey "Voting and Registration Supplement," November 2004 (www.icpsr.umich.edu/icpsrweb/RCMD/studies/04272/version/2) and November 2008 (www.icpsr.umich.edu/icpsrweb/RCMD/studies/25643/version/1).

2. Current Population Survey turnout rates tend to be slightly inflated by the tendency of some respondents to overreport their voter participation, but that should not affect the time trends discussed here.

3. Note that there are some slight differences in shares of the electorate as measured by the Current Population Survey Voter Supplement and by the National Election Pool exit polls.

4. The data shown in figures 3-5 and 3-6 draw from the 2010 Current Population Survey annual demographic supplement taken in March 2010.

5. This survey of adults in the six Mountain West states was conducted August 23 through September 1 by Gerstein and Agne Strategic Communications. Overall sample size was 2,000; sampling was adjusted to ensure at least 250 respondents in each state. See Bowman and Teixeira, chapter 5, for a more thorough discussion of the survey and an overview of its results for the total populations of these states. Hispanic-white comparisons presented here were possible for the aggregated six-state region and for four individual states: New Mexico, Arizona, Nevada, and Colorado.

6. The remaining respondents either did not know or did not answer.

7. These tabulations and those in figure 3-10 exclude the 3 percent of respondents who either did not know or did not answer.

four

The Political Attitudes
of the Millennial Generation
in the Mountain West

Scott Keeter

The politics of the American West are frequently described as paradoxical—an uneasy, awkward marriage of rugged frontier ideals and rapid demographic change. But change is at the heart of the frontier spirit, and opportunity is a core motivation of the many Americans settling in the West. Young people are at the center of this change, especially in the Mountain West region where the population tilts young. And young adults in the region are politically distinctive, just as they are in the rest of the country. This chapter will examine the political attitudes and behavior of the youngest generation of adults in the Mountain West, comparing them with their elders in the region and with young people living elsewhere in the nation.

Today's young adults have come of age during a politically turbulent and polarized period in American politics. During much of the second half of the past decade, the Republican Party was in disfavor, largely because of the public's unhappiness with the presidency of George W. Bush and some of the actions of the Republican congresses of the period. More recently, the nation's economic troubles have led to similar public unhappiness with Democratic stewardship of the country. President Barack Obama's approval ratings have slumped, though not yet to the depths reached by his predecessor. But the Democratic Party suffered a resounding defeat in the 2010 midterm elections, erasing many of the gains the party had built in Congress in the 2006 and 2008 elections.

As these political events have unfolded, the nation also has been under-going slow but significant changes in its demographic composition and in some key social values, including tolerance of diversity. In the view of many political observers, the combination of the political, demographic, and social changes has left a strong imprint on the youngest generation of adults, the Millennials—so called because many of them came of age politically near or after the turn of the twenty-first century. They are significantly more diverse ethnically and racially than older Americans. And beginning with the 2004 presidential election, members of this generation have exhibited a significant tilt toward the Democratic Party, providing Democratic presidential and congressional candidates with stronger support than any other age group. This pattern reached a peak in 2008, when Millennial voters supported Barack Obama's candidacy by a 66 percent to 32 percent margin on election day. Even though support for the Democrats has waned since 2008 among both younger and older Americans, younger voters show stronger support.

The Democratic tendency among young people nationally is rooted in political attitudes and values that differ sharply from those held by older voters. The young are more politically liberal in a host of ways: they support a more activist government, the social safety net, regulation, environmental protection, and the health care reform legislation passed in 2010. They also are more accepting than older people of immigration, same-sex marriage, and interracial dating and marriage. They are significantly less likely than older people to identify with a religious tradition. The product of these attitudes has been a higher level of affiliation with the Democratic Party and a greater propensity to describe their political ideology as liberal.

All of these distinctive characteristics of young people nationally are also present among young adults in the Mountain West. As this chapter will show, the attitudes and values of young people in the region are nearly indistinguishable from those of young people elsewhere. Where young people in the region differ from young people in the rest of the country is in their party affiliation and voting behavior. Like their older counterparts in the Mountain West, young people in the region are significantly more Republican—but still less Republican than their elders.

This analysis draws on survey data from several sources, including Pew Research Center surveys conducted since 2000, the Pew Forum on Religion & Public Life's 2007 U.S. Religious Landscape Survey, U.S. Census postelection surveys of voter registration and turnout, the National Election Pool's 2008 and 2010 exit polls, and the Brookings Mountain West 2010 survey of adults in the region. Details for these sources may be found in the appendix to this chapter.

Figure 4-1. Party Affiliation and Leaning for Voters Aged 18–29

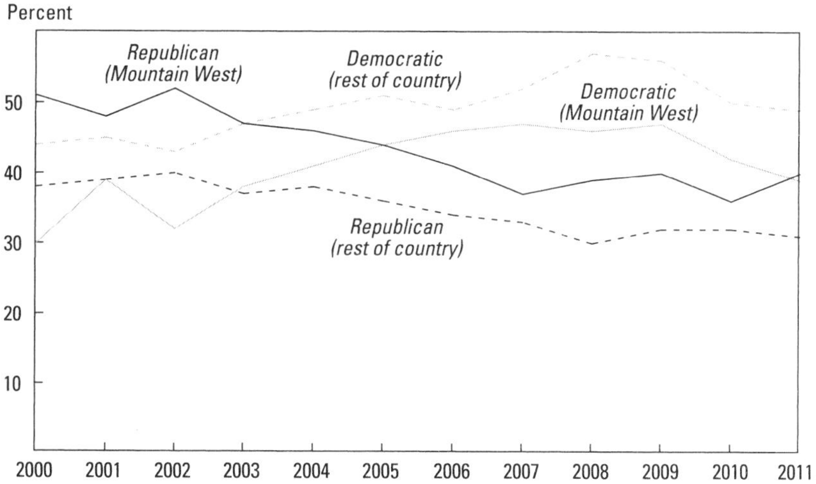

Source: Compilation of national polls conducted 2000–11 by the Pew Research Center for the People & the Press.

Party Affiliation and the Vote

As the twenty-first century dawned there was little difference nationally in the party affiliation of younger and older people. In the Mountain West, young people ages 18 to 29 were actually somewhat less Democratic than those 30 and older. Republicans and independents who leaned Republican in the region outnumbered Democrats among young people by a 51–30 percent margin, exceeding the 47–39 percent margin among those 30 and older. In the rest of the United States, Democrats outnumbered Republicans among young people by 44–38 percent. (See figure 4-1.)

Following the 2002 elections, which were generally good for the Republican Party, Democratic Party affiliation began to grow among young adults, both in the Mountain West and the rest of the country. By 2005 Democratic and Republican affiliation among the young was equal in the region, and by 2007 the Democratic number among young residents of the Mountain West was 10 points higher than the Republican number (47 percent to 37 percent). In 2008 young residents of the region favored the Democratic Party by 46 percent to 39 percent, while those in the rest of the country were Democratic by a huge 57–30 percent margin.

Economic troubles have blunted the Democratic advantage nationally and in the region, but Democratic affiliation among the young—though

Figure 4-2. Party Affiliation by Age in the Mountain West

Percent

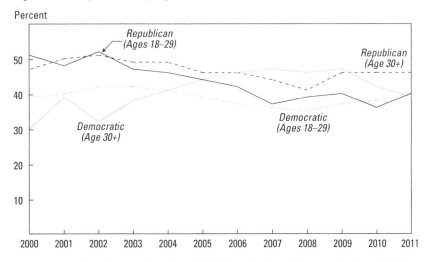

Source: Compilation of national polls conducted 2009–11 by the Pew Research Center for the People & the Press.

lower than in 2008—still matches Republican affiliation in the Mountain West (39 percent Democratic and leaning, 40 percent Republican and leaning); elsewhere the Democratic margin in 2011 is a much larger 49 percent to 31 percent.

Compared with younger people, fewer older people in the Mountain West were Republican as the decade began, but this quickly changed. By 2003 Republican Party affiliation was slightly higher among older residents, and the gap has been widened in much of the rest of the decade. In 2010, 46 percent of those 30 and older in the region were Republican or leaned Republican, compared with just 36 percent of those 18–29. With the decline of Democratic identification among the young over the past two years, the percentage of younger and older people in the region affiliating with or leaning to the Democratic Party is now the same (39 percent). (See figure 4-2.)

Young voters in the Mountain West were slightly more supportive of Barack Obama's presidential bid than were older voters in the region, but their support was nowhere near as strong as that of their counterparts elsewhere. Just 51 percent of those 18–29 in the region voted for Obama, compared with 67 percent in the rest of the country. Still, 51 percent was slightly higher than the 47 percent Obama got among voters 30 and older in the region. (See table 4-1.)

The age pattern seen in the election persists today in evaluations of Obama's performance in office. Young residents of the region are somewhat

Table 4-1. 2008 Presidential Vote, by Age[a]

Percent

Candidate	Ages 18–29		Ages 30+		Total		
	MW	Other	MW	Other	MW	Other	All
Obama	51	67	47	50	48	53	53
McCain	47	31	51	48	50	45	46
Other/Don't know	2	2	2	2	2	2	1
Sample size	1,807	3,530	7,437	13,595	9,471	14,066	

Source: Mountain West results are from merged state exit polls by the National Election Pool; other results are from National Election Pool national exit poll.

a. MW = Mountain West; Other = rest of country. "All" is actual election result and not part of the survey.

Table 4-2. Attitude toward President, by Age, 2010[a]

Percent

Attitude	Ages 18–29		Ages 30+		Total		
	MW	Other	MW	Other	MW	Other	All
Approve	44	56	36	44	37	46	45
Disapprove	44	32	56	47	54	45	45
Other/Don't know	12	12	8	9	9	9	9
Sample size	192	3,000	1,163	16,071	1,371	19,388	20,759

Source: Compilation of national polls conducted in 2010 by the Pew Research Center for the People & the Press.

a. MW = Mountain West; Other = rest of country.

more supportive of Obama than those 30 and older (44 percent approval vs. 36 percent). But young people outside the region are considerably more supportive of the president (56 percent approval), as are those 30 and older (44 percent approval). (See table 4-2.)

While the pro-Democratic tendency of young people has been evident in the Mountain West, even if not to the same degree as in the rest of the country, young people in the region are nearly identical to young people in the rest of the country on broader measures of political values.

One key indicator of political sentiment is ideological identification—whether a person identifies as conservative, moderate, or liberal in his or her political views. In the population overall, far more people say they are conservative than liberal. But among young people ages 18–29, about equal numbers identify as liberal and conservative. This is true in the Mountain West and in the rest of the country. (See table 4-3.)

Table 4-3. Political Ideology, by Age, 2009–10[a]

Percent

Ideology	Ages 18–29		Ages 30+		Total	
	MW	Other	MW	Other	MW	Other
Conservative	27	28	45	41	41	38
Moderate	42	38	33	34	35	35
Liberal	27	27	17	19	19	20
Other/Don't know	4	7	5	6	5	6
Sample size	245	3,720	1,474	20,384	1,747	24,522

Source: Compilation of national polls conducted in 2009–10 by the Pew Research Center for the People & the Press.

a. MW = Mountain West; Other = rest of country.

These tendencies appear in more concrete questions about political issues and values. Young people, whether in the region or elsewhere, are more liberal on many questions about the scope of government and especially on social issues.

On a broad question about the size of government asked in 2007 by the Pew Forum on Religion & Public Life, fewer young people than older people in the region—and in the rest of the country—favored the idea of a smaller government providing fewer services. Residents of the Mountain West were slightly more favorable to the idea of a smaller government than those elsewhere (47–42 percent). But just 29 percent of those under 30 in the region favored the idea, compared with 53 percent of those 30 and older. (See table 4-4.)

One specific manifestation of activist government is the social safety net. In 2007, 62 percent of Americans agreed with a statement that government should do more to help the needy even it means going deeper in debt. Among young adults, however, 68 percent agreed. Moreover, there was no difference on this question in the views of young people in the Mountain West and those elsewhere. Older people, whether in the region or not, were less supportive, with 56 percent in the Mountain West and 61 percent elsewhere favoring more government aid to the needy.

Social Issues

Young people in the Mountain West also mirror their age counterparts in opinions on two key social issues: homosexuality and abortion. As with

Table 4-4. Opinions on Government, by Age, 2007[a]

Percent

Opinion	Ages 18–29		Ages 30+		Total		
	MW	Other	MW	Other	MW	Other	All
I prefer . . .							
Smaller government with fewer services	29	26	53	46	47	42	43
Larger government with more services	65	67	35	42	42	47	46
Other/Don't know	6	7	13	12	11	11	11
Government . . .							
Should do more to help the needy	68	68	56	61	58	62	62
Can't afford to do more	26	27	34	30	32	29	29
Other/Don't know	7	7	11	9	10	9	9
Stricter environmental laws and regulations . . .							
Are worth the cost	65	63	58	60	59	61	61
Cost too many jobs and hurt the economy	28	31	33	30	32	30	30
Other/Don't know	8	6	9	10	8	9	9
Sample size	293	3,949	1,821	28,632	2,167	33,389	35,556

Source: Pew Forum on Religion & Public Life's U.S. Religious Landscape Survey, 2007.
a. MW = Mountain West; Other = rest of country.

young people nationally, those in the region tend to be significantly more tolerant of homosexuality than older adults. Asked in 2007 whether homosexuality should be accepted or discouraged by society, a sizeable majority of young people, both in the region and elsewhere (62 percent and 63 percent), said it should be accepted. Barely half of older people agreed (49 percent in the region, 47 percent elsewhere).

On abortion younger and older adults are much more similar in their opinions, both in the Mountain West and elsewhere. Young people are about evenly divided on whether abortion should be legal in all or most instances (47 percent legal, 48 percent illegal in the region, 49 percent and 47 percent elsewhere). Older adults tilt slightly in a pro-choice direction, with half of those 30 and older in the region favoring legal abortion (compared with 44 percent who say most or all abortions should be illegal). Outside the region, supporters of legal abortion outnumber opponents 52–41 percent. (See table 4-5.)

Table 4-5. Attitudes toward Homosexuality and Abortion, by Age, 2007[a]

Percent

Attitude	Ages 18–29		Ages 30+		Total		
	MW	Other	MW	Other	MW	Other	All
Homosexuality should be . . .							
Accepted	62	63	49	47	52	50	50
Discouraged	29	30	40	42	37	40	40
Other/Don't know	9	8	12	11	11	10	10
Abortion should be . . .							
Legal in all/most cases	47	49	50	52	49	51	51
Illegal in all/most cases	48	47	44	41	45	42	42
Other/Don't know	5	4	6	7	6	6	6
Sample size	293	3,949	1,821	28,632	2,167	33,389	35,556

Source: Pew Forum on Religion & Public Life's U.S. Religious Landscape Survey, 2007
a. MW = Mountain West; Other = rest of country.

Religious Affiliation and Commitment

One politically relevant way the Mountain West is different from the rest of the country is in its religious makeup. The area is significantly less Protestant, though arguably its Christians are no less conservative than elsewhere in the nation. The region is, however, somewhat more secular and unaffiliated than the country as a whole. These distinctive characteristics are clearly evident in the members of its Millennial generation as well. (See table 4-6.)

White evangelical Protestants—a mainstay of the Republican Party—make up slightly more than one in five Americans. In the Mountain West, they are only 13 percent of adults. And they are only 7 percent of young people in the region. Because there are fewer African Americans in the region than elsewhere in the country, black Protestants make up only a tiny fraction of the population (2 percent versus 9 percent elsewhere).

But the absence of evangelicals is more than offset by the sizeable Mormon population, which is just as politically conservative on many issues. Overall, 14 percent of adults in the region affiliate with the Church of Jesus Christ of Latter-day Saints, including 18 percent of those ages 18–29. Elsewhere in the country, Mormons make up only about 1 percent of the population.

Roman Catholics are about as prevalent in the region as they are elsewhere in the country, but the Catholic population is more racially diverse in the Mountain West. Non-white Catholics (mostly Hispanic) slightly outnumber

Table 4-6. Religious Affiliation and Attendance, by Age[a]

Percent

Affiliation	Ages 18–29		Ages 30+		Total	
	MW	Other	MW	Other	MW	Other
Protestant	27	45	40	55	37	53
White non-Hispanic evangelical	7	13	14	22	13	20
White non-Hispanic mainline	9	14	17	19	15	18
Black non-Hispanic Protestant	2	10	2	9	2	9
Other Protestant	9	8	7	5	7	6
Catholic	18	21	21	24	21	23
White non-Hispanic Catholic	5	11	10	17	9	16
Other Catholic	13	10	12	7	12	7
Mormon	18	1	13	1	14	1
Other religion	5	6	5	5	5	5
Unaffiliated	30	26	18	14	21	16
Attendance at religious services						
Once a week or more often	32	30	37	40	36	38
1–2 times a month/a few times a year	34	39	29	32	30	34
Seldom or never	34	31	33	26	33	27
Sample size	716	10,636	4,342	64,109	5,135	76,113

Source: Compilation of national polls conducted 2009–10 by the Pew Research Center for the People & the Press.

a. MW = Mountain West; Other = Rest of country. "Don't know" responses are not shown. Categories will not sum to 100 percent due to rounding.

white non-Hispanic Catholics in the region (by 12–9 percent), and do so by a wider 13–5 percent margin among young adults.

Much as is the case among all adults, young residents of the Mountain West are somewhat less likely to affiliate with a religious tradition at all. And like young people across the country, they are more likely than their elders to be unaffiliated. The unaffiliated are among the Democratic Party's strongest supporters. Consistent with their lower levels of affiliation in the region, adults in the Mountain West are somewhat less likely than adults elsewhere to attend religious services. But this pattern is somewhat less evident among young people.

Political Engagement and Voting

The Millennial generation made its mark with higher than average voter turnout in the 2004, 2006, and 2008 elections. Still, its level of engagement

Table 4-7. Political Engagement, by Age[a]

Percent

Measure of engagement	Ages 18–29		Ages 30+		Total		
	MW	Other	MW	Other	MW	Other	All
Voter registration							
Registered to vote	51	59	78	82	72	77	76
Not registered or not certain	49	41	22	18	28	23	24
Sample size	730	10,823	4,378	64,490	5,185	76,695	81,880
I follow government and public affairs . . .							
Most of the time	31	33	57	56	51	52	52
Some of the time	40	35	28	28	30	29	29
Now and then/hardly at all	28	30	14	16	18	18	18
Other/Don't know	2	1	1	1	1	1	1
Sample size	293	3,949	1,821	28,632	2,167	33,389	35,556

Sources: Voter registration data are from a compilation of national polls conducted 2009–10 by the Pew Research Center for the People & the Press; question on interest in government and public affairs is from the Pew Forum on Religion & Public Life's U.S. Religious Landscape Survey, 2007.

a. MW = Mountain West; Other = Rest of the country.

fell far below that of older adults, as is typically the case in American politics. Overall, adults in the Mountain West are slightly less likely to be registered to vote—a difference that is larger among young adults. But residents of the region—whether young or old—are no different from residents of the rest of the country in the percentage who say they follow government and public affairs most of the time. (See table 4-7.)

Postelection surveys by the U.S. Census measure voter turnout, and the nonprofit organization CIRCLE analyzes these to compare younger and older adults (see table 4-8). Despite a relatively high national turnout figure of 51 percent for young adults in 2008 (ages 18–29, the Millennial generation), turnout in most of the Mountain West states slipped below this mark: 49 percent in Nevada, 47 percent in Arizona and New Mexico, and just 37 percent in Utah. Only in Colorado did a 52 percent turnout among young people match the national average. (As with all surveys of voter turnout, this voting supplement to the Current Population Survey likely overstates actual turnout levels.)

Part of the explanation for these varying rates is found in demography and part in politics. In 2008 Colorado, New Mexico, and Nevada were all focal points for Democratic Party mobilization, which tended to increase

Table 4-8. Voter Turnout, by Age

Percent

State	2008		2010	
	18–29	30+	18–29	30+
National	51	67	24	51
Arizona	47	64	31	54
Colorado	52	73	30	58
New Mexico	47	67	21	50
Nevada	49	63	24	47
Utah	37	60	17	46

Source: Data from 2008 and 2010 Current Population Survey Voting and Registration Supplement, compiled by the Center for Information and Research on Civic Learning and Engagement (CIRCLE) at Tufts University, Medford, Massachusetts.

turnout. The larger Hispanic population in the latter two states may have held down overall turnout, but they were able to match states with much less diverse populations in the region. For their part, Arizona and Utah fell below the national average. In Utah, which was not contested at the presidential level, overall turnout was at 60 percent for adults 30 and older and only 37 percent for those 18–29.

As is always the case in off-year elections, turnout rates in 2010 were much lower than in 2008 and the fall-off in youth voting was particularly steep. Nationally, just 24 percent of young people 18–29 turned out, compared with 51 percent of those 30 and older. But the effects of political mobilization can also be seen in the 2010 election. The Mountain region featured several high-profile gubernatorial and U.S. Senate races. Perhaps as a result, young people in Arizona and Colorado exceeded the national turnout average, and those in Nevada matched it. New Mexico lagged slightly behind the national average, and Utah fell far below, as it did in 2008.

Opinions on Current Issues

Thanks to a comprehensive Brookings Mountain West survey conducted among 2,000 adults in the region between August 23 and September 1, 2010, we can examine opinions among residents on several current issues facing the country as well as their broader political values (see table 4-9). The survey interviewed a minimum of 251 adults in each of the six states in the region and included enough young people (N = 307) that their opinions can

Table 4-9. Opinions on Current Issues, by Age
Percent

Opinion	18–29	30–64	65+	All
Arizona immigration law . . .				
Goes too far	49	34	25	36
Is about right	36	47	48	45
Does not go far enough	14	16	24	17
Other/Don't know	1	3	3	3
Same-sex marriage				
Should be allowed	57	43	25	43
Should not be allowed	39	49	65	49
Other/Don't know	5	8	10	7
Obama health care plan				
Support	45	37	37	39
Oppose	47	57	58	55
Other/Don't know	8	6	5	6
Health care reform law . . .				
Is an important first step in lowering costs and ensuring access	52	44	42	45
Will lead to higher costs and taxes and must be changed significantly or repealed	45	53	55	53
Other/Don't know	4	3	3	3
Financial reform legislation				
Favor	54	52	49	52
Oppose	33	39	40	38
Other/Don't know	14	9	11	10
Direction of the country				
Right direction	32	22	22	24
Wrong track	58	68	69	66
Other/Don't know	11	10	10	10
Direction of the state				
Right direction	42	34	40	37
Wrong track	48	57	49	54
Other/Don't know	10	9	11	9
Sample size	307	1,210	446	2,000

Source: Brookings Mountain West survey, 2010.

be compared with those of older adults. Among other topics, the survey's respondents were asked about health care reform and the overhaul of the regulatory system for Wall Street banks, the new Arizona immigration law, same-sex marriage, and the general direction of the country and the states in the region.

As has been the case nationally, young residents of the Mountain West (those ages 18–29) are more positive about the direction of the country than are older adults. About one-third (32 percent) say the country is generally going in the right direction, while 58 percent say it's off on the wrong track. Older adults are somewhat less positive, with 22 percent of those 30–64 and 65 and older saying we are on the right track.

Opinions about the direction of their state are somewhat more favorable and not so clearly related to age. Overall, 37 percent say their state in going in the right direction, with 54 percent saying it's off on the wrong track. Among young adults, 42 percent say the direction is right.

Residents of the region render a somewhat negative judgment on perhaps the most controversial accomplishment of the first two years of the Obama administration and the Democratic Congress, health care reform. A 55 percent majority opposes the health care reform plan, while 39 percent support it. Among young residents of the region, opinion is divided (45 percent support, 47 percent oppose). Yet, asked if the measure should be changed significantly or repealed, only 45 percent of young respondents indicate that it should be. Majorities of other age groups favored significant change or repeal.

The region's public is more positive regarding another important legislative achievement of the past two years, financial reform. A 52 percent majority favors the reform package, while 38 percent oppose it. Opinion on this issue does not vary significantly by age, with young people supporting it at about the same rate as other age groups.

On two highly contentious social issues, younger residents of the region are more socially liberal, just as they are in the rest of the nation. Asked whether the new Arizona immigration law goes too far, does not go far enough, or is about right, a plurality of the region's residents (45 percent) says it's about right. But among young adults, a 49 percent plurality says the law goes too far. Older residents (those 65 and older) are more likely than others to say the law does not go far enough (24 percent versus 16 percent and 14 percent for adults 30–64 and 18–29, respectively).

And on the question of same-sex marriage, a solid majority of 57 percent of young adults in the region says that it should be permitted; just 39 percent disagree. A plurality of those 30–64 opposes same-sex marriage (49 percent oppose, 43 percent favor), while a 65 percent majority of adults 65 and older opposes allowing gays and lesbians to marry legally.

The Mountain West region has a reputation for both environmentalist sentiment and libertarian views on federal government regulation of natural resources and development. Majorities in the poll strongly endorsed the idea that state officials should make protection of the environment and natural resources a top priority, with only small age differences on this question. The poll also posed three questions about specific aspects of this issue using so-called balanced alternative questions, which pose two statements and ask respondents which comes closer to their own view. Young people were more supportive of specific aspects of environmental protection than were older adults. Asked to choose between state investments in clean and renewable energy or coal and nuclear, young residents of the region by nearly three to one (71–28 percent) opted for the former. Majorities of other age groups did so too, but not by such lopsided margins.

Similarly, a clear majority of young people (57 percent) supported the idea of government regulation of development and growth, while older age groups were more divided on the question. Pluralities of those ages 30–64 and 65 and older supported regulation of development and growth, but nearly as many agreed that government regulation unfairly restricts property rights and limits economic growth.

Overall, slightly more in the poll agreed that climate change is a real threat with potentially disastrous consequences (51 percent) than supported the view that it is an unsupported theory used to justify radical energy policies (44 percent). Compared with those ages 65 and older (43 percent of whom say climate change is real), slightly more young people (55 percent) take that position. (See table 4-10.)

General Views of Government

Using balanced alternative questions, the Mountain West survey probed views on three general questions about the government (table 4-11). Residents of the region were evenly divided (48 percent each) on the question of whether government should ensure equal opportunity and basic security, or strictly limit its role in individuals' lives and let them live with the consequences. Young adults were no different from others in their response on this item. But young people were more supportive than the oldest group of adults in endorsing the importance of government regulation in helping workers and consumers.

On a general question about the impact of immigrants on society (as opposed to a specific immigration policy issue), young respondents to the poll also were more likely than the oldest respondents to choose the view that immigrants strengthen the economy and enrich the culture, rather than that they are a burden.

Table 4-10. Opinions on Climate Change, Energy Policy, and Development, by Age
Percent

Opinion	18–29	30–64	65+	All
Climate change is . . .				
A real threat with potentially disastrous consequences	55	51	43	51
Just a theory designed to support radical energy policies	40	44	49	44
Other/Don't know	5	5	8	5
State energy policy is better off . . .				
Investing in clean renewable energy solutions	71	64	56	64
Investing in proven technologies like clean coal and nuclear energy sources	28	29	36	30
Other/Don't know	1	7	9	6
Regulation of development				
We need government regulation to prevent overdevelopment and plan growth	57	49	49	51
Government regulation of development unfairly restricts property rights and limits economic growth	38	45	43	43
Other/Don't know	5	6	8	6
Sample size	307	1,210	446	2,000

Source: Brookings Mountain West survey, 2010.

The 2010 Elections

The 2010 midterm elections brought a resounding Republican victory in much of the country, though Democrats had reason to cheer some of the results in Nevada and Colorado. No estimate of the Millennial vote for House of Representatives in the region is available, but the Brookings Mountain West pre-election survey provides one gauge of the likely pattern of support. In general the findings are consistent with the results of previous elections. Among registered voters, the poll found a slight plurality of young people favoring Democratic candidates for the House (45–40 percent), while older voters favored Republican candidates. Among those who said they were almost certain to vote, 46 percent of young people favored Republican candidates and 43 percent supported Democratic candidates. And—as in other parts of the country—young people were significantly less likely than older ones to say they were certain to vote. (See table 4-12.)

The region featured several key statewide races. Exit polling was not conducted in New Mexico and Utah, and the sample size of young voters was too small in Colorado to permit an estimate of the direction of the youth

Table 4-11. Opinions on Political Issues, by Age

Percent

Opinion	18–29	30–64	65+	All
Role of government				
Government should provide security such as food, housing, and medical care	50	46	49	48
Government should strictly limit its role in individuals' lives	48	49	45	48
Other/Don't know	2	5	6	4
Government regulation . . .				
Is necessary to protect workers and consumers	60	54	49	55
Prevents economic growth by stifling innovation and investment	34	40	44	39
Other/Don't know	6	6	8	6
Federal taxes				
I don't mind paying federal taxes because we have a responsibility for the common good	57	52	53	53
I don't like paying federal taxes because government in Washington is wasteful and inefficient	40	40	40	40
Other/Don't know	3	8	7	7
Impact of immigrants				
Immigrants strengthen our economy and enrich our culture	57	53	45	52
Immigrants are a burden because they take jobs and government benefits	40	40	44	41
Other/Don't know	4	7	11	7
Sample size	307	1,210	446	2,000

Source: Brookings Mountain West survey, 2010.

vote there. But in both Arizona and Nevada, young people were significantly less likely than older voters to cast a ballot for Republican candidates for U.S. Senate and governor (table 4-13). In Arizona, incumbent senator John McCain won a small majority of 53 percent among voters under age 30 (Democratic candidate Rodney Glassman got 38 percent), but McCain did better among all other age groups. Incumbent Arizona governor Jan Brewer broke even with her Democratic opponent Terry Goddard among young voters (47 percent each), but decisively won other age groups.

In Nevada, majorities of young voters supported Democratic candidates Harry Reid for Senate and Rory Reid for governor. Harry Reid also won a 56 percent majority among voters 30–44, but broke even or lost among

Table 4-12. Affiliation of Registered Voters and Prospective House Vote, by Age
Percent

Affiliation/vote	18–29	30–64	65+	All
Registered voters				
Republican	40	52	52	50
Democratic	45	41	40	41
Other/Don't know	14	7	8	9
Sample size	238	1,132	433	1,803
"Almost certain" to vote				
Republican	46	55	55	54
Democratic	43	40	37	40
Other/Don't know	12	5	8	7
Sample size	138	927	371	1,436

Source: Brookings Mountain West survey, 2010.

older voters. Perhaps contributing to Reid's good showing among young people was the strong support he received among Latino voters, who were 15 percent of the total electorate in Nevada and who tend to be significantly younger on average than non-Latino voters.

Conclusion

Young people in the Mountain West present something of a political puzzle. They match their age counterparts elsewhere in key political values and attitudes, as well as in politically relevant characteristics such as secularism and racial and ethnic diversity. And yet they are significantly more Republican in their political affiliation and voting than their age cohort nationally. Thus they share a Republican tilt with older counterparts in the region, who are somewhat more conservative than older adults elsewhere but far more Republican in their voting patterns. Still, the Democratic Party has managed to battle the Republican Party to a draw among young residents of the region and even held a significant lead during several years of the last decade.

The region's young population is more racially and ethnically diverse than in most of the rest of the nation, providing potential support to the Democratic Party. At the same time, young people exceed their older counterparts in the region and young people elsewhere in the percentage that are unaffiliated, atheist, or agnostic. But the presence of the large Mormon population among the young—18 percent, nearly matching the national percentage

Table 4-13. Vote in Arizona and Nevada U.S. Senate and Governor Elections, 2010, by Age

Percent

Election	18–29	30–44	45–64	65+	All
Arizona U.S. Senate					
McCain	53	59	62	57	59
Glassman	38	32	33	37	35
Arizona governor					
Brewer	47	53	59	53	55
Goddard	47	43	40	44	42
Nevada U.S. Senate					
Angle	30	40	48	53	45
Reid	58	56	47	44	50
Nevada governor					
Sandoval	30	52	58	59	53
Reid	61	41	38	37	42

Source: 2010 National Election Pool exit polls, as reported by CNN (www.cnn.com/ELECTION/2010/results/polls.main/).

of white evangelicals among all adults—provides a solid bloc of conservatives and Republicans that offsets the Democratic tendencies of the young in many parts of the region. Added to the mix is the fact that the young Latino population is large and growing.

As the 2012 election approaches, most forecasters expect a very close presidential election—similar to 2000 and 2004. Much of the Electoral College map is likely to be locked up well in advance and relatively evenly balanced, barring a strong surge by one party of the other. But most observers also expect that at least three of the six states of the Mountain West—Colorado, Nevada, and New Mexico—will be highly competitive. While the total electoral vote from these three states is relatively small, they could provide the margin of victory in a tight race. Two of these three states will also feature highly competitive races for the U.S. Senate, which could determine whether the Democratic Party holds or loses its majority there. It is possible, though not yet probable, that Arizona could have a competitive Senate race as well.

The presence of competitive races and the concomitant strong efforts to mobilize voters—including young voters—likely means that the Millennial generation will be a factor in the outcome of the races in the region and thus perhaps the nation as well. More generally, the signs are that there will be a vibrant and competitive political culture among the emerging generation of the Mountain West—a culture that may perpetuate the paradoxical nature of the region. It will likely be more Democratic in its vote than previous generations, but its political distinctiveness will also be felt—and perhaps more dramatically—beyond the polling place. The libertarian instinct will survive in this generation but will go hand in hand with support for environmental protection and the regulation that accompanies it. The region will be more welcoming to immigrants and less likely to fight a political war over cultural differences on social issues. In this respect, its conservatives may be more true to Western roots and libertarian tendencies than the older generations of the region. A new politics of the West awaits a generation willing to shape it.

Appendix

This chapter draws on survey data from several sources. Details for these sources are available at the following websites:

Brookings Mountain West survey of Mountain West states, 2010 (http://brookingsmtnwest.unlv.edu/publications/public-opinion-survey.html).

Center for Information and Research on Civic Learning and Engagement (CIRCLE), August 17, 2009, "The Youth Vote in 2009" (www.civicyouth.org/PopUps/FactSheets/FS_youth_Voting_2008_updated_6.22.pdf).

Center for Information and Research on Civic Learning and Engagement (CIRCLE), April 15, 2011, "The Youth Vote in 2010: Final Estimates Based on Census Data" (www.civicyouth.org/wp-content/uploads/2011/04/The-CPS-youth-vote-2010-FS-FINAL1.pdf).

National Election Pool exit polls conducted by Edison Media Research, 2008 and 2010. Surveys from 2008 are available from the Roper Center. Surveys reported by CNN.com in 2010 (www.cnn.com/ELECTION/2010/results/polls.main/).

Pew Forum on Religion & Public Life's U.S. Religious Landscape Survey, conducted May 8–August 13, 2007 (http://religions.pewforum.org/pdf/report-religious-landscape-study-appendix4.pdf).

Pew Research Center for the People & the Press aggregated surveys conducted 2000–11. Surveys have been combined as noted in the tables and figures. All surveys employed a standard telephone survey methodology described at http://people-press.org/methodology/about/. Interviewing dates, samples sizes, and other details for individual surveys can be found at http://people-press.org.

five

The Mountain West Today

A Regional Survey

Karlyn Bowman and Ruy Teixeira

What does it mean to live in the Mountain West today? What issues are most and least important to the region's residents? Do Arizona, Colorado, Idaho, Nevada, New Mexico, and Utah have a collective identity, or are their state-level differences too great? Is there an identifiable Mountain West personality? Results from the 2010 Brookings Mountain West Survey allow us to begin to answer those questions.

This chapter provides an overview of this survey, with results for key questions broken out by state. We conclude by taking a look at how ongoing demographic shifts may affect the public opinion profile of the region going forward. The survey, which was conducted from August 23 through September 1, 2010, by Gerstein and Agne Strategic Communications, looked at the views of adults in Arizona, Colorado, Idaho, Nevada, New Mexico, and Utah. The overall sample size was 2,000, with sampling adjusted to ensure a minimum of around 250 interviews per state. The specific sample sizes per state were 512 in Arizona, 478 in Colorado, 248 in Idaho, 260 in Nevada, 251 in New Mexico, and 251 in Utah.

The survey was not intended to tell us about possible electoral outcomes in 2010 and 2012 but to take the pulse of the region on key issues and values and to create a portrait of the present-day Mountain West. Some of the key findings include the following:

—Strong majorities of Mountain West residents see themselves as more likely than other Americans to have a number of characteristics, such as making environmental protection a top priority, engaging in outdoor activities and recreation, feeling the impact of illegal immigration, supporting the development of renewable energy sources, expressing patriotic pride, feeling skeptical of the federal government's power, engaging in volunteer activities, and joining a church.

—The top-ranked characteristic was engaging with the outdoors and the third-ranked was supporting renewable energy. Consistent with that ethos, by more than 2 to 1 regionwide and with strong majorities in every state, Mountain West residents felt that their state was better off "investing in wind and solar energy solutions that will generate clean, renewable energy sources and jobs for years to come" than "investing in proven technologies like clean coal and nuclear energy sources because they are guaranteed to produce jobs now."

—The second-ranked characteristic was dealing with the effects of immigration. Across the region and in five of the six states, immigration was also the area where the most residents wanted to see more federal government involvement. Across the region and in every state, majorities of Mountain West residents felt that the new Arizona immigration law was either about right or did not go far enough. But across the region and in every state, residents also felt that immigrants made a positive contribution to the country and supported a path to citizenship for illegal immigrants.

—A strong majority regionwide and in every state felt that the Second Amendment rights of Americans to keep and bear arms are under attack. And nearly half of regional residents agreed with a libertarian-style statement that government should strictly limit its role in individuals' lives rather than promote opportunity and provide security.

—But strong majorities across the region also said that they wanted more federal and state government involvement in areas like protecting the environment, promoting renewable energy sources, cracking down on crime and drugs, guaranteeing quality public education, and creating jobs. The latter two areas were also the ones that overall and in most states were the top two issues that residents wanted their state elected officials to address.

—Mountain West residents do not appear to be as tax-sensitive as would be suggested by a libertarian stereotype. Regionwide and in every state, majorities or pluralities felt that their federal taxes were "about right" and said that they did not mind paying federal taxes "because we each have a responsibility to contribute to the common good and to support those who can't support themselves."

—On some controversial policy issues like health care reform, financial regulatory reform, the economic stimulus, and gay marriage, Mountain West residents are in synch with national attitudes. Regionwide, residents oppose the new health care reform law, support the new financial regulations, are distinctly unenthusiastic about the economic stimulus plan, and oppose gay marriage, just as the national public does. But there is some important variation within the region. New Mexico, for example, supports the health care reform law, Utah opposes the new financial regulations, and Colorado and Nevada support gay marriage.

A Political Portrait

Our survey took a close look at the political views of Mountain West residents. We tested views on prominent political figures and institutions, recent controversial policy debates (health care, financial regulation, and immigration), and federal involvement in a range of policy issues. Many of the results in this survey look very much like national results for the same period. In the survey, for example, 41 percent approved of the job that the president was doing while 54 percent disapproved, including 43 percent who disapproved strongly. In the late August–early September 2010 ABC News/Washington Post poll, slightly more, 46 percent nationally, approved of the job that Obama was doing while 52 percent disapproved. The high level of strong disapproval seen in the Mountain West was also present in the national polls. Thirty-eight percent in the national ABC/Post poll disapproved strongly of the president's performance.

We also asked respondents how favorable or unfavorable, on a scale of 0 to 100, their views of some public figures were (0–49 was scored as unfavorable, 51–100 as favorable, and 50 as neutral). In this exercise, views of Barack Obama and George W. Bush were similar in the Mountain West as a whole, with Obama viewed slightly more favorably but also slightly more unfavorably—that is, fewer people were neutral about Obama. Two states, Idaho and Utah, had the strongest negative views of the president (table 5-1). Sarah Palin's overall favorable rating was 10 percentage points lower than the president's, but her unfavorable rating was identical. Only in Utah did even four in ten respondents rate her favorably.

Gallup reported that Congress's approval rating nationally for the first half of 2010 had averaged 20 percent, down from 30 percent in 2009, the first year of the 111th Congress. In the Mountain West at the time of this survey, slightly more, 26 percent, approved of the job that Congress was doing (table 5-2). Once again, Idaho and Utah stand out in terms of exhibiting especially low levels of approval. Neither Democrats nor Republicans in Congress fared

Table 5-1. Attitudes toward Selected Public Figures

Percent

Attitude	Total	Arizona	Colorado	Idaho	Nevada	New Mexico	Utah
Obama							
Favorable	41	38	44	29	46	51	32
Unfavorable	49	49	46	63	41	43	60
Bush							
Favorable	38	40	35	40	33	36	46
Unfavorable	46	45	49	43	50	53	36
Palin							
Favorable	31	31	27	38	30	30	40
Unfavorable	49	49	54	43	50	53	40

Source: Brookings Mountain West Survey, 2010.

well in the poll. Thirty percent in the region had a favorable view of the Democrats (51 percent unfavorable) and 32 percent a favorable view of the Republicans in Congress (also 51 percent unfavorable). Job approval of both parties in Congress was also low across the nation. In a late August 2010 Gallup poll, 33 percent approved of the job that Democrats in Congress were doing while 32 percent approved of the job that Republicans were doing.

Despite the equally unfavorable views of Democrats and Republicans in Congress, Mountain West residents are clearly leaning Republican in their party identification. Overall, 38 percent identified with or leaned toward the Democrats while 51 percent identified with or leaned toward the Republicans. They also said that they would support Republican candidates (49 percent) for the House of Representatives over Democratic candidates (40 percent).

Fewer residents in the region were familiar with the Tea Party movement at the time of this survey (77 percent) than with the major parties. Views of the Tea Party regionwide were evenly split, at 34 percent (table 5-3). The late August–early September 2010 Quinnipiac University national poll found that 30 percent had a favorable opinion of the movement and 31 percent an unfavorable opinion. In a separate question in the Quinnipiac poll, 12 percent said that they considered themselves part of the movement. The responses to these two national questions had been stable since April 2010.

Related to the Tea Party is the issue of support for third-party candidates. We included an item about support for an emerging third party in our series on distinctive aspects of Mountain West residents. Of the characteristics

Table 5-2. Attitudes toward U.S. Congress

Percent

Attitude	Total	Arizona	Colorado	Idaho	Nevada	New Mexico	Utah
Approve	26	26	29	20	30	26	22
Disapprove	68	64	66	73	69	71	73

Source: Brookings Mountain West Survey, 2010.

Table 5-3. Attitudes toward Tea Party Movement

Percent

Attitude	Total	Arizona	Colorado	Idaho	Nevada	New Mexico	Utah
Favorable	34	36	30	40	35	32	36
Unfavorable	34	27	40	27	40	40	27
Don't know[a]	23	27	21	25	16	18	24

Source: Brookings Mountain West Survey, 2010.

a. Wording was "If you have never heard of a name, or don't know enough to rate them, please just say so."

tested, this was the characteristic deemed least likely to be distinctive of the Mountain West: about as many said that regional residents were less likely than other Americans to embrace a third party (38 percent) as said that they were more likely to do so (42 percent).

Turning to national issues, the poll examined three of 2010's hottest policy debates. After telling survey participants that President Obama had signed legislation restructuring the American health care system in March, we asked them whether they supported or opposed the new health care reform law. Thirty-nine percent supported it while 55 percent were opposed (table 5-4). Opposition was especially sharp in Idaho and Utah, where two-thirds disapproved. Only in one state, New Mexico, did support outweigh opposition.

In most national polls at the time, opposition to the new law outweighed support (though there was more support nationally in some polls for reforming it than repealing it). To take just one example, when the Gallup Organization asked in late August 2010 whether people approved or disapproved of the health care overhaul passed by Congress, the results were nearly identical to those in this survey. Thirty-nine percent approved while 56 percent disapproved.

Negative views of the health care law can also be seen in another question that asked people to choose between two views of the legislation. Forty-five

Table 5-4. Attitudes toward New Health Care Reform Law

Percent

Attitude	Total	Arizona	Colorado	Idaho	Nevada	New Mexico	Utah
Support law	39	38	42	28	43	50	26
Oppose law	55	54	52	66	50	48	67

Source: Brookings Mountain West Survey, 2010.

percent regionally chose the statement "The new health care reform signed by President Obama may need to be fixed, but it is an important first step in lowering costs and making affordable health care available to all Americans." But 52 percent chose the response "The new health care reform law will lead to higher taxes and massive cuts to Medicare while doing little to rein in skyrocketing costs and must be significantly changed or repealed."

In most national polls at the time, there was solid majority support for greater regulation of the financial institutions. In a Gallup poll taken in late August 2010, 61 percent nationally approved of the legislation Congress passed to increase regulation of banks and major financial institutions while 37 percent disapproved. When asked in the Mountain West survey whether they favored or opposed the new financial reform that "increases federal regulation over banks, Wall Street investors, and other financial institutions," 52 percent said that they favored it while 38 percent were opposed (table 5-5). Support was highest in Colorado and New Mexico and lowest in Utah.

Using a split-sample methodology, we asked our survey participants whether we needed more, less, or about the same level of involvement from the federal government in addressing a number of issues (Split A in table 5-6).[1] Solid majorities opted for more federal government involvement on seven of nine issues. The largest majorities in favor of more federal involvement were those supporting involvement in immigration, followed by jobs and economic growth, stopping crime and drugs, and promoting renewable energy.

There were two areas where less than a majority of Mountain West residents called for more federal involvement. One was health care, where just 48 percent called for more federal involvement, perhaps because people had made up their minds about the health care law, believed that the necessary level of government involvement had been achieved, or were aware of the legislation's price tag. Note, however, that even on this question, the number calling for less federal involvement (31 percent) was still less than the number calling for more involvement. That contrasts with the other

Table 5-5. Attitudes toward New Financial Reform Regulations

Percent

Attitude	Total	Arizona	Colorado	Idaho	Nevada	New Mexico	Utah
Favor reform	52	54	55	48	53	55	40
Oppose reform	38	35	34	43	39	38	49

Source: Brookings Mountain West Survey, 2010.

item—promoting the role of faith in public life—where only a small proportion wanted more government involvement. Just 19 percent in the region wanted more government involvement in faith in public life, far less than the 54 percent who wanted less.

We also found that even when people were reminded that "government is currently facing record deficits, and increased spending would require larger deficits, increased taxes, or spending cuts in other areas" (split B), public opinion on more federal government involvement changed very little. That suggests that the Mountain West public's interest in more government involvement in key areas is fairly robust (of course, raising taxes to support increased government activity in any of these areas would still remain a challenging political task).

The state variation in the table shows some interesting patterns.[2] Idaho residents are clearly the least supportive of more government involvement. For example, only 28 percent wanted to see more involvement in preserving clean air, and in two areas, promoting renewable energy and creating jobs and economic growth, Idaho was the only state where less than half the public wanted to see more government activity. In contrast, Nevada residents were most likely to call for more federal government involvement. Areas where Nevada residents topped all other states in support for more involvement included dealing with illegal immigrants living here (80 percent), creating jobs and economic growth (79 percent), promoting renewable energy (72 percent), preserving clean air (69 percent), and guaranteeing quality public education (65 percent).

Immigration

Immigration was on the front burner in most of 2010, especially for residents of the Mountain West. We asked survey respondents about certain characteristics that made the region distinctive. Seventy-five percent said that

Table 5-6. Percent of Respondents Favoring More Federal Government Involvement in Selected Issues, Splits A and B[a]

Issue	Total	Arizona	Colorado	Idaho	Nevada	New Mexico	Utah
Preserving the cleanliness of our air							
Split A	56	60	57	28	69	58	44
Split B	55	63	50	38	64	61	41
Guaranteeing a quality public education							
Split A	59	64	57	50	65	58	55
Split B	57	60	57	50	63	61	47
Promoting renewable energy sources							
Split A	61	64	57	45	72	67	54
Split B	58	65	54	46	69	58	45
Cracking down on crime and drugs in our communities							
Split A	62	66	56	52	69	70	59
Split B	57	63	51	50	65	63	47
Making affordable health care available to everyone							
Split A	48	54	48	32	48	54	36
Split B	49	56	54	31	52	52	28
Stopping the flow of illegal immigrants across our borders							
Split A	74	77	74	64	76	67	74
Split B	74	71	72	75	78	72	78
Dealing with the millions of illegal immigrants living here							
Split A	69	75	58	64	80	58	79
Split B	71	71	69	73	71	71	74
Creating jobs and economic growth							
Split A	68	70	69	43	79	77	52
Split B	72	63	51	63	57	57	
Promoting the role of faith in our public life							
Split A	19	19	15	14	23	34	19
Split B	25	27	24	25	25	38	13

Source: Brookings Mountain West Survey, 2010.
a. Categories "About the same level of involvement" and "Less involvement" are not shown.

Table 5-7. Attitudes toward Arizona's Immigration Law
Percent

State	Attitude		
	Goes too far	About right	Not far enough
Total	36	45	17
Arizona	35	44	18
Colorado	42	40	16
Idaho	28	49	20
Nevada	35	45	18
New Mexico	36	47	14
Utah	30	50	15

Source: Brookings Mountain West Survey, 2010.

residents of the Mountain West were more likely to feel the impact of illegal immigration than people in other regions. Only 15 percent said that they were less likely to feel the impact.

That was the second most important characteristic separating regional residents, in their view, from the rest of the country (number one was engaging in outdoor activities and recreation, discussed in the environment section of the chapter). It should be stressed that this opinion extends beyond partisan or demographic lines and is relatively consistent regardless of a respondent's position on how to address the immigration issue (discussed below); no matter how respondents felt about the response to illegal immigration, they agreed that residents of this region have a unique understanding of the issue because of their role on its front lines. As we see throughout this survey, the simplistic storylines that often surround the immigration issue do not match the reality of attitudes toward it in this region. Regional attitudes are complex; they do not reflect the rigid orthodoxy of the debate in Washington.

Another question in our survey told respondents that the state of Arizona "recently passed a law that gives the police the power to question anyone they suspect is in the country illegally, requires people to produce documents verifying their status if asked, and allows officers to detain anyone who cannot do so." When asked whether this law goes too far in dealing with the issue of illegal immigration, does not go far enough, or is about right, 36 percent in the region said that it went too far, 45 percent said that it was about right, and 17 percent said that it did not go far enough (table 5-7). In a national survey in May and July 2010, CBS News told people that "as you may know, the state of Arizona recently passed a law that gives the police the power to question someone they have already stopped, detained, or arrested about their legal status in the country. The law requires people to produce documents verifying their status if asked." The survey then asked a question about respondents' view of the law that was similar to this one. In May, 28 percent said that the law went too far in dealing with the issue of illegal immigration, 52 percent said that it was about right, and 17 percent said that it did not go far enough. In July responses were 23, 57, and 17 percent, respectively.

In the question series on more, less, or the same level of federal involvement in various issues (described above), the two largest majorities in favor of more government involvement were on the issues of stopping the flow of illegal immigrants across the border (74 percent) and dealing with the millions of illegal immigrants already here (69 percent). That suggests the depth of concern about the immigration issue in these states.

National polls in 2010 showed that most Americans believed dealing with immigration is a national issue, but they also told pollsters that Arizona was right to act in the absence of federal government action. When asked in a separate question in this survey whether their *state* government should be more involved in stopping the flow of illegal immigrants across the border, 63 percent of respondents said yes. As for dealing with those already here, a similar number (62 percent) said that they wanted their state government more involved.

Two pairs of statements in the survey probed attitudes about immigrants and about immigration reform. In the first statement pair, 52 percent chose the statement "As they have for generations, immigrants today continue to enrich our culture and strengthen our economy," while 40 percent viewed immigrants today "as a burden on our country because they take our jobs and use government benefits." There were only small differences in responses by state. Arizonans, for example, split 54 to 39 percent on this question.

Most Americans are not punitive in their views about immigration, and that is true in the Mountain West despite residents' high level of concern about the issue. In the second statement pair, 58 percent chose the statement that "illegal immigrants who have been living and working in the United States for years, and who do not have a criminal record, should be allowed to start on a path to citizenship by registering that they are in the country, paying a fine, getting fingerprinted, and learning English." Thirty-eight percent endorsed the other statement, that there should be "no amnesty, social services, or other benefits given to illegal immigrants who have broken the laws of our country by coming here illegally in the first place." Views were remarkably similar across the states in the region.

The State of the States

People are usually more optimistic about conditions in their states than they are about national conditions, and the responses in this survey follow that pattern. The question of whether the nation is on the right track or heading in the wrong direction was first asked in the early 1970s by the Roper Organization. In most years, when the question was asked in national surveys, the country was seen to be going in the wrong direction. The level of national pessimism reflected in answers to this question in 2010 was toward the high end of commonly negative responses, and that pessimism is mirrored in the states that we surveyed. Two-thirds of respondents said that things in the country were going in the wrong direction; only a quarter thought that they were on the right track. Those results were very similar to national responses at the time of our survey.

Residents of the Mountain West were more optimistic about their states than the nation as a whole, but they could hardly be described as enthusiastic. Just 37 percent said that things in their state were going in the right direction, while 54 percent said that they had gotten pretty seriously off on the wrong track (table 5-8). This question produced some stark differences among states, with the level of pessimism in Nevada (76 percent) far surpassing any of the other states in the region. In contrast, Utah residents were more optimistic (56 percent) than pessimistic (36 percent). Views of adults in Nevada about the performance of their governor also were much more negative than were views of adults in other states, as table 5-9 shows. Nevada and New Mexico residents also gave majority disapproval to their governors. On the other hand, Utah, Idaho, and Arizona gave their governors solid majority approval. The latter finding is striking since Arizona residents also were so pessimistic about the direction of their state.

The verdict on the economic stimulus passed in 2009 was decidedly negative in the Mountain West. Just 37 percent of residents believed that the stimulus plan "helped avert an even greater economic crisis and is making investments that will ultimately help create jobs and economic growth," while 59 percent said that it "produced few jobs and wasted billions of taxpayer dollars, increased the deficit, hurt American business, and weakened our economy."

In our survey, respondents were asked to rate policy priorities for their state on a scale of 1 to 10, with 10 being extremely important and zero not at all important. Given widespread economic pessimism, it is hardly surprising that creating new jobs and promoting economic growth was the top issue

Table 5-8. Attitudes toward Direction in Which State Is Going

Percent

Attitude	Total	Arizona	Colorado	Idaho	Nevada	New Mexico	Utah
Right direction	37	34	41	41	17	30	56
Wrong track	54	58	48	45	76	59	36

Source: Brookings Mountain West Survey, 2010.

Table 5-9. Attitudes toward State Governor

Percent

Attitude	Total	Arizona	Colorado	Idaho	Nevada	New Mexico	Utah
Approve	48	56	44	58	32	43	55
Disapprove	39	34	42	32	59	52	21

Source: Brookings Mountain West Survey, 2010.

that respondents in the region (and in five of the six states) wanted their elected officials to address. Overall, this issue received a mean rating of 8.7, with 69 percent giving it a very high rating of 9 or 10 (table 5-10).

Second overall and in four of the six states was improving state schools (mean of 8.5, with 62 percent giving the issue a rating of 9 or 10), and third was fighting crime (mean of 8.5, with 58 percent giving a rating of 9 or 10). Also rated highly were reducing federal government spending (8.0 mean, 56 percent rating 9-10), reducing illegal immigration (7.7 mean, 53 percent rating 9-10), moral decline (7.7 mean, 52 percent rating 9-10), and protecting the environment (8.0 mean, 51 percent rating 9-10). Reducing taxes, limiting federal government power, and promoting alternative energy sources were less highly rated, and by far the least highly rated was congestion/overdevelopment. The latter finding is perhaps surprising given the high profile of this issue in some campaigns and communities in the Mountain West.

In our survey, people were asked whether they felt the need for more, less, or about the same level of involvement from their state government in addressing a number of issues (Split C in table 5-11).[3] The questions paralleled exactly the questions that we asked about more, less, or the same amount of federal government involvement. Solid majorities opted for more state government involvement on seven of nine issues, the same pattern that we observed in the federal government series. But there were some important

Table 5-10. Percent of Respondents Believing that State Officials Should Make Selected Issues a Top Priority[a]

Issue	Total	Arizona	Colorado	Idaho	Nevada	New Mexico	Utah
Jobs and growth	69	75	68	52	69	70	62
Schools	62	70	55	59	64	70	54
Crime	58	72	46	49	57	63	54
Federal government spending	56	56	53	56	60	51	62
Illegal immigration	53	64	42	45	57	53	51
Moral decline	52	56	45	50	52	53	60
Environment	51	54	49	38	55	58	40
Health care	47	51	46	32	52	56	38
Taxes	43	44	41	38	45	47	42
Limiting power of the federal government	42	41	39	46	42	45	50
Alternative energy	40	47	35	30	48	46	27
Congestion/over-development	26	27	25	18	32	30	22

Source: Brookings Mountain West Survey, 2010.

a. Percent of respondents giving 9–10 points to an issue on a scale of 1 to 10, with "10" indicating that it is "extremely important" for state elected officials to make the issue a top priority. The full wording for each category is as follows: creating new jobs and economic growth; improving state schools; fighting crime and drugs in our communities; reducing federal government spending; reducing the flow of illegal immigrants into the United States; standing up to our country's moral decline; protecting our environment and natural resources; ensuring access to affordable health care; reducing taxes; limiting the power of the federal government; promoting alternative energy sources like wind and solar; reducing congestion and opposing overdevelopment.

differences. One was that support for more state government involvement was somewhat stronger in most areas than support for more federal government involvement (already fairly high). Another was that the largest majorities in support of more state involvement were on the issues of jobs/economic growth (67 percent) and guaranteeing quality public education (66 percent) rather than immigration (62–63 percent). In addition, promoting renewable energy sources (65 percent) and cracking down on crime and drugs (65 percent) also ranked higher on more involvement than immigration.

As with the federal government questions, there were two areas where less than a majority of Mountain West residents called for more involvement by their state government. One was health care, where 49 percent called for more state involvement, but the number calling for less state government involvement (29 percent) was still less than the number calling for more involvement. Far below health care was promoting the role of faith in

Table 5-11. Percent of Respondents Favoring More Federal Government Involvement in Selected Issues, Splits C and D[a]

Issue	Total	Arizona	Colorado	Idaho	Nevada	New Mexico	Utah
Preserving the cleanliness of our air							
Split C	58	66	54	47	57	58	58
Split D	53	54	49	34	72	64	38
Guaranteeing a quality public education							
Split C	66	71	59	69	59	88	60
Split D	67	68	62	64	81	76	59
Promoting renewable energy sources							
Split C	65	71	57	58	67	72	61
Split D	58	64	51	56	69	75	39
Cracking down on crime and drugs in our communities							
Split C	65	81	51	52	62	67	66
Split D	61	64	48	70	75	69	55
Making affordable health care available to everyone							
Split C	49	54	49	37	43	58	39
Split D	50	55	41	41	67	54	45
Stopping the flow of illegal immigrants across our borders							
Split C	63	64	54	67	76	69	62
Split D	68	69	69	73	64	73	65
Dealing with the millions of illegal immigrants living here							
Split C	62	64	58	58	62	62	70
Split D	66	65	65	67	64	68	69
Creating jobs and economic growth							
Split C	67	72	63	58	60	78	62
Split D	70	77	65	64	76	79	54
Promoting the role of faith in our public life							
Split C	23	25	17	20	23	17	36
Split D	25	29	16	17	31	28	29

Source: Brookings Mountain West Survey, 2010.

a. Categories "About the same level of involvement" and "Less involvement" are not shown here.

public life; here just 23 percent in the region wanted more state government involvement, while 50 percent wanted less.

We also found that even when people were reminded that "[the state] has been forced to make significant cuts in the state's budget due to current economic conditions, government is currently facing record deficits, and increased spending would require increased taxes or spending cuts in other areas" (split D), public opinion on more state government involvement shifted only modestly. That suggests that the Mountain West public's interest in more state government involvement in key areas is strong and not easily shaken (again, raising taxes to support increased government activity in any of these areas would still remain a challenging political task for governors and legislators).

It is clear from this survey that residents of the Mountain West want Washington and their states to do many things, none of which can be accomplished easily or inexpensively. That may explain the only middling level of concern about taxes (see previous question), despite the region's reputation for anti-tax sentiment. Several other results from this survey bear on the issues of taxes. Since 1947 the Gallup Organization has asked people whether the federal taxes that they pay are too high, too low, or about right. Hardly anyone ever says that they are too low. For most of the long history of the question, people have said that their federal income taxes are too high. But on national surveys on several occasions in the past decade, people have said that they are about right. In this survey, 41 percent of residents of the Mountain West said that the federal income taxes that they paid "this year" were too high, but 53 percent said that they were about right (table 5-12). Just 2 percent said that they were too low. Those sentiments varied surprisingly little across the region, with residents in every state more likely to say that their federal taxes were about right than to say that they were too high. When asked about the property taxes that they paid, 43 percent said that they were too high and 46 percent said that they were about right. But departing from the overall pattern, residents of two states—Arizona and Utah—were more likely to say that their property taxes were too high than about right.

Also in the survey, 53 percent said that they did not mind paying federal taxes "because we each have a responsibility to contribute to the common good and to support those who can't support themselves," while 40 percent said that they did not like paying federal taxes "because the government in Washington is wasteful, inefficient, and doesn't do anything for people like me." Only in Utah were the results close, with 49 percent saying that they did not mind paying federal taxes and 46 percent saying that they did not like

Table 5-12. Attitudes toward Amount of Federal and State Taxes

Percent

Attitude	Total	Arizona	Colorado	Idaho	Nevada	New Mexico	Utah
Federal income taxes							
Too high	41	40	42	38	41	41	45
About right	53	54	52	54	55	54	47
Property taxes							
Too high	43	46	40	40	43	41	46
About right	46	43	49	52	45	53	39

Source: Brookings Mountain West Survey, 2010.

paying them. Again, this somewhat belies the common image of the region as embracing a libertarian stance on taxes. In another question in the survey, 51 percent agreed with the statement that "the gap between rich and poor should be reduced, even if it means higher taxes for the wealthy," while 46 percent disagreed. Agreement with the statement was between 53 and 56 percent in Arizona, Colorado, Nevada, and New Mexico but only 45 percent in Idaho and 39 percent in Utah.

The Environmental Ethos of the Mountain West

One of the defining characteristics of the Mountain States region in our survey was the belief that people in the region were more likely to engage in outdoor activities and recreation than people in other areas. Eighty-five percent gave that response—the highest response for any characteristic tested—with more than 90 percent responding that way in Idaho, Utah, and Colorado (table 5-13). In addition, 61 percent said that residents of the region were more likely than residents of other regions to make environmental protection a top priority. Once again there were some notable differences by state, with nearly eight in ten in Colorado giving that response but only five in ten in Idaho and Nevada. A third question, about supporting the development of renewable energy sources such as wind and solar power, confirmed Coloradans' more intense interest in these issues: 83 percent in Colorado saw this as a defining regional characteristic, while 75 percent did so for all the Mountain West states that we surveyed.

Note, however, that the environment wasn't as high a priority for state officials to address as the more traditional issues of jobs, crime, and

Table 5-13. Percent of Respondents Believing that Mountain West Residents Are More Likely than Other Americans to Have Selected Characteristics

Characteristic	Total	Arizona	Colorado	Idaho	Nevada	New Mexico	Utah
Likely to engage in out-door activities and recreation	85	78	91	93	76	86	93
Likely to make environ-mental protection a high priority	61	55	79	50	50	59	53
Likely to support devel-opment of renewable energy sources	75	77	83	66	76	75	58

Source: Brookings Mountain West Survey, 2010.

schools (see table 5-11). Fifty-one percent put the issue at points 9 and 10 on a 10-point scale in terms of top priorities for the state. Seven in ten gave that response about job creation, for example. On the question of federal government activity, environmental issues did not have the same intensity as immigration issues and jobs, but majorities still said that they wanted the government to do more to preserve the cleanliness of our air, water, and other natural resources (56 percent) and, in a separate question, to promote renewable energy sources (61 percent). When asked about state activity in those areas, majorities in favor of more involvement were somewhat larger (58 percent and 65 percent, respectively). But interestingly, the percentage of Coloradans calling for more federal or state involvement in these areas was not especially high, despite their view that environmental and renewable energy issues are central to the Mountain West ethos (see table 5-6).

Another question that asked people whether they agreed more with one statement than another found that by a decisive 64 to 30 percent, residents of the region felt that their state was better off "investing in wind and solar energy solutions that will generate clean, renewable energy sources and jobs for years to come" than "investing in proven technologies like clean coal and nuclear energy sources because they are guaranteed to produce jobs now." Majorities in favor of the first statement were strong in each state, with the highest percentage in New Mexico (71 percent) and the lowest in Utah (56 percent).

As for climate change, 51 percent said that they agreed with the statement that "climate change is a real threat with potentially disastrous consequences,

Table 5-14. Attitudes toward Climate Change

Attitude	Total	Arizona	Colorado	Idaho	Nevada	New Mexico	Utah
A real threat	51	56	51	42	51	54	39
Just a theory	44	39	45	53	44	40	53

Source: Brookings Mountain West Survey, 2010.

and we must take steps now to reduce the damage created by fossil fuels and other pollutants" while 44 percent said that the statement that "climate change is just a theory based on unproven science that is designed to support radical energy policies that will increase costs for American families and business" came closer to their view (table 5-14). Majorities of residents in Idaho and Utah chose the "just a theory" response.

Political Ideology and Views of Government

The survey asked which of four labels best described the respondents' "political perspective"—progressive, liberal, libertarian, or conservative; those who initially said "moderate" were asked which of the labels they would choose if they had to pick one. The results are shown in table 5-15 (the 2 percent of respondents who stuck with the moderate label after the follow-up question are omitted from the table). As the table shows, while "conservative" was easily the most popular label (48 percent), there were some substantial differences by state, with 60 percent in Utah, 57 percent in Idaho, but just 41 percent in New Mexico describing themselves as conservative. Combining the progressive and liberal categories yields 38 percent on the left, with the highest proportion in New Mexico (46 percent) and the lowest in Utah (25 percent). These figures differed from the most recent national figures (a Center for American Progress/Hart Research survey in May 2010), in which there were nearly as many progressives/liberals (40 percent) as conservatives (42 percent).

The number of libertarians (7 percent) was the same, however. The ranks of self-identified libertarians in each state were small. But another question in the survey that asked people which of two statements came closer to their view produced an even split regionally (table 5-16) between the more liberal/progressive idea that "government should promote economic opportunity and provide for minimum measures of security such as food, housing, medical care and old age protection" (47 percent) and the more libertarian idea

Table 5-15. Percent of Respondents' Having a Particular Self-Described
Political Philosophy

Philosophy	Total	Arizona	Colorado	Idaho	Nevada	New Mexico	Utah
Progressive	16	15	18	8	16	21	11
Liberal	22	22	24	20	23	25	14
Libertarian	7	5	6	9	10	5	9
Conservative	48	50	44	57	44	41	60

Source: Brookings Mountain West Survey, 2010.

that "government should strictly limit its role in individuals' lives so they are left alone to pursue their lives as they please and to deal with the consequences of their actions on their own" (48 percent). The latter idea generated exceptionally high support (60 percent) in Utah.

Another question in the survey asked whether residents of the region were more likely than Americans elsewhere to feel "skeptical of the federal government's power and reach." A strong majority (64 percent) of those surveyed believed that this libertarian-leaning sentiment was an identifying characteristic of Mountain West residents. On the other hand, another question, which asked whether federal government regulations "are necessary to keep businesses in check and protect workers and consumers" or whether such regulations "prevent economic growth by stifling innovation and investment," elicited a solid 55–39 majority in favor of the first statement. A weaker majority was in favor of the idea that state government regulation is needed to prevent overdevelopment and strategically plan growth (51 percent) rather than the idea that state government regulation unfairly restricts property rights and limits economic growth (43 percent). Government programs for the poor elicited a less sanguine view of government's role. By 60-34, Mountain West residents believed that such programs "undermine individual initiative and responsibility."

Cultural and Social Issues

The survey also tested the Mountain West public's view of some cultural and social issues. Again showing a libertarian-style sentiment, 64 percent in the survey agreed with the statement that "the Second Amendment rights of all Americans to keep and bear arms are under direct threat in our country today" (table 5-17). Majorities in Idaho, New Mexico, and Utah strongly

Table 5-16. Attitudes toward Government Intervention in Public and Individual Issues
Percent

Attitude	Total	Arizona	Colorado	Idaho	Nevada	New Mexico	Utah
Government should promote economic opportunity and provide minimum measures of security	47	52	46	46	48	52	34
Government should strictly limit its role in individuals' lives	48	44	48	51	48	43	60

Source: Brookings Mountain West Survey, 2010.

Table 5-17. Attitudes toward Second Amendment Rights of all Americans to Keep and Bear Arms
Percent

Attitude	Total	Arizona	Colorado	Idaho	Nevada	New Mexico	Utah
Agree that rights are under direct threat in our country today	64	61	57	76	68	77	70
Agree strongly	44	37	38	56	47	56	54

Source: Brookings Mountain West Survey, 2010.

agreed with the statement. Thirty-four percent of the region's residents owned one or more guns or rifles.

Sixty percent of adults in the region thought that their fellow residents of the Mountain West were more likely to join a church or other organized religious community than Americans in other regions. However, Mountain West residents also said that they were averse to mixing politics and religion, with 58 percent agreeing that the country had gone too far in that direction. Strong majorities in every state but Utah agreed with that statement. In addition, a direct question about religious practice yielded just 35 percent who said that they attend religious service every week or almost every week (the rate was by far the highest in Utah). At the other end of the spectrum, 32 percent said that they never attended at all (table 5-18). Forty-nine percent of Protestants described themselves as "born again," including

Table 5-18. Frequency of Church Attendance[a]

Percent

Frequency	Total	Arizona	Colorado	Idaho	Nevada	New Mexico	Utah
Attend church more than once a week/every week	35	35	29	40	27	30	58
Never attend church	32	34	34	25	38	28	20

Source: Brookings Mountain West Survey, 2010.

a. Not all categories are shown.

65 percent in New Mexico, 56 percent in Nevada, 52 percent in Idaho, and 51 percent in Utah.

On the issue of gay marriage, 43 percent said that same-sex marriages should be recognized by law with the same rights as traditional marriages, with 49 percent disagreeing. Two states in the region, Colorado and Nevada, had majorities or pluralities in favor of gay marriage, while Idaho and Utah had large majorities against (table 5-19). Fifty-seven percent of the youngest age cohort (18–29 year olds) in the survey said that gay marriage should be recognized by law, as did a plurality of those ages 30–39 years. All other age groups opposed legal recognition. This is a familiar pattern in national polls, where the youngest age cohort is most receptive to legally recognized gay marriage. In most national surveys taken at the time of this survey, the public as a whole drew the line at gay marriage. That is no longer the case. In a handful of surveys conducted in 2011, majorities of Americans have supported gay marriage.

Another question in the survey also probed the social conservatism of the Mountain West. People were asked whether they agreed with the statement "If financially able to do so, it is better for a woman to stay at home and take care of the household than to hold a job outside the home." A quarter of those in all states strongly agreed with the statement, but 30 percent strongly disagreed (table 5-20). Overall 44 percent agreed with statement while 47 percent did not, with majority agreement only in the conservative states of Idaho and Utah.

Finally, the survey found that an impressive 61-37 majority agreed with the idea that "cultural institutions, the arts, and public broadcasting play an important role in society and should receive government support." There were strong majorities across every state in favor of this proposition, somewhat surprising in light of the conservative cultural stance of some of the states.

Table 5-19. Attitudes toward Same-Sex Marriage
Percent

Attitude	Total	Arizona	Colorado	Idaho	Nevada	New Mexico	Utah
Same-sex marriages should be recognized by law with the same rights as traditional marriages	43	49	52	32	48	45	30
Should not be recognized	49	50	43	62	41	51	64

Source: Brookings Mountain West Survey, 2010.

Demographic Change and Public Opinion in the Mountain West Region

By and large, Mountain West residents display the demographic variation in attitudes common in American politics today. For example, single people have a more liberal take on issues like health care, financial regulation, and support for government action than their married counterparts. Rather than rehearse all such demographic differences, we think that it is more interesting to consider specific survey demographics that connect most directly to the processes of demographic change that are transforming the Mountain West region.

In this context, one critical demographic is youth, the rising Millennial generation that will exert increasing influence on the political and attitudinal complexion of the Mountain West going forward. In our survey, the views of 18–29-year-olds were definitely distinct from those of older residents of the region. They were markedly more sympathetic to the new health care reform law; more sympathetic to immigrants and immigration reform; more supportive of increased government involvement, especially in areas like renewable energy, environmental protection and education; more supportive of free trade; and far more supportive of gay marriage. In chapter 4 of this volume, Scott Keeter discusses Millennials and their attitudinal profile in more detail.

Another way to look at demographic change and attitudes is to focus on three groups that are heavily implicated in demographic trends in the Mountain West (see chapter 1 in this volume): the white working class (defined here as those without a four-year college degree), white college graduates, and minorities. Together they tell a very interesting story about how public opinion may evolve in the region in the future.

Table 5-20. Attitudes toward Women Working outside the Home

Percent

Attitude	Total	Arizona	Colorado	Idaho	Nevada	New Mexico	Utah
Agree that it is better for a woman to stay at home and take care of the household	44	43	40	53	39	38	61
Strongly agree	25	24	20	23	24	22	42

Source: Brookings Mountain West Survey, 2010.

The white working class is the most conservative of these three groups, significantly more conservative than white college graduates in a number of important ways, including support for health care reform (27 percent white working class versus 39 percent white college graduates), financial regulatory reform (43 percent versus 55 percent), and gay marriage (39 percent versus 46 percent).

The contrast is especially strong with respect to immigration. Only 42 percent of white working-class residents agreed that "as they have for generations, immigrants today continue to enrich our culture and strengthen our economy," while 62 percent of white college graduates agreed. And while 50 percent of the white working-class respondents thought that "illegal immigrants who have been living and working in the United States for years, and who do not have a criminal record, should be allowed to start on a path to citizenship by registering that they are in the country, paying a fine, getting fingerprinted, and learning English," 65 percent of white college graduates did so.

The white working class also appears to be more tax-sensitive. Half of the group viewed their federal taxes as "about right" while 60 percent of white college graduates agreed with that assessment. And while 46 percent of the white working-class respondents said that they did not mind paying federal taxes "because we each have a responsibility to contribute to the common good and to support those who can't support themselves," 59 percent of white college graduates concurred. The contrast was also strong on free trade. Just 44 percent of white working-class residents but 60 percent of white college graduates thought that free trade was good for America "because it creates new markets for our goods and services and lowers costs for consumers."

In terms of interest in more government involvement in addressing issues, white working-class and college graduate residents differed little on education, energy, and the environment. However, on crime/drugs and on jobs/

economic growth, white working-class interest in more government involvement is substantially higher than among white college graduates. Both of these groups, however, differed from minority residents, who are primarily Hispanic, in their appetite for increased government action. Minorities were 14 percentage points higher than either of the two groups on increased federal government involvement in protecting the environment, 18 points higher on education, and 24 points higher on health care. And 57 percent of minorities favored the idea that government should promote economic opportunity and provide security over the idea that government should strictly limit its role in individuals' lives. Minorities were also more strongly in favor of financial regulatory reform (61 percent) and health care reform (53 percent) than either of the two other groups.

On several other issues, minorities were more liberal than working-class whites, but no more liberal than college-educated whites. Their level of support for gay marriage, for example, is about the same as that of white college graduates. And, intriguingly, minority support for the idea that immigrants enrich our culture and strengthen our economy and for providing a path to citizenship for illegal immigrants was about on the level of white college graduates' support but no higher. Both groups also expressed about the same level of agreement with the statement that they did not mind paying federal taxes because taxes are used to provide for the common good. However, minorities were less likely than white college graduates and about as likely as white working-class respondents to say that their federal and property taxes were about right. Minorities also were less supportive of free trade than white college graduates. However, their support was still higher than support among the white working class.

Chapter 1 in this volume shows that across the region, the general pattern of change reveals a decline in the white working-class share of eligible voters balanced by a rise in the white college graduate and, especially, minority share of eligible voters. These changes are substantial: the white working-class share is declining at a rate of about half a percentage point a year in each state except Nevada, where it is declining a full percentage point a year. That means that over time we can expect the views of white working-class residents to become less influential in the Mountain West and the views of white college graduate and minority residents to become more influential. Such a shift could entail the following changes:

—more support for government involvement in most areas—especially education, energy, the environment, and health care—and more support for government regulation

—less tax sensitivity

—a warmer attitude toward immigrants and toward providing a path to citizenship for illegal residents

—more support for free trade

—less support for socially conservative positions such as opposing gay marriage (this, like most other changes here, will be reinforced by the effects of generational change).

We hasten to add that these changes will occur only gradually and that the views of the Mountain West public will remain complicated and nuanced, just as described in the body of this report. However, this analysis suggests that those views should not be considered static; there are some predictable effects of demographic change that both parties will have to contend with going forward.

Another feature of possible changes in public opinion is that they are likely to be disproportionately concentrated in the largest, typically fast-growing metros in the region—Phoenix, Arizona; Denver, Colorado; Boise, Idaho; Las Vegas, Nevada; Albuquerque, New Mexico; and Salt Lake City, Utah—areas where the white working class tends to be declining rapidly, with minorities and white college graduates taking their place. These areas, compared to the rest of their states, already lean in the direction described in the list of potential changes above, a tilt that will be enhanced by these ongoing demographic shifts.[4] (See chapter 2 in this volume for a detailed discussion of unfolding political shifts in these metro areas.)

Conclusion: Looking toward 2012

Our survey found that New Mexico, Nevada, and Colorado residents are more liberal than those in Arizona, who, in turn, are more liberal than those in Utah and Idaho. This diversity coexists uneasily with the unifying characteristics and views described above. It will be interesting to see whether the demographic changes described here create more unity in the Mountain West region or wind up accentuating the differences. Whatever the outcome, it seems safe to say that the parties will face very challenging political terrain where nothing should be taken for granted and where conventional stereotypes about the Mountain West should be treated very, very cautiously.

The challenges to the parties will be highlighted in the upcoming 2012 election. In 2010, the GOP did very well in the region, capturing the U.S. House popular vote in every state save New Mexico and gaining a total of seven seats (two in Colorado, two in Arizona, and one each in Idaho,

Nevada, and New Mexico). Underscoring the highly competitive nature of the Mountain West, in the rest of the West (Alaska, California, Hawaii, Montana, Oregon, Washington, and Wyoming) there was no net change in the partisan distribution of House seats. Republicans also gained a governorship in New Mexico with Susana Martinez. However, they failed in their bids to take Senate seats from Democrat Michael Bennet in Colorado and Democratic majority leader Harry Reid in Nevada.

But 2012 could bring different results. A presidential contest is likely to produce heavier turnout among rising demographics such as minorities and the young, and that should benefit Democrats. The latter are likely to heavily target Colorado, Nevada, and New Mexico—the three most liberal states, as noted above—and all states that Barack Obama carried in 2008. As our survey shows, there are plenty of attitudes and issues in the Mountain West, especially in these three states, that an activist government–oriented campaign can tap. Of course, the state of the economy in the Mountain West has to be counted as a big plus for whoever opposes Obama. And as our survey and the results of the 2010 election both show, there are also strong libertarian-leaning sentiments that the GOP nominee can attempt to mobilize.

Our survey was not designed to tell us how this struggle between the parties is likely to turn out. But it does, we think, shed considerable light on the complexities of public opinion that both parties will have to negotiate in the Mountain West. They would be well advised to pay close attention to those complexities as they make their play for the region's sympathies. Perhaps victory will go to the party that does the best job of listening to rather than stereotyping the region's diverse population.

Notes

1. Data on support for more, the same, or less federal and state government involvement was gathered using a split-sample methodology. We read each respondent a list of nine major issues facing the country today and asked half of the respondents whether they felt that "we need more involvement, about the same level of involvement, or less involvement from the federal government in addressing each issue." The other half were asked whether "we need more involvement, about the same level of involvement, or less involvement from state government in [state] in addressing each issue." In addition, half of each of the groups were also reminded of the deficits facing our federal and state governments and the fact that any increased spending would require either tax increases, further spending cuts in critical programs, or higher deficits (only for those asked about the federal government). This produced a four-way split of respondents in this series.

2. However, the state figures should be treated with some caution because of small sample sizes generated by the split-sampling exercise. We include them because they are

interesting and seem generally plausible when compared with the state-level variation seen on full sample questions.

3. Again, state figures in the table for this series should be treated with some caution because of small sample sizes generated by the split-sampling exercise. We include them because they are interesting and seem generally plausible when compared to the state level variation seen on full sample questions.

4. Demographic shifts in these metro areas are discussed in considerable detail in chapter 1 of this volume.

six

Reapportionment and Redistricting in the Mountain West

DAVID F. DAMORE

During the first decade of the twenty-first century, no region in the United States experienced anything like the political and demographic changes that occurred in the six states of the Mountain West: Arizona, Colorado, Idaho, Nevada, New Mexico, and Utah. Collectively, these states grew at unprecedented levels that resulted in populations that are more demographically diverse than before and increasingly urbanized—all of which helped to transform a region that was a traditional Republican stronghold into a partisan battleground. To be sure, those changes were more prevalent in some states (for example, Arizona, Colorado, Nevada, and New Mexico) than others (for example, Utah and Idaho). Moreover, a good deal of the ground that the Democrats gained in the Mountain West during the decade was blunted by the outcomes of the 2010 election. Consequently, the Democrats' ability to use reapportionment and redistricting to solidify their gains in 2011 is likely to be limited; it is the Republicans who are better positioned to minimize the effects (at least temporarily) of the demographic forces working against the party in the region.

Against this backdrop, I investigate how political and demographic changes are likely to affect the drawing of the maps for congressional and state legislative districts in the six states of the Mountain West, devoting particular attention to the likely implications of redistricting in both the nation and these states. Thus, while the region is poised to become a more significant player on the national stage, the continued urbanization and diversification of the Mountain West reflected in the 2011 maps is likely to further reshape these states' internal political dynamics.

The chapter first gives an overview of reapportionment and redistricting and uses examples from the region's history to illuminate these processes. To provide further context to the six states examined here, it then summarizes the outcomes and controversies surrounding the 2001 redistricting across the region and analyzes the regional political and demographic changes manifested in the 2010 census. Next, an assessment of how those factors will affect the maps that ultimately are implemented in each state is presented. The chapter concludes with a discussion of the likely implications of the 2011 reapportionment and redistricting at the state and national levels in the coming decade.

Reapportionment and Redistricting Politics

Perhaps no use of the data collected from the decennial census engenders more controversy than using it to determine the redistribution of seats in state legislatures and the U.S. House of Representatives to account for population shifts (reapportionment) and the ensuing drawing of boundaries for state legislative and congressional districts (redistricting). Because the process of transforming raw population counts and geographic spaces into political representation affects the behavior of legislators and voters and influences electoral and policy outcomes at the national and state levels, redistricting is often characterized by conflict and uncertainty, pitting the goals of political parties against the ambitions of individual politicians, be they incumbents or potential challengers.[1] Despite the significance of these processes for electoral competition and representation, the interests of the public are typically absent from the deliberations on them.

Since the passage of the 1929 Reapportionment Act, the size of the House of Representatives has been set at 435 members. The reapportionment of House seats therefore is the quintessential zero-sum game—what one state gains, another loses.[2] After the 2001 census, the 435th House seat was awarded to North Carolina, which bested Utah by fewer than 900 citizens.[3] Because of the state's growth since 2000, Utah did gain a fourth seat after the 2010 census, as did Nevada. Arizona also gained its ninth House seat. Thus, starting with the 2012 election, the Mountain West will have forty-one Electoral College votes and twenty-nine seats in the House of Representatives.

While Congress standardized the method of reapportionment in the 1940s, equivalent standards for redistricting did not emerge for another quarter-century. Unhindered by requirements for compactness, contiguousness, and equality—the hallmarks of contemporary redistricting—map drawers created districts of unequal sizes and irregular shapes. These practices persisted because of the unwillingness of the federal courts to intervene in what was viewed as a state political process. With states able to devise their own standards, redistricting prior to the 1960s often resulted in maps that were malapportioned (for example, districts had unequal populations) and gerrymandered (for example, lines were drawn for political purposes). In the South, gerrymandering was used to undercut the voting power of African Americans.[4] The more significant consequence in the West was malapportionment that skewed representation toward rural interests. Various measures of malapportionment suggest that Nevada had by far the most inequitable distribution of seats in the region.[5] By one metric, in 1955 a majority of the upper chamber of the Nevada legislature could be elected by just over 12 percent of the population.[6]

These arrangements persisted until federal judicial intervention in the 1960s that led to the "one person, one vote" holding in *Baker* v. *Carr* (396 U.S. 186, 1962) and in that case's progeny, for example, *Wesberry* v. *Sanders* (376 U.S 1, 1964). As a result, there was an unprecedented wave of redistricting during the mid-1960s that eradicated malapportionment.[7] Judicial intervention also obligated states to regularly redraw boundaries and put the judiciary directly into the fray by allowing supervising state courts to set the reversion plans if the political branches failed. Prior to these reforms, when the executive and legislative branches were unable to compromise, states often continued using the existing plans. New Mexico, for instance, used its 1911 redistricting plan until 1949. The net effect of these rulings, coupled with ongoing political changes, eliminated a pro-Republican bias and altered the career calculations of incumbents and challengers alike.[8] However, at the state level, the expectation of a policy shift from rural to urban interests failed to materialize.[9]

State autonomy over redistricting was further constrained by the passage of the Voting Rights Act in 1965. Specifically, section 2 of the act permits and in some instances requires states to create majority-minority districts to protect against minority vote dilution, and section 5 requires redistricting plans in some locales to be precleared by the Department of Justice.[10] Of the six states in the Mountain West, only Arizona is subject to preclearance owing to its status as a former Confederate territory and its history of using English-language literacy tests to disenfranchise Spanish-speaking and Native American residents. However, as discussed below, the Mountain

Table 6-1. Redistricting-Related Characteristics of the Mountain West States

State	Growth 2000–10[a] (percent)	Upper chamber size	Lower chamber size	Determinant of size of legislature	Professionalism ranking[b]	Redistricting authority	Term limits
Arizona	24.6	30	60	Statute	10	Commission	Yes
Colorado	16.9	35	65	Constitution	14	Commission/ Legislature[c]	Yes
Idaho	21.1	35	70	Constitution	29	Commission	No[d]
Nevada	35.1	21	42	Statute	30	Legislature	Yes
New Mexico	13.2	42	70	Constitution	39	Legislature	No
Utah	23.8	29	75	Constitution	46	Legislature	No[d]

a. Data are from the U.S. Census Bureau, "State and County Quick Facts" (http://quickfacts.census.gov/qfd/index.html).

b. Data are from Peverill Squire, "Measuring Legislative Professionalism: The Squire Index Revisited," *State Politics and Policy Quarterly* 7, no. 2 (2007): 211–27.

c. Maps for the Colorado legislature are drawn by the Colorado Reapportionment Commission, while the Colorado legislature draws the maps for the state's seats in the U.S. House of Representatives.

d. Voter-initiated and -approved term limits in Idaho and Utah were repealed by the state legislature.

West's booming Hispanic population has meant that section 2 has become an important consideration in many states in the region.

Besides these constraints, a number of regional quirks add important wrinkles to reapportionment and redistricting in the Mountain West, summarized in table 6-1. First, the states in the region are the fastest growing in the country. Between 2000 and 2010, the four states with the largest percent gain in population (Nevada, Arizona, Utah, and Idaho) were located in the Mountain West, and population growth in all six states exceeded the national average. Thus, while the districts may be equal in size when maps are approved, this equity is short-lived. For instance, after the 2000 census, each of Nevada's three U.S. House districts was populated with 666,088 people. However, by the end of the decade, the size of the districts had swelled to 820,442 (1st District), 835,896 (2nd District), and 1,044,213 (3rd District).[11] At the time of the 2010 midterm election, Nevada's 3rd District was by far the most populated in the country.

Second, the region's legislative chambers are quite small. Excluding Nebraska (which has a unicameral structure), the average size of the lower and upper houses of the other 49 state legislatures are 110 and 39.22 seats respectively. Only the forty-two-member New Mexico Senate exceeds the national average chamber size. The largest lower house in the region, Utah's seventy-five-seat House of Representatives, is thirty-five seats below the national average. The combination of small chambers and large geographic spaces (Utah is the smallest state in the region, but the twelfth-largest state in the country) results in very large rural districts. This dynamic also helps to explain the region's history of malapportionment, which often awarded seats by county regardless of population. And while legislative size is not immutable, to increase the size of the legislatures in Colorado, Idaho, and New Mexico would require those states to amend their constitutions.[12] The lower chamber of the Utah legislature could be expanded, as it is presently below its constitutional cap.[13] Arizona and Nevada set the sizes of their legislatures by statute. However, given the antigovernment, libertarian nature of these states, it is unlikely that legislators would risk the political backlash of voting to expand the size of state government.[14]

Third, state legislatures in the region have low levels of professionalism (measured in terms of time in session, staff resources, and compensation). Looking at the most commonly used metric of legislative professionalism in the political science literature, the Squire Index (for 2003), reveals that only one Mountain West state, Arizona, is in the top ten. Colorado is ranked 14. Idaho and Nevada are ranked 29 and 30 respectively, while New Mexico is 39 and Utah is 46.[15] Similarly, the National Conference of State Legislatures (NCSL) rates the Idaho, Nevada, New Mexico, and Utah legislatures as citizen legislatures characterized by small staffs, low compensation, and part-time status, and it rates the Arizona and Colorado legislatures as hybrid legislatures (they are slightly better compensated, have relatively more staff, and are in session two-thirds of full time).[16] The degree to which legislative professionalism promotes better equipped and stronger competitors in the policymaking process suggests that legislative outputs in the Mountain West may fall below the norms of states with more professional legislators. [17]

Fourth, while only twenty-four states have the initiative process, whereby citizens can either directly or indirectly place statutes or constitutional amendments on the ballot, five of those states are in the Mountain West. The only exception is New Mexico. The consequences for redistricting are twofold. First, initiative proponents have sought to use the process to remove control of reapportionment and redistricting from state legislatures. Two such provisions, one in Colorado in 1974 and one in Arizona in 2000, successfully passed, placing those responsibilities in the hands of commissions. Idaho, too, uses a commission, which was created by a voter-approved legislative referendum in 1994. Second, the initiative has been used to establish term limits in all five of the region's initiative states (the legislatures in Idaho and Utah subsequently repealed those limits).[18] The degree to which term limits erode professionalism[19] may further undercut the capabilities of the region's legislatures and shift influence to states' executive branches.[20] Also, because term limits alter state legislators' time horizons and career paths,[21] term-limited legislators may view redistricting not as an opportunity to promote the electoral safety of their current post but to position themselves to compete for other offices, typically those with broader constituencies.[22]

The picture that emerges is of a region that has increased its share of U.S. House seats and Electoral College votes due to its growth. At the same time, the legislative institutions within these states have not kept pace, as indicated by small chamber sizes and limited professionalism. Citizen activism, through the initiative process, has further constrained many of these legislatures by stripping their authority over redistricting or by limiting the number of terms that legislators may serve.

The 2001 Redistricting of the Mountain West

The political and demographic transformations that occurred in the Mountain West between 2000 and 2010 took place within the maps that resulted from the 2001 redistricting in the region's six states. Across the region, there was notable variation in the capabilities of the map drawers and in the level of acrimony that redistricting generated.

Arizona

The 2001 Arizona redistricting was the first completed by the Arizona Independent Redistricting Commission (AIRC). Before passage in 2000 of Proposition 106, which created the AIRC, redistricting was handled by the Arizona legislature. The commission consists of five appointed members: four partisans chosen by the party leaders of each legislative chamber and a nonpartisan chosen by the other four members who serves as chair. The AIRC's "mission is to administer the fair and balanced redistricting of the Congressional and Legislative districts for the State of Arizona"—the only commission in the region that is charged with drawing competitive redistricting plans.[23] However, the AIRC's experiences in 2001 demonstrate how difficult it can be to transform broad normative principles into political reality.

The Arizona legislature is structured so that the state is divided into thirty districts, each of which is represented by two members of the lower chamber and one state senator. Because Arizona grew by over 71 percent between 1990 and 2000, the state was apportioned two new U.S. House seats, for a total of eight. In addition, the 2001 redistricting had to reapportion state legislative seats to account for the increased concentration of the state's population in Maricopa County and to ensure that the Hispanic vote was not diluted.

While Arizona Republicans held just a 5 percent voter registration advantage at the time of the 2000 general election, at the time of the 2001 redistricting the partisan composition of Arizona's congressional delegation and state government heavily favored the GOP. Specifically, the Republicans controlled both seats in the U.S. Senate, the governorship, and five U.S. House seats, and they enjoyed a two-to-one advantage in the lower chamber of the Arizona legislature. Arizona Democrats claimed shared control of the evenly divided upper chamber of the Arizona legislature and just one of the state's six U.S. House seats.

The commission's approval of its redistricting plan in early November of 2001 was a disappointment for Democrats. Because of the need to create districts that would not dilute minority voting power (in accordance with section 2 of the Voting Rights Act), ten of the thirty state legislative districts in the commission's plan were Hispanic majority. A consequence of the change, coupled with the relative density of Democratic voters in the state's urban centers, was the diminishment of Democratic support in the surrounding districts.

The AIRC's approval, however, was anything but final. The first issue to come to light was that the commission had used faulty data to draw its maps. That disclosure slowed the preclearance process of the Department of Justice (DOJ) and, along with a legal challenge to the competitiveness of the map, caused the 2002 election to take place under interim maps. Eventually, the DOJ rejected the AIRC's first maps. The second set of maps gained DOJ approval in early 2003. However, a 2004 legal challenge brought by the Democrats resulted in the second set of maps being thrown out due to lack of competitiveness. Thus, it was not until May of 2004 that Arizona had a plan that could withstand legal scrutiny.

Colorado

If the process in Arizona in 2001 was the height of dysfunction, Colorado's was not far behind. By design, the process in Colorado is convoluted, as redistricting works on two tracks. The Colorado general assembly draws the boundaries for the state's U.S. House seats, and the Colorado Redistricting Commission (CRC) oversees the process for state legislative districts. The commission consists of eleven members. Four are picked by the party leaders of the general assembly; three are selected by the governor; and four are chosen by the chief justice of the Colorado supreme court. According to the CRC's website, the commission's charge is to draw geographically compact and contiguous districts that do not deviate by more than 5 percent and that keep communities of interest intact.[24] Because of the inexact ratio of seats of the lower and upper chambers of the general assembly, separate maps are drawn for each.

During 2001, the Democrats controlled the thirty-five-member upper chamber of the legislature, while the Republicans controlled the governorship and the sixty-five-member lower chamber. The state's congressional delegation leaned to the GOP, with the Republicans controlling both U.S. Senate seats and four of the state's six House seats.[25] Because the state grew by nearly 31 percent during the 1990s, with the bulk of the growth occurring in Denver and its suburbs, Colorado was apportioned a seventh U.S. House seat after the 2000 census.

Colorado's redistricting was slowed because of a delay in the state's receipt of the necessary data from the U.S. Census Bureau. The Colorado general assembly therefore was unable to begin the redistricting of the state's House seats until a special session was held. Leading up to the special session, members of both parties filed lawsuits requesting that the process be handled by the courts. Thus, while state legislators were developing their maps, the same legislators, as well as Colorado governor Bill Owens, were actively courting judicial intervention. In January 2002, a state court judge took control of the process and selected a Democratic compromise plan over a more partisan Republic plan. Meanwhile, the state legislative maps that had been approved by the CRC in fall 2001 became the source of another set of legal challenges, with the Republicans getting the state supreme court to invalidate the CRC's state senate map. The revised state legislative maps and the judicially approved map for Colorado's seats in the House of Representatives were used for the 2002 election.

That, however, was not the end of the legal wrangling. After capturing control of the state senate in 2002 and unifying the Colorado general assembly and governorship under Republican control, the GOP sought to push through another set of maps for the state's U.S. House seats that were more favorable to the party. The Democrats filed suit, claiming that the Republicans had violated the Colorado constitution by drawing maps twice for one redistricting cycle. That claim was followed by partisan squabbling about who would defend the new GOP plan in court. The state's Democratic attorney general, Bill Salazar, refused and even went so far as to sue the Republican secretary of state, Donetta Davidson, to prevent implementation of the new congressional map. Ultimately, the Colorado supreme court threw out the Republicans' second set of congressional maps in a decision that was upheld by the U.S. Supreme Court.

Idaho

Like Arizona, Idaho is a state that entrusts all of its redistricting to an independent commission, Idaho's Citizen Commission for Reapportionment (ICCR). The commission consists of six members; four are chosen by party leaders of the Idaho legislature, and one member is chosen by each of the state chairs for the Democratic and Republican parties. In addition to the mandates of equal population for House seats and legislative districts that vary less than 10 percent, Idaho's redistricting guidelines forbid drawing oddly shaped districts for any reason (for example, partisanship or incumbent protection), discourage the division of counties, require the preservation of communities of interest, and do not allow districts to overlay other legislative districts.[26] For the state legislature, Idaho is divided into thirty-five districts, from each of which one senator and two members of the lower chamber are elected.

Clearly, Idaho is a Republican stronghold.[27] At the time of the 2001 redistricting all four members of the state's congressional delegation (two U.S. House members and two senators) were Republicans, as was the governor. The GOP also had overwhelming majorities in both chambers of the Idaho legislature. Consequently, the partisan strife that characterized the 2001 processes in Arizona and Colorado was absent; instead, the main obstacle facing the ICCR was addressing uneven patterns of growth that resulted in large population gains in Boise relative to those in the rest of the state (during the 1990s, Idaho grew by 28.5 percent). Specifically, Idaho's increased urban concentration threatened the districts of rural legislators. The first two plans approved by the ICCR were struck down in court because of population deviations that exceeded 10 percent. On the third try, the commission was able to produce maps that were upheld by the courts.

Nevada

Akin to that in other states in the region, the 2001 redistricting in Nevada had to address geographic population discrepancies in drawing the state's U.S. House and state legislative districts. During the 1990s, Nevada's population increased by 66 percent, and by the end of the decade, roughly seven in ten Nevadans resided in Clark County. Nevada therefore was apportioned a third House seat after the 2000 census, and because of uneven patterns of population growth, the clout of southern Nevada in the Nevada legislature would increase.

Despite the political mischief that growth and a new House seat might provoke, particularly in a swing state,[28] the redistricting process in Nevada went relatively smoothly,[29] aided by a number of factors. Split partisan control of the Nevada legislature (the Democrats held the assembly and the Republicans were in the majority in the senate) meant that neither party could implement a partisan gerrymander. Also, because the state's Republican governor, Kenny Guinn, stayed out of the process, the legislators did not have to worry about executive interference. In addition, while the state's Hispanic population did organize and pressed for greater representation, its lobbying efforts were largely ineffective.

The drawing of legislative districts in Nevada was also eased by three structural factors. First, Nevada allows for multi-member state senate seats, each of which is twice as large as the other senate seats and is represented by two senators who run in alternating elections.[30] Second, while the Nevada legislature consists of forty-two assembly districts and twenty-one senate seats, the boundaries for assembly seats can be drawn without regard for the overlying senate districts. Third, the size of the Nevada legislature can be increased by law. The Republicans originally proposed expanding the legislature by two assembly seats and one senate seat to protect the seats of rural incumbents.

In the end, these factors facilitated a plan that resulted in the most typical redistricting outcome: incumbent protection for both parties.[31] The major point of controversy was the drawing of the state's new U.S. House district. A Republican state senator, who would go on to hold the seat until 2008, forced a special session in order to exact a district that was more favorable to the GOP. In exchange, the Republicans dropped their expansion proposal. Given the centrality of geography and partisanship in Nevada politics, the interests of Hispanics got little attention in the process. Despite constituting 20 percent of the population in 2000, after the 2002 midterm election, Hispanics held just 5 percent of seats in the state legislature.[32]

New Mexico

The New Mexico legislature oversees the state's redistricting and employs guidelines that are similar to those used in most other states (for example, equally populated congressional districts; minimal population deviations for state legislative seats; contiguous and compact districts; and no dilution of minority voting strength). The legislature can preserve existing districts and consider the residence of incumbents.[33] Separate maps are drawn for the New Mexico house (seventy seats) and senate (forty-two seats) and for the state's three seats in the U.S. House of Representatives.

Voter registration figures from 2000 indicate that 53 percent of voters in New Mexico were Democrats, 33 percent were Republicans, and 12 percent registered as nonpartisans. However, at the time of the 2001 redistricting, the GOP controlled the governorship, two of the state's three seats in the U.S. House of Representatives, and one U.S. Senate seat. The Democrats' main source of strength was in the state legislature, where the party held large majorities in both chambers. Like the other states in the region, New Mexico experienced significant growth (20.1 percent) during the 1990s that further concentrated the state's population in its largest city, Albuquerque.

Redistricting in New Mexico begins with recommendations from the eighteen-member Redistricting Committee, which consists of state legislators from both chambers and both political parties. Individual legislators also can propose their own maps or put forth plans created by outside groups. In 2001, redistricting took place in a special session characterized by partisan rancor as the Democrats sought to ensure their continued control of the New Mexico legislature and to draw two of the state's three U.S. House districts so that they were favorable to their party.

Not surprisingly, New Mexico's Republicans cried foul and two sets of maps passed by the Democratic legislature were vetoed by the Republican governor, Gary Johnson. Because Johnson refused to call a second special session, New Mexico's redistricting battle went to the courts. Ultimately, a state district court signed off on a plan that made minimal changes to the state's three U.S. House districts. Further, the court ruled that because white voters did not vote as a block and therefore were unable to defeat the minority's preferred candidate, none of New Mexico's U.S. House seats had to be drawn as a majority-minority district. However, the same standard did not hold for the map for the state legislature's lower chamber. Here, a state court ruled that part of the plan approved by the New Mexico legislature did not provide equal electoral access for the Navajo and Jicarilla Apache nations; the court therefore redrew the plan for the state's northwestern quadrant. The remainder of the plan for the lower chamber that had been passed by the legislature but vetoed by the governor was upheld and implemented. During the ensuing regular session, the state senate districts were finally drawn after the Democrats passed a compromise bill that was signed by Governor Johnson.

Utah

Like Idaho, Utah is a heavily Republican and ethnically homogenous state.[34] Because Republicans held significant majorities in both chambers of the state legislature and controlled the governorship, the party was in position to implement a partisan redistricting in 2001. Moreover, data from the 2000 census indicate that 85 percent of Utahans were white, slightly less than the percentage in the region's most homogenous state, Idaho (88 percent white); as a result, redistricting in Utah is unencumbered by the need to protect minority voting power. The main goal of redistricting for Utah's Republicans, therefore, was to undermine the electoral safety of the state's lone Democratic member of Congress, Representative Jim Matheson (the GOP controlled Utah's other two U.S. House seats and its two U.S. Senate seats) and to further entrench Republican dominance in the state legislature. On both counts, Utah's Republicans were successful. Matheson's 2nd District was made less Democratic by the exchange of more liberal urban voters with conservative rural voters.[35] In the state legislature, Republicans were able to strengthen their party's position by packing and overpopulating the districts of Democratic incumbents and underpopulating GOP districts.[36] The net effect was that Democratic voters were distributed as inefficiently as possible.

The main point of controversy in Utah in 2001 was over the state not being apportioned a fourth U.S. House seat, despite a population increase of over 30 percent. That led to Utah challenging the U.S. Census Bureau in federal court on two fronts: that the Census Bureau undercounted Utah's population by not considering Mormon missionaries living abroad and that the Census Bureau used illegal statistical estimates for part of the 2000 count. On both counts, Utah lost in federal courts. Utah's appeal on the second claim to the U.S. Supreme Court was rejected.[37]

Lessons Learned from 2001

Review of the 2001 redistricting in the six states of the Mountain West, the outcomes of which are summarized in table 6-2, reveals a number of insights. First, clearly the use of independent commissions is no panacea as the three states in the region that used commissions had parts of their commission-drawn plans thrown out in court. Indeed, even in Idaho, a state dominated by one party, it took the ICCR three rounds to develop maps that would withstand judicial scrutiny. In contrast, there were no legal challenges to the maps drawn by state legislators in Nevada and Utah.

Table 6-2. Summary of Redistricting Outcomes in the Mountain West States, 2001

State	Litigation	Issue	Outcome
Arizona	Yes	Initial preclearance denied and lack of competitiveness challenged (final resolution 5/04).	Effective Republican gerrymander
Colorado	Yes	Initial CRC Senate and U.S. House maps and 2003 U.S. House redistricting invalidated (final resolution 6/04).	Democratic leaning
Idaho	Yes	Excessive population variation for state legislative districts. Third plan accepted by Idaho supreme court.	Favorable to Republicans and rural interests
Nevada	No	Partisan composition of Nevada's 3rd District and legislative expansion (resolved in special session).	Bipartisan incumbent protection
New Mexico	Yes	Reversion plan set by state court for U.S. House map and some state legislative districts redrawn by a state court to ensure electoral access for Native American communities.	Democratic leaning
Utah	Yes	U.S. Census Bureau undercounted Utah's population by not including Mormon missionaries and used illegal statistical estimates for part of the 2000 count (both cases dismissed in federal court).	Republican gerrymander

Source: Author's summary, various sources.

Second, mapmakers across the region were afforded different degrees of latitude in drawing boundaries as redistricting guidelines across the states varied considerably. For instance, in New Mexico the residency of incumbents could be taken into account, while Idaho forbids consideration of their residency. Similarly, for state legislative districts, Idaho allows for twice as much interdistrict population variation as Colorado. Further, in Arizona, the state's redistricting commission is charged with drawing balanced districts, while the commissions in Idaho and Colorado have no such requirement. Also, while Colorado, Nevada, New Mexico, and Utah allow the districts for the lower chamber of their state legislatures to be drawn without regard for the boundaries of their upper chambers, Arizona and Idaho require two lower chamber districts to be nested within the boundaries of a state senate district. Map drawing in Arizona and New Mexico was further constrained by those state's significant minority populations.

Third, as New Mexico Democrats learned, implementing a partisan gerrymander is difficult. In an increasingly competitive region, the conditions under which such plans can be realized are rare (the state must be a noncommission state and one party must have control of the state government). In the end, only Utah Republicans were able to use redistricting for obvious partisan gain.

A Region in Flux

The issues and controversies surrounding the 2001 redistricting of the Mountain West serve as a precursor to the region's 2011 redistricting battles. Indeed, the disputes that came to the fore in 2001—whether partisan, geographic (urban versus rural), or racial—are exerting even greater influence in 2011. For instance, map drawers were able to minimize the loss of rural seats across the region by preserving the core of rural districts and then stretching them to pick up parts of urban areas. That will be more difficult to accomplish in 2011 given the small legislative chambers and increased urbanization throughout the region. Also, while protection of minority voting rights was a significant factor in Arizona and New Mexico in 2001, these considerations are again affecting maps drawn in those states as well as Nevada and Colorado. And with the exceptions of Idaho and Utah, the states in the region are now more Democratic than in 2001. I focus on the three variables—diversity, density, and partisanship—to place the region's 2011 reapportionment and redistricting in context.

More Diverse Populations

As the data presented in table 6-3 indicate, since 2000 all six Mountain West states became more ethnically diverse. The first three columns of table 6-3 capture the increase in the nonwhite population in each state, and the latter three columns document the growth of the Hispanic populations throughout the region. In both regards, Idaho and Utah, which remain overwhelmingly white, are outliers. At the same time, both states did see increases in their nonwhite populations that were similar to the increase in Colorado. For all three states, increased diversity was driven primarily by growth among Hispanics. On the other end of the spectrum is Nevada, where the nonwhite population increased by over 11 percent, with the 2010 census classifying better than 45 percent of Nevadans as nonwhite. While the bulk of this growth was among Hispanics, the Silver State recorded large increases in its Asian and Pacific Islander populations. Arizona, too, witnessed significant minority growth, while growth in New Mexico was slightly less. Nonetheless, by the decade's end, roughly three of five New Mexicans were nonwhite and nearly half of the state's population was Hispanic.

Table 6-3. Change in Population Diversity in the Mountain West States, 2000–10
Percent

State	Nonwhite population			Hispanic population		
	2000	2010	+/–	2000	2010	+/–
Arizona	36.2	42.2	+6	25.3	29.6	+4.3
Colorado	26.5	30	+3.5	17.1	20.7	+3.6
Idaho	12	16	+4	7.9	11.2	+3.3
Nevada	34.8	45.9	+11.1	19.7	26.5	+6.8
New Mexico	55.3	59.5	+4.2	42.1	46.3	+4.2
Utah	14.7	19.6	+4.9	9	13	+4

Source: Data from the U.S. Census Bureau, "State and County Quick Facts" (http://quickfacts.census.gov/qfd/index.html).

Increased Population Density

A second aspect of population growth between 2000 and 2010 in the Mountain West was increased concentration in the region's population centers. The data presented in table 6-4 summarize the growth in each state's largest U.S. census metropolitan statistical area (MSA) and the change in the share of each state's population within its largest MSA. Of the six MSA's featured, the greater Las Vegas area experienced the most rapid growth. By 2010, nearly three in four Nevadans lived in the Las Vegas metro area—the most highly concentrated population in the region. The patterns were similar in Arizona, where in 2010 roughly two in three Arizonans lived in the Phoenix MSA, which grew by nearly 30 percent. In contrast, the Salt Lake City and Denver MSAs grew more slowly than the state average; therefore the share of the Colorado and Utah populations residing in these MSAs decreased slightly after 2000. Albuquerque experienced the largest overall increase as a share of total population: the Albuquerque MSA increased by nearly 25 percent, and 44 percent of New Mexico's population is concentrated in the Albuquerque MSA. While Idaho remains the state in the region with the least dense population, population growth in the Boise MSA (32.64 percent) significantly outpaced Idaho's total population growth (21.1 percent). By decade's end, nearly 40 percent of all Idahoans resided in and around Boise.

Partisan Swings

The increases in diversity and density throughout the region correlated with greater support for the Democratic Party.[38] To capture the dynamics, the

Table 6-4. Change in Population Density in the Mountain West States, 2000–10
Percent unless otherwise shown

State	U.S. census metropolitan statistical area	National rank	Growth 2000–10	Population share 2000	Population share 2010	+/-
Arizona	Phoenix–Mesa–Glendale	14	28.94	63.38	65.59	+2.21
Colorado	Denver–Aurora–Brooomfield	21	16.71	50.65	50.57	−.08
Idaho	Boise–Nampa	86	32.64	35.92	39.33	+3.41
Nevada	Las Vegas–Paradise	30	41.38	69.19	72.25	+3.06
New Mexico	Albuquerque	57	24.41	40.11	44.08	+3.97
Utah	Salt Lake City	50	16.03	43.38	40.67	−2.70

Sources: Data are from the U.S. Census, "American Fact Finder" (http://factfinder2.census.gov/faces/nav/jsf/pages/index.xhtml); Office of Management and Budget, *Bulletin 10-02*, "Update of Statistical Area Definitions and Guidance on Their Uses," December 1, 2009 (www.whitehouse.gov/sites/default/files/omb/assets/bulletins/b10-02.pdf).

strength of the Democratic vote in the 2000 through 2010 elections for each state in the region is plotted in figure 6-1. The metric used here, the Major Party Index, was developed by Ceasar and Saldin and combines a party's electoral support in the most recent presidential, gubernatorial, U.S. Senate, and U.S. House contests and the share of the seats that the party controls in both chambers of the state legislature.[39]

These data demonstrate that the Mountain West, in general, has become more hospitable to the Democratic Party since 2000. At the same time, the Democrats made few to no inroads into the Republican bastions of Idaho and Utah. Indeed, using this metric, Idaho and Utah have some of the lowest Democratic strength scores of any of the fifty states. On the other hand, the Democrats were able to make significant gains in Colorado, Nevada, and New Mexico, effectively flipping those states from Republican leaning in 2000 to Democratic leaning in 2010. The party's performance in Arizona was highly variable, moving in concert with the vicissitudes of the national political environment.

The 2010 downturn depicted in figure 6-1, however, suggests that Democratic gains in the Mountain West remain fragile. To more precisely assess just how large a setback the 2010 election was for the Democrats in the region, table 6-5 summarizes the Democratic losses at the federal and state levels. While the Republicans gained one governorship (in New Mexico) in 2010, the Democrats lost seats in ten of the region's twelve state legislative chambers. At the federal level, despite close elections in Colorado and Nevada, none of the region's U.S. Senate seats changed parties in 2010. In contrast, the

Figure 6-1. Democratic Party Strength in the Mountain West States, 2000–10

Major Party Index score

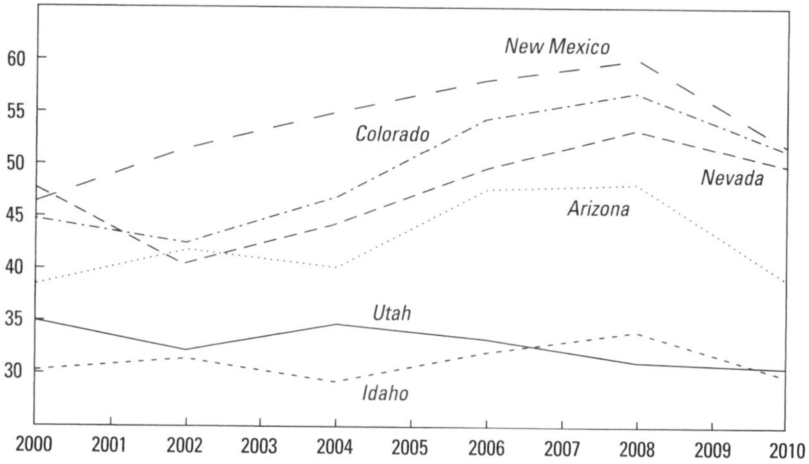

Source: Data are Ceasar and Saldin's Major Party Index measure of state party strength, with higher values indicating greater Democratic strength in the electorate. Data for years 2000 through 2008 are from "Major Party Index Data" (http://scholar.harvard.edu/saldin/data). Data for 2010 were calculated by author.

Democrats suffered the loss of seven House seats in 2010 (of a total of twenty-six in the region). Not surprisingly, many of the House seats that the GOP picked up in 2010 had swung to the Democrats in either 2006 or 2008—the better Democratic years of the decade. Perhaps the most volatile seat was in Nevada's 3rd District. Since its creation in 2001, the seat has been held by three different politicians, going Republican in 2002, 2004, and 2006; Democratic in 2008; and Republican again in 2010, but by less than 2,000 votes.

Table 6-6 summarizes the impact of the 2010 election on the partisan composition and control of the region's state governments moving into the 2011 redistricting. Prior to the 2010 election, the GOP controlled the executive and legislative branches in Arizona, Idaho, and Utah and the Democrats had unified control in Colorado and New Mexico. After the 2010 election, the Republicans maintained control of Arizona, Idaho, and Utah, while the Democrats' loss of the governorship in New Mexico and of the majority (by one seat) in the lower chamber of the Colorado general assembly left the party without unified control in any of the states of the region. In Nevada, the status quo of a Democrat-controlled legislature and Republican-controlled governorship was unaltered.

Therefore, there are no opportunities for the Democrats to engineer a partisan gerrymander in 2011. Fortunately for the Democrats, in two of three

Table 6-5. Impact of the 2010 Election in the Mountain West States

State	Governorship	Upper chamber	Lower chamber	U.S. House	U.S. Senate
Arizona	Republican hold	–2 Democrats	–5 Democrats	–2 Democrats	Republican hold
Colorado	Democratic hold	–1 Democrat	–5 Democrats	–2 Democrats	Democratic hold
Idaho	Republican hold	No change	–5 Democrats	–1 Democrat	Republican hold
Nevada	Republican hold	–1 Democrat	–2 Democrats	–1 Democrat	Democratic hold
New Mexico	Republican pickup	No change	–8 Democrats	–1 Democrat	No race
Utah	Republican hold	–1 Democrat	–5 Democrats	No change	Republican hold

Sources: Data are from the National Conference of State Legislatures, "2010 State and Legislative Partisan Composition Prior to the Election," January 31, 2011 (www.ncsl.org/documents/statevote/2010_Legis_and_State_pre.pdf) and "2011 State and Legislative Partisan Composition," November 1, 2010 (www.ncsl.org/documents/statevote/2010_Legis_and_State_post.pdf).

states—Arizona and Idaho—where the Republicans have unified control, the maps are drawn by commissions, which may provide the Democrats with better outcomes than plans drawn by their opponents. Democratic prospects for gaining any meaningful foothold in Utah are generations away, if then.

2011 Redistricting Overview

The 2011 redistricting takes place in arguably the most hostile political environment in recent history, in which partisan antipathy has been further inflamed by recall and special elections across the country. Trust in government is at an all-time low,[40] public disenchantment with the two major political parties is on the rise,[41] and increasingly, citizens are using the initiative process to either restrict or remove legislative control over redistricting. Most notably, in 2011 California became the thirteenth state to use a commission for all or some of its redistricting. Redistricting in 2011 also takes place for the first time in a fully digital age—an evolution that facilitates public input to a greater degree than during prior cycles. Across the country, more citizens are taking an interest in the process and many have gone so far as to draw their own maps.[42]

In the Mountain West, all six states developed comprehensive websites that provide access to redistricting data and allow citizens to examine proposed maps and, in some instances, to build and submit their own. In addition, public hearings have been held throughout the states by either commissioners or legislators. In this regard, the process in 2011 more closely observes "the principles for transparency and public participation" developed by the Brookings Institution and the American Enterprise Institute.[43] At the same time, it

Table 6-6. Partisan Control in the Mountain West States, 2010 and 2011

	2010			2011		
State	Legislative control	Governor's party	State control	Legislative control	Governor's Party	State control
Arizona	Republican	Republican[a]	Republican	Republican	Republican	Republican
Colorado	Democratic	Democratic	Democratic	Divided	Democratic	Divided
Idaho	Republican	Republican	Republican	Republican	Republican	Republican
Nevada	Democratic	Republican	Divided	Democratic	Republican	Divided
New Mexico	Democratic	Democratic	Democratic	Democratic	Republican	Divided
Utah	Republican	Republican[a]	Republican	Republican	Republican	Republican

Sources: Data from National Conference of State Legislatures, "2010 State and Legislative Partisan Composition Prior to the Election" and "2011 State and Legislative Partisan Composition."

a. Governor took office through succession in 2009.

is unclear what influence the public will have, particularly in states where the process is controlled by self-interested state legislators and where public hearings were held well in advance of the unveiling of legislatively proposed maps. As the Brookings Institution's redistricting maven, Michael McDonald, noted in the context of Utah, "lawmakers may turn out to be 'wolves in sheep's clothing,' when it comes to following through on public input."[44]

By fall 2011, redistricting was completed in three states in the region: Idaho, Nevada, and Utah.

Map drawing for Colorado's U.S. House seats and all of New Mexico's redistricting had shifted to state courts. The outcome in Arizona was uncertain owing to the decision of the governor, Jan Brewer, with the backing of Republicans in the legislature, to remove the nonpartisan chair of the Arizona Independent Redistricting Commission shortly before the commission was to have completed its work. Therefore, while I am unable to make a definitive statement regarding the redistricting outcomes in all six Mountain West states in 2011, the discussion that follows offers insights into the key issues in each state and predictions of what the eventual maps are likely to look like in the three states where the process has not been completed.

Arizona

The redistricting in Arizona in 2011 was the second one handled by the Arizona Independent Redistricting Commission. Given the commission's struggles in 2001, it began work amid criticism of its composition, calls for its abolishment, and an investigation into a claim by the Arizona attorney general that the AIRC had violated state procurement and open meeting laws.

Over the summer, the commission held twenty-four public meetings, with more conducted after the AIRC's initial maps were unveiled. In the end, map drawing in Arizona will center on three considerations.

First, given Arizona's growth, which further concentrated the state's population in urban centers (see table 6-4), representation of rural interests is in the balance. Rural districts could be saved if the Arizona legislature were expanded. If that is not done, then the ratio of state senators to citizens would be 1 to 213,067 and the ratio of citizens to state house members would be 106,534 to 1—easily the most lopsided ratios in the region. To date, the AIRC has signaled no interest in increasing the number of seats in the state house. Consequently, the representation of rural interests in the Arizona legislature as well as in the state's nine U.S. House seats will be diminished regardless of the partisan contours of the map.

Second, as noted above, map drawing in Arizona is constrained by the state's large minority populations, which include not only significant Hispanic communities but also a large number of Native Americans. Satisfying section 2 of the Voting Rights Act therefore is likely to conflict with the AIRC's task of drawing "fair and balanced" maps. Akin to that in 2001, the outcome in 2011 is likely to be the creation of a large number of majority-minority districts, which would make Arizona's plans less likely to draw the ire of the DOJ. At the same time, Arizona filed a lawsuit in federal court challenging the Voting Rights Act's preclearance requirement (which was reauthorized by Congress with strong bipartisan support in 2006).

Third, assuming that the federal courts uphold Arizona's preclearance requirement, the final maps are likely to look like a partisan gerrymander that benefits the GOP. By drawing a large number of majority-minority districts to ensure compliance with section 2 of the Voting Rights Act, the AIRC is likely to pack those districts with a large number of Democratic voters. Democratic support in the surrounding areas is likely to be diminished as a result.

The outcome in Arizona is likely to follow the contours of redistricting in another section 2 region, the South. In both instances, the provisions of the Voting Rights Act have the perverse effect of increasing symbolic representation for minority groups while decreasing the number of legislators that may be receptive to minority interests.[45] Thus, while Republicans hold a 4.35 percent registration advantage over the Democrats (as of July 2011), Arizona is likely to end up with state legislative and U.S. House maps that are more favorable to the GOP than that figure would suggest. Despite these considerations, late in the process Arizona Republicans sought to undermine the AIRC's work by removing the commission's nonpartisan chair, Colleen

Mathis, on the grounds that she was skewing the process in a manner favorable to the Democrats and that the commission's work was being improperly conducted.[46] Governor Brewer and her allies in the Arizona legislature also sought but ultimately failed to remove the AIRC's two Democratic members. In addition to putting Arizona's redistricting process in limbo by creating legal challenges and requiring the recruitment of a new commission chair, the actions of Arizona Republicans undercut the will of the citizens of Arizona, who voted in 2000 to create the commission in order to remove partisan politics from the redistricting process.

Colorado

As noted above, Colorado uses a commission (the Colorado Redistricting Commission) for redistricting state legislative seats and the Colorado general assembly draws the maps for the state's seven U.S. House seats. Although the Democrats increased their traction in Colorado during the prior decade (see figure 6-1), the state was one of two in the Mountain West where the urban core as a share of total population decreased since 2000 (see table 6-4). Whereas in most states equalizing population across districts generally works to the advantage of Democrats in that districts become more urban, in Colorado the seats in and around Denver need to be stretched into rural areas to equalize their populations.

For the state's seven U.S. House seats, Democrats in the legislature proposed significant alterations to existing district lines, the goals being to keep urban centers intact and increase overall competitiveness. As might be expected in a legislature characterized by divided partisan control, the Republicans saw things differently and put forth maps that were more protective of rural interests and that were skewed in favor of the GOP. After exchanging two rounds of maps, the Democrat-controlled upper chamber and the Republican majority in the lower chamber failed to reach a compromise by the end of the regular legislative session. The unwillingness of the Democratic governor, John Hickenlooper, to call a special session required the redistricting of Colorado's U.S. House seats to be completed in state court.

In addition to the maps proposed by the parties, plans were submitted to the court by groups representing Hispanic interests and by the Pueblo County district attorney. Given the conflicting goals in the plans proposed by the various litigants, it is difficult to determine exactly how the court will rule. However, if history is a guide, the Democrats may end up carrying the day. As discussed above, in 2001, Colorado courts largely sided with the Democrats. If the legal challenges over the state's House districts ultimately is decided by the Colorado supreme court, the Democrats may be victorious owing to a five-to-two partisan advantage in the composition of the court.

The drawing of the maps for state legislative districts also has been hindered by partisanship. The CRC, consisting of ten partisan representatives and chaired by a nonpartisan commissioner, began its work in May with a series of public hearings. The primary task facing the CRC was equitably repopulating state legislative districts that had grown at varying rates during the prior decade. In August 2011, the CRC approved its preliminary plan, based on a Democratic proposal, along party lines. The maps drew criticisms from both parties, with Democrats charging that the plan would weaken minority representation and hinder the Democrats' ability to regain the lower chamber of the legislature[47] and Republicans complaining that the maps were unconstitutional because they split rural municipalities.[48]

In an attempt to overcome partisan gridlock, the nonpartisan chair of the CRC presented revised state legislative maps in September. The new CRC maps combine parts of Democratic and Republican proposals and create thirty-three competitive seats (out of a total of 100) and twenty-four seats with Hispanic populations of 30 percent or more (while putting the Ute Mountain Ute and Southern Ute tribes in separate districts). The maps were approved by the CRC, with some Republican commissioners dissenting. If approved by the Colorado supreme court, the maps would give both parties a chance to control both state legislative chambers. At the same time, because competitiveness is not a criterion that the CRC is obligated to consider, the plan may attract legal challenges if competitiveness is seen as trumping the CRC's charge of producing districts that are compact and contiguous and keep communities of interest intact.

Idaho

After being impaneled in June 2011, Idaho's redistricting commission (Idaho's Citizen Commission for Reapportionment) began holding public hearings as the first step in a process that had to be completed within ninety days. The commission's main task is to equitably repopulate the state's two U.S. House districts and thirty-five state legislative districts (each of which elects one state senator and two members of the lower chamber) to account for the increased urbanization of the state. Specifically, thirteen of the thirty-five state legislative districts exceed "the ideal size," and nine seats with Democratic incumbents are undersized. Because the size of the Idaho legislature cannot be enlarged without amending the state's constitution, the likely result will be the movement of rural Republican voters into urban Democratic districts, further weakening the Democrats' position in the state. The lines for Idaho's 1st House district also need to be adjusted to shed roughly 50,000 citizens.

The ICCR's task was made more difficult by the passage of a state law in 2009 that allows state legislative districts to cross county lines only if the counties are linked by a highway. Note that in 2001 the ICCR struggled to draw districts with appropriate population differences even without such a constraint. To draw districts with equal populations that comply with the new law would mean sacrificing the residency of incumbents. The ICCR's preliminary maps (one set drawn by Democratic and one by Republican commission members), released in August, equalized district populations by pairing (drawing into the same district) roughly a third of all state legislators. However, because of the difficulty of satisfying the constitutional requirement limiting county splits and the state law constraining how geographic areas can be combined, the ICCR failed to reach an agreement before its September 6 deadline.

The inability of the ICCR to finalize a redistricting plan prior to its constitutionally imposed deadline put Idaho's 2011 redistricting in uncharted waters.[49] The assumption of most was that in response to two legal challenges stemming from the ICCR's inability to complete the process, the Idaho supreme court would order the commission to reconvene, appoint special masters to oversee the process, or simply draw the maps itself. However, the supreme court dismissed the legal challenges by noting that the Idaho constitution does not give the court authority to act without an approved plan on which to rule. Adding to the tumult, ICCR commissioners are prohibited from serving multiple terms. Because the term for the original commissioners expired, the 2011 Idaho redistricting was completed by a second set of commissioners in less than three weeks. Given the partisan composition of Idaho, the final maps unsurprisingly benefit the GOP while being somewhat more urban oriented—a regional anomaly to say the least. At the same time, because of Idaho's strict requirement that limits the division of cities and counties, the map for the state legislature placed a number of incumbents in the same district, including one district that contains the residences of five incumbents.

Nevada

Nevada's 2011 redistricting focuses on three concerns: the shifting of northern state legislative seats to southern Nevada to account for Clark County's outsized growth since 2000 and the redrawing of many of the seats in Clark

County to account for significant population disparities; accommodation of the state's booming and increasingly engaged Hispanic communities; and the drawing of the state's newly awarded fourth U.S. House seat. These issues are similar to those that confronted the state during the prior redistricting. However, in 2001, the Nevada legislature was able to overcome partisan divisions to develop a map that drew no legal challenges. In 2011, however, the divide between the Democrat-controlled legislature and the state's Republican governor, Brian Sandoval, proved to be too large. After two Sandoval vetoes of maps passed by the legislature on party line votes and Sandoval's refusal to call a special session, Nevada's redistricting was overseen by a state court judge.

The main point of contention is partisan differences in how section 2 of the Voting Rights Act should be implemented to accommodate Nevada's minority populations. Governor Sandoval and Republicans in the legislature claimed that section 2 requires the use of race as the basis for drawing a Hispanic U.S. House seat—a position at odds with the holding in *Shaw* v. *Reno* (509 U.S. 630, 1993), which allows race to be taken into consideration but does not allow it to be the predominant factor. Democrats and many Hispanic activists countered that packing Hispanics into a single House district would marginalize their influence in Nevada's other three U.S. House districts and that race-based redistricting in Nevada is unnecessary because white voters in Nevada do not vote as a block, as evidenced by the fact that Hispanic candidates won ten state legislative seats, the attorney generalship, and the governorship in 2010 without such accommodations.

At a late September hearing, the supervising state court judge essentially punted on the legal questions surrounding the applicability of section 2 and, with no legal directions on where to begin, turned the process over to three special masters. Despite the uncertainty of the special masters' charge, they produced maps that, after some minor tweaking by the supervising state court judge, gained the support of Republican and Democratic litigants for an agreement that effectively ended Nevada's 2011 redistricting. In drawing the final maps, the special masters rejected the GOP's claim that section 2 of the Voting Rights Act required a majority Hispanic district. As a consequence, two of Nevada's U.S. House seats are Democratic leaning, one is safely Republican, and the fourth is a swing district. With respect to the Nevada legislature, the representation of urban interests will increase as parts of or all of forty-seven of the sixty-three seats in the Nevada legislature are located in the Democratic stronghold of Clark County.

New Mexico

Redistricting in New Mexico lagged significantly behind that in the other Mountain West states. By summer's end 2011, the eighteen-member Redistricting Committee had completed its public hearings and made its nonbinding recommendations to the New Mexico legislature. The legislature began haggling over maps for the state's three U.S. House seats, forty-two-seat state senate districts, and seventy-member state house of representatives during a September special session.

The 2011 process has been very much a rerun of the partisan gridlock that engulfed the state's 2001 redistricting debate. Once again, the Democrats sought to use their control over both chambers of the New Mexico legislature to implement a plan that would preserve their majorities and draw the boundaries for the state's three U.S. House seats in a manner favorable to the party. However, the legislature failed to approve the map for the state's three U.S. House seats prior to the end of the special session, and the plans for the state legislature that were passed on party line votes were vetoed by Republican governor Susana Martinez.

So, once more, New Mexico's divided state government coupled with the state's history of litigating redistricting plans (in 2001 map drawing and court battles cost the state roughly $3.5 million) means that redistricting will be completed in state court. While the Republicans may be able to gain some concessions through the courts, the supervising state court will likely be working from the maps drawn by the Democrats. Moreover, of the six states in the Mountain West, New Mexico is the most Democratic (see figure 6-1). Thus, as in 2001, the likely outcome in New Mexico is a redistricting plan that will be favorable to the Democrats and that will further consolidate the influence of the state's urban population.

Utah

Redistricting in Utah, despite that fact the state is as close to being a one-party state as there is, has drawn the most public anger in the region. For instance, a January 2011 poll found that nearly three-quarters of Utah's population favored creating an independent redistricting commission.[50] However, an initiative that would give control of redistricting to a citizen-based commission failed to qualify for the ballot in the spring.

Critics contend that despite holding seventeen field hearings throughout the state and receiving more than 160 citizen-generated maps, the Joint

Redistricting Committee—a nineteen-member committee consisting of legislators from both parties and chambers of the Utah legislature that develops the preliminary maps—ignored the public.[51] Whereas the main concern of the various citizen groups that have been active in the process is keeping communities intact, the legislators who actually draw the maps are more interested in protecting incumbents and, in the case of the GOP, further weakening the Democratic opposition.

The main source of contention is the urban/rural composition of the state's four U.S. House seats. Republicans prefer a plan that divides the state's population center (Salt Lake City) into three or four districts, each of which is joined to a number of rural counties—a plan that, not coincidentally, would crack the only part of the state where Democrats are able to compete. The Democrats, in contrast, prefer three urban districts along the Wasatch Front and one large rural district—a plan that would allow the party to maintain the 2nd District and potentially compete in the other two urban-centric seats. Similarly, maps for state legislative districts pushed by Republicans would increase the number of seats hospitable to the party and, in many instances, carve out districts that protect incumbents from potential primary challengers by dividing communities into multiple districts.

In the end, because of growth patterns favorable to the GOP coupled with Republican control of the Utah legislature and governorship, the proposed Republican plan carried the day. Consequently, the 2011 redistricting in Utah will result in another partisan gerrymander that offers little hope for the state's Democrats beyond threats of legal action. Indeed, Democrats in Utah are so depleted that they were unable to get the Republicans even to agree to include recognition and protection of minority communities of interest in Utah's redistricting guidelines. Therefore, despite constituting nearly 20 percent of the state's population, minorities received no consideration in Utah's 2011 redistricting.

Implications and Conclusions

Redistricting is often regarded as the most political activity in the United States, and the process in the Mountain West in 2011 certainly fit that bill—a point underscored by the summary of the likely 2011 redistricting outcomes presented in table 6-7. In the swing states where legislators drew the maps (for example, Colorado, Nevada, and New Mexico) but the state government was divided, partisan considerations loomed large, with the result that all of these states concluded all or parts of their redistricting in the courts. The

Table 6-7. Summary of Likely Redistricting Outcomes in the Mountain West States, 2011

State	Litigation	Issue	Likely outcome
Arizona	Yes	Federal challenge to preclearance requirement; state legislature challenges to AIRC regarding open meeting and procurement laws and removal of AIRC chair.	Favorable to Republicans and more urban oriented
Colorado	Yes	Reversion plan set by state court for House maps. Competitive and Hispanic-friendly map adopted by CRC.	Competitive
Idaho	Yes	Inability to resolve constitutional and statutory space constraints prior to expiration of original ICCR term of office (process completed by new commissioners).	Favorable to Republicans and slightly more urban oriented
Nevada	Yes	Reversion plan set by state court and applicability of section 2 of Voting Rights Act.	Democratic leaning and more urban oriented
New Mexico	Yes	Reversion plan to be set by state court.	Democratic leaning
Utah	No	Division of communities of interest.	Republican gerrymander

Source: Author's summary, various sources.

conflicts between Arizona's preclearance requirement and the AIRC's commitment to drawing competitive districts have partisan consequences as well, a point illustrated by the removal of the nonpartisan commissioner by Arizona Republicans. In one-party Idaho and Utah, the politics of space were at issue. Geographic constraints on district boundaries imposed through statute and the Idaho constitution ensured that more rural seats were preserved and that the growing influence of urban interests was checked. In Utah, state legislators moved in the opposite direction by opting to carve up the very communities from which they are elected.

While the level of interparty competition accounts for much of the difference in the types of conflict that redistricting engenders across the region, some of the difference also stems from the incentives that redistricting offers ambitious politicians. In the term-limited states where interparty competition is high, the goal of individual legislators is to maximize partisan considerations in order to create the most opportunities for their future electoral prospects. In Utah and Idaho, where legislators repealed voter-imposed term limits, seniority and careerism remain the key to power. For these legislators the nooks and crannies of the physical spaces that compose their districts are of great import. In the case of Utah, that means tweaking district boundaries to eliminate potential primary challengers, while in Idaho undercutting the effects of urbanization will help to sustain the careers of rural incumbents.

Another school of thought, however, argues that the most typical redistricting outcome is not partisan gain or loss or incumbent protection but an uncertainty that shakes up the state political environment and facilitates political renewal.[52] In the case of the Mountain West, there certainly is evidence to support that claim. The biggest wild card, of course, is growth. While the economic downturn slowed migration to the region, the six states of the Mountain West remain poised to keep expanding in a manner that will further concentrate and diversify their populations. The degree to which the new arrivals become politically active may very well tilt the region's swing states one way or the other by the end of the decade. A second source of uncertainty is the region's large number of nonpartisans. While redistricting is often framed as a zero-sum game played between Democrats and Republicans, the electoral hopes for either party hinges on its ability to attract the support of the region's expanding nonpartisan demographic. At the time of the 2010 election, nonpartisan registrants constituted over 30 percent of Arizona's voters, 26 percent of the Colorado electorate, and around 15 percent of voters in Nevada and New Mexico (Idaho and Utah do not report partisan registration figures). Therefore, because of the uncertainty inherent in redistricting, particularly in fast-growing states with weak political institutions, plans that may favor one party on implementation may have very different effects by decade's end.

Reapportionment and redistricting in the Mountain West will also have more definitive implications at the state and national levels. Most notable is that regardless of which party gains an electoral advantage through redistricting in each state, the undisputed loser will be rural interests. Because of seniority, the political acumen and agility of individual politicians, and an undying nostalgia for the small-town ethos, rural legislators in the region have long exerted an influence over policy outcomes that exceeds their numbers.[53] Those days are waning. The combination of term limits, small legislative chambers, and fast-growing urban populations will decrease the number of entrenched rural legislators and the number of stand-alone rural seats. Consequently, urban interests should be able to better align state policy with demographic reality over the coming decade. In Idaho and Utah that may translate (eventually) into less obsequious catering to ranching interests, while in Colorado and Nevada the mining industry may find itself with fewer protectors in the state legislatures than it is accustomed to having.

The void created by the demise of rural legislators will be filled by minorities. During the prior decade, Hispanic state legislators increased their numbers in every state in the region except Idaho. Even in Utah the number of

Hispanic legislators increased from one in the 2003 session to five in 2011.[54] To date, the increased political activism of Hispanic communities has benefited Democrats primarily. Democratic outreach and recruitment efforts have been aided by the hard-line rhetoric and policies championed by many Mountain West Republicans—for example, Arizona's 2010 Support Our Law Enforcement and Safe Neighborhoods Act (SB 1070) and Utah's 2011 Utah Illegal Immigration Enforcement Act (HB497). The more moderate tone on such issues taken by Hispanic Republican governors in Nevada (Brian Sandoval) and New Mexico (Susana Martinez), however, indicate that the GOP in the region is not necessarily monolithic on this front. More generally, depending on growth patterns, by 2020 Nevada and perhaps Arizona may join New Mexico as states with majority-minority populations. Thus, with or without section 2 of the Voting Rights Act, minority legislators, primarily Hispanics, will increase their ranks significantly. The only question is whether all of these politicians will be taking office with a "D" next to their names or whether some will be elected as Republicans.

Nationally, the impact of reapportionment and redistricting is a mixed bag. Even with the addition of three seats after the 2010 census, it is unlikely that the clout of the Mountain West in the U.S. House of Representatives will increase. With a combined twenty-nine seats, the region's House delegation is just over half as large as that of its powerful western neighbor, California. Moreover, the region's House membership will continue to be split along partisan lines for the coming decade, and given the competitiveness of many House races in the region, it may be difficult for any but the safest Mountain West representatives to accrue the requisite seniority to become players in the House.

Instead, the Mountain West's hopes for influencing the national agenda lie in the U.S. Senate and its status as a presidential election battleground. Yet even in the Senate, with its inherent small-state bias, the Mountain West's clout is likely to decline in the near term. Certainly, having the Senate majority leader, Nevada's Harry Reid, hailing from the region is an invaluable asset. However, two of the other longest-serving senators from the region, Arizona's John Kyl and New Mexico's Jeff Bingham, have announced their retirement and will not seek reelection in 2012. The 2012 reelection of another old-guard senator, Orrin Hatch, is no guarantee given a potential Tea Party primary challenge. In 2010, the Tea Party denied Utah's three-term senator Bob Bennett the Republican nomination. The 2011 resignation of Nevada's scandal-plagued John Ensign also cost the region a senior voice. Thus, after the 2012 election the only senators from the region who will have served longer than one term are Reid, Arizona's John McCain, Idaho's Mike Crapo, and, presumably, Hatch.

Perhaps the arena where the region is likely to garner the most attention is in the three presidential elections in the next ten years. Colorado, Nevada, and New Mexico were all battleground states in 2004 and 2008, with Republican George W. Bush narrowly winning all three in 2004 and Democrat Barack Obama flipping them blue in 2008 by wider margins. Obviously, Idaho and Utah will remain out of reach for the Democrats in statewide contests for some time. However, Arizona is likely to become the region's fourth swing state in the near future. During the prior decade, Arizona elected a centrist Democratic governor (Janet Napolitano) and the party increased its House seats from two in 2002 to a high of five in 2008, before losing two seats in 2010. Thus, continued investment in Arizona and throughout the region will allow the Democrats to further expand the number of Mountain West states in play while forcing the GOP to spend resources to defend turf that it once could safely call its own.

Notes

1. Andrew Gelman and Gary King, "Enhancing Democracy through Legislative Redistricting," *American Political Science Review* (September 1994): 541–59.

2. To bring more precision to reapportionment, in 1941 Congress mandated that Huntington's Method of Equal Proportion be used as the standard for the reapportionment of House seats after each census.

3. Utahans were able to enjoy a bit of schadenfreude after the 2010 census as it was North Carolina that lost out to Minnesota for the 435th House seat.

4. Charles S. Bullock III, *Redistricting* (Lanham, Md.: Rowan and Littlefield, 2010).

5. Ibid., pp. 31–32.

6. Manning J. Dauer and Robert G. Kelsay, "Unrepresentative States," *National Municipal Review* (December 1955): 571–75, 581.

7. As a consequence of these court decisions, congressional seats within a state must be equally populated, while the size of state legislative districts can vary up to 10 percent. States may mandate less interdistrict population variation than the federal standard.

8. Republicans outside of the South were able to win roughly 6 percent more House seats than the party's aggregate vote share; see Gary W. Cox and Jonathan N. Katz, *Elbridge Gerry's Salamander: The Electoral Consequences of the Reapportionment Revolution* (Cambridge University Press, 2002).

9. Analysis of agriculture, regulatory, and transportation policies suggests that such a shift did occur at the federal level; see Mathew D. McCubbins and Thomas Schwartz, "Congress, the Courts, and Public Policy: Consequences of the One Man, One Vote Rule," *American Journal of Political Science* (May 1988), pp. 388–415.

10. Bullock, *Redistricting*.

11. Legislative Counsel Bureau, "United States House of Representatives Districts: 2010 and 2000 Populations," August 2011 (www.leg.state.nv.us/Division/Research/Districts/Reapp/2011/Tables/PopulationCongressionalDistrictsInNevada2010.pdf).

12. A 1966 ballot initiative amended the Colorado constitution to limit the size of the state senate to thirty-five and the size of the assembly to sixty-five seats. A 1976 amendment to the New Mexico constitution capped the upper chamber at forty-two and the lower chamber at seventy seats. Article III, section 2, of the Idaho constitution states: "Following the decennial census of 1990 and in each legislature thereafter, the senate shall consist of not less than thirty nor more than thirty-five members. The legislature may fix the number of members of the house of representatives at not more than two times as many representatives as there are Senators." Both chambers of the Idaho legislature are at their maximum constitutionally allowable sizes.

13. Article IX, section 2, of the Utah constitution states: "The Senate shall consist of a membership not to exceed twenty-nine in number, and the number of representatives shall never be less than twice nor greater than three times the number of Senators." The Utah senate is at its maximum size of twenty-nine seats, but the state house of representatives could be expanded beyond its current size of seventy-five.

14. During the 2001 redistricting negotiations in Nevada, Republican legislators proposed to expand the size of the Nevada legislature to preserve the seats of rural districts. Ultimately, GOP legislative leaders backed away from the proposal in return for a more favorable drawing of the state's new third congressional seat. For an extended discussion, see David F. Damore, "The 2001 Nevada Redistricting and Perpetuation of the Status Quo," *American Review of Politics* (Summer 2006): 149–68.

15. Peverill Squire, "Measuring Legislative Professionalism: The Squire Index Revisited," *State Politics and Policy Quarterly* 7, no. 2 (2007): 211–27.

16. National Conference of State Legislatures, "Full- and Part-Time Legislatures," August 2011 (www.ncsl.org/?tabid=16701).

17. Squire, "Measuring Legislative Professionalism: The Squire Index Revisited."

18. Term limits went into effect in 1998 in Colorado, in 2000 in Arizona, and in 2010 in Nevada. Colorado and Arizona limit legislative service in each chamber to eight years. Nevada limits legislators to twelve total years of service in each chamber.

19. Thad Kousser, *Term Limits and the Dismantling of State Legislative Professionalism* (Cambridge University Press, 2005).

20. John M. Carey and others, "The Effects of Term Limits on State Legislatures: A New Survey of the Fifty States," *Legislative Studies Quarterly* (February 2006): 105–34.

21. Ibid.

22. Jennifer A. Steen, "The Impact of State Legislative Term Limits on the Supply of Congressional Candidates," *State Politics and Policy Quarterly* (Winter 2006): 430–47.

23. Arizona Independent Redistricting Commission, "Mission," August 2011 (www.azredistricting.org).

24. The Official State Portal, "Redistricting in Colorado," August 2011 (www.colorado.gov/cs/Satellite/CGA-ReDistrict/CBON/1251581769173).

25. Partisan registration data for Colorado prior to 2004 are unavailable. To assess the level of party competition in the state, one can look at the presidential vote. Republican presidential candidate George W. Bush won Colorado with 50 percent of the vote

in 2000 and 52 percent of the vote in 2004. Democrat Barack Obama carried Colorado in 2008 with nearly 54 percent.

26. Idaho Legislature, "Redistricting Guidelines," August 2011 (http://legislature.idaho.gov/redistricting/guidelines.htm).

27. The Idaho office of the secretary of state does not report partisan voter registration figures. In 2000 and 2004, Republican presidential candidate George W. Bush won 67 percent and 68.4 percent of the vote respectively. GOP nominee John McCain won 61 percent of the vote in 2008.

28. At the time of the 2000 general election, Republican voters outnumbered Democratic voters by 838. Nevada's congressional delegation was evenly split, with each party controlling one House and one Senate seat.

29. Damore, "The 2001 Nevada Redistricting and Perpetuation of the Status Quo."

30. The 2001 plan reduced the number of senators serving in multi-member districts from eight to four.

31. Gelman and King, "Enhancing Democracy through Legislative Redistricting."

32. Damore, "The 2001 Nevada Redistricting and Perpetuation of the Status Quo."

33. New Mexico Legislature, "A Guide to State and Congressional Redistricting in New Mexico," August 2011 (www.nmlegis.gov/lcs/lcsdocs/reddocs/134250.pdf).

34. The Utah office of the secretary of state, like that in Idaho, does not report partisan voter registration figures. Using the presidential vote as a measure of party competition indicates little traction for the Democrats. George W. Bush won the state with 69 percent and 72 percent of the vote in 2000 and 2004 respectively, and John McCain received 62 percent support in 2008.

35. The partisan gerrymandering engineered by the Utah legislature was so blatant that it drew the scorn of Republican U.S. Representative Jim Hansen (whose district was made less safe because of the redrawing of Matheson's 2nd District); he commented that "if there was ever an argument for letting someone other than the legislature do redistricting, this is one," quoted in Bryson Baird Morgan, "Assessing the Partisan Impact of the 2001 Utah State Legislative Redistricting Plan," senior honors thesis, University of Utah, December 2007.

36. Morgan, "Assessing the Partisan Impact of the 2001 Utah State Legislative Redistricting Plan."

37. Utah Representative Chris Cannon introduced a bill in 2001 that would withhold part of the Census Bureau's budget unless the bureau developed a plan to count all Americans living abroad for the 2011 census.

38. See chapter 2 in this volume.

39. James W. Ceasar and Robert P. Saldin, "A New Measure of Party Strength," *Political Research Quarterly* (June 2005): 245–56.

40. Pew Research Center, "Public Trust in Government: 1958–2010," August 2011 (http://people-press.org/2010/04/18/public-trust-in-government-1958-2010).

41. Pew Research Center, "Distrust, Discontent, Anger, and Partisan Rancor," August 2011 (http://people-press.org/2010/04/18/section-4-congress-and-the-political-parties).

42. For instance, the website DrawCongress.org, overseen by the Columbia University Law School, seeks nonpartisan maps for all 435 House seats.

43. See Micah Altman and others, "Principles for Transparency and Public Participation in Redistricting," August 2011 (www.brookings.edu/opinions/2010/0617_

redistricting_statement.aspx), and Micah Altman and Michael McDonald, "Pulling Back the Curtain on Redistricting," *Washington Post,* July 9, 2010 (www.washingtonpost. com/wp-dyn/content/article/2010/07/08/AR2010070804270.html).

44. Lisa Riley Roche, "Drawing Boundaries: Will Public Have Influence in Redistricting Process?" August 6, 2011 (www.ksl.com/?sid=16700175).

45. See Kevin A. Hill, "Congressional Redistricting: Does the Creation of Majority Black Districts Aid Republicans?" *Journal of Politics* (May 1995): 384–401, and David Lublin, *The Paradox of Representation: Racial Gerrymandering and Minority Interests in Congress* (Princeton University Press, 1999).

46. The law creating the Arizona Independent Redistricting Commission allows commission members to be removed by the governor with two-thirds support in the thirty-member state senate for "substantial neglect of duty, gross misconduct in office, or inability to discharge the duties of office."

47. Tim Hoover, "Colorado Legislative Districts Get Tentative OK, Draw Criticism," *Denver Post,* July 19, 2011 (www.denverpost.com/news/ci_18504045).

48. Peter Marcus, "Reapportionment Commission Wrangles over Districts," *Colorado Statesman,* July 15, 2011 (www.coloradostatesman.com/content/992923-reapportionment-commission-wrangles-over-districts).

49. The ICCR did finalize a redistricting plan seventeen days after the commission was disbanded. But because the commission's legal authority has expired, the plan has the same weight as the other eighty-two maps submitted by the public.

50. Lee Davidson, "Utahans Want Independent Redistricting Commission," *Salt Lake Tribune,* January 30, 2011 (www.sltrib.com/sltrib/politics/51146379-90/commission-county-districts-independent.html.csp).

51. Lee Davidson, "Critics Say Lawmakers Don't Listen on Redistricting," *Salt Lake Tribune,* July 27, 2011(www.sltrib.com/sltrib/politics/52272034-90/committee-congressional-lake-listening.html.csp).

52. Gelman and King, "Enhancing Democracy through Legislative Redistricting."

53. William Yardley, "Some Rural Lawmakers Defy Power Erosion," *New York Times,* July 13, 2011 (www.nytimes.com/2011/07/14/us/politics/14farm.html?pagewanted=1&sq=rural legislators&st=cse&scp=2).

54. National Conference of State Legislatures, "Latino Legislators Overview," August 2011 (www.ncsl.org/default.aspx?tabid=22391).

Contributors

Karlyn Bowman
American Enterprise Institute

David F. Damore
University of Nevada–Las Vegas

William H. Frey
Brookings Institution

Scott Keeter
Pew Research Center

Robert E. Lang
Brookings Institution, University of Nevada–Las Vegas, and the Lincy Institute

Thomas W. Sanchez
Virginia Tech

Ruy Teixeira
Century Foundation and the Center for American Progress

Index